OFF ROAD HANDBOOK
with back country travel tips
by Bob Waar

Editors: Bill Fisher
             Carl Shipman

Typesetting: Debbie McMillian

Book Design: Josh Young

Book Assembly: Nancy Fisher
                 Ellen L. Duerr

Cover Photo: Jim Forbes

ISBN 0-912656-15-8

Library of Congress Catalog
Number 74-83546

H. P. Books Number 34

© 1975 Printed in U.S.A. 1-75

H. P. BOOKS
P. O. Box 5367
Tucson, Arizona 85703

INTRODUCTION TO OFF-ROADING

This "thing" of running a vehicle off the road just for grins—to get away from it all—has to be one of the most exhilarating experiences in the motor vehicle's relatively short history.

For those of you who are not a part of the Southern California "scene," perhaps a bit of history might interest you before you begin digging into the following pages. Shortly before WW II, a handful of motorcyclists began spending their weekends zipping around in the desert area near Los Angeles. From this evolved the American version of Enduros and Cross Country or Hare and Hound racing. Before the gang hung up their helmets to become better acquainted with Uncle Sam, several of each type of event had been held in the Southern California desert.

Concurrent with the motorcycle activity was the development of dune buggies. In the beginning they were just that: Cutdown versions of older-model cars chugged around the sand dunes at Pismo Beach, California and Yuma, Arizona. During the war, GIs came to know a ubiquitous, slab-sided, underpowered military vehicle called the Jeep. At the end of the war, motorcyclists went back to their fun and games in the deserts and more and more Jeeps began showing up in the boonies. Often, the flathead four-cylinder engine had been replaced with a healthier engine. Jeep kept right on producing Jeeps—for civilians as well as the military. Slowly other manufacturers began to turn out off-road-oriented vehicles. Tire manufacturers began providing rubber designed to be run primarily off-road. By the mid-'60s, the amount of leisure time and money had grown to have considerable clout—even more manufacturers introduced vehicles to get their share of a growing market. The first Mexican 1000 along the length of the Baja peninsula in October of 1967 brought the hard core of the hotrod cult into the activity and the technological advances that came in the next several years were overwhelming. Off-road racing is now sanctioned by several organizations and the sport is very popular—primarily in the Southwest and the Midwest. For the most part

the technology behind the racing is quite sophisticated. A large and healthy off-road equipment industry has been spawned. Four-wheel-drive recreational vehicles and trucks have become a status symbol.

Four wheelers are popular—no doubt about it, but for every four wheeler (4WD) there are a half-dozen two-wheel-drive (2WD) pickups grinding down a wash loaded with a cooler, kids and some bedrolls. Thousands of Americans enjoy getting off the beaten path for a few hours or days. We are a healthier people for it—get off road a little; you'll see why.

THANKS

No book of this type is ever put together by just one man. Many men and organizations have been extremely helpful and encouraging as this book went together over a two-year period. Special thanks go to Bill Janowski and crew of DataMotive in Reno who worked from sunup till "dark-thirty" getting all of the tire testing done and the data compiled. Dick Cepek loaned us more than a thousand dollars worth of tires and wheels for the tire testing section. He said he wanted to see a book full of meaty information about off-roading. We hope we have done Tom and Dick Cepek justice on that request with this volume. Vic Hickey literally turned his shop over to us—providing equipment, answering questions, giving us total freedom to reprint from his booklet on how to use a winch. Thanks, Vic. Wayne Thoms and Jim Williams of Chevrolet Public Relations arranged for the Blazer shown in the tire-test section and provided all sorts of information appearing throughout the book. Dick Goold owns a repair shop specializing in 4WD equipment—as a result he sees a lot of broken and abused hardware. We picked his brain, used his shop and drank his coffee. We always felt safe with him in the desert at night—he snores loud enough to keep away all the critters.

Others helped and asked that their names not be mentioned. Thanks to all of you!

Once you go off-road you'll go back again and again. Sunset is one reason why.

If I seem to be an old maid when it comes to preventive maintenance, forgive me, I've broken—and had to repair—a lot of equipment out in the boonies. Experiences such as chaining up a broken frame, or tricycling with a broken front spindle, last a long time. They're fun to romance about around the campfire, but damned unfunny at the time they occur. So my old-maidish admonition to you is to be safe, be sane.

Have fun out there. Take nothing but pictures . . . leave nothing but footprints.

Bob Waar

One last romp in the sands of Pismo before chow time. Get an off-road buddy—you'll have twice the fun.

Hey Ma, We Forgot The TV!—A lot off off-roaders take far too much gear with them—too much food, camping gear, spare parts and tools. A strange thing occurs when the average off-road enthusiast realizes he has four wheels and an engine to carry his junk. He begins to make vast lists of items which can somehow be jammed in. Then he adds on all of the parts that could possibly break. Add on huge amounts of oil, gas, water and—and— the list grows and grows. You wind up not using half the junk you take and it's always in the way of everything you do use.

Go light. Start thinking like a bike rider or back-packer. Experienced back-packers don't take unnecessary things with them—at least not after the first time. Start thinking of weight as "the enemy." Buy or borrow these two books and learn the joy of equipping yourself with the minimum amount of things: *The Complete Walker* (the joys and techniques of hiking and backpacking), by Colin Fletcher, published by A. A. Knopf, 1969; *Going Light With Backpack or Burro,* by David Brower, published by the Sierra Club.

OFF-ROAD FUN

You probably had a pretty good idea of what you were going to do with your off-road rig before you bought it—we'll mention some areas you might not have thought of.

CLUBS

In many areas of the country four-wheel-drive clubs are active. Normally they have an outing a month plus one or more meetings a month. Several times a year they'll probably get together with another club for longer outings on holiday weekends. Club politics are usually low key and the sole object is go off the road and have good safe, family-oriented fun. Through a club a novice off-roader can increase his knowledge about vehicles and how to drive them off-road. Chances are you'll soon learn about the best (and worst) repair shops in the area and also the best places to fish, hunt and camp. Some clubs offer their services and vehicles to local law-enforcement agencies and as a consequence provide loads of help in locating those who get lost in rugged terrain. Search and rescue operations are the long suit of 4WD clubs in many areas.

Some clubs specialize in organizing competition events—such as hill climbs, sand drags and a host of low-speed driving skill games. In some cases a vehicle must be radically (and expensively) modified before it can be competitive. In other cases, being competitive depends entirely on being a good off-road driver.

In joining a local off-road club—local chamber of commerce or the sheriff's office can probably tell you if one exists in the area—you might find a guy that lives around the block from you is a member. Lasting friendships are formed this way. Don't let the thought of organized fun scare you away from a club—there are often real benefits in joining.

HUNTING & FISHING

An off-road rig can get you into hunting and fishing locations previously inaccessible to you. In a case like this, hunting and fishing might be the real recreation in your life while the off-roading is just a means to that end.

Breathe wrong and the seesaw will tilt. Gals love this activity—and do they get excited!

Off-roaders' version of barrel racing—driver negotiates a marked course while the passenger either removes or places a tennis ball on a stick. When husbands and wives team up, the verbal exchange gets pretty funny, even hilarious at times.

If you like a little companionship when making an off-road trip, a club is a good place to start. One- and two-day outings are plentiful, fun and safe.

At large off-road meets, clubs conduct interesting activities. Blindfold race isn't very fast—driver is blindfolded, passenger gives directions in and out of traffic cones and pucker brush. Fun!

Hill climbing is just one of many active competition areas open to the avid off-roader. Some clubs specialize in one form of competition or another.

Clubs camping together have a lot of fun—share in camp chores, food expenses, and in getting one another unstuck. The stamp sign was obviously put up so campers arriving late could quickly identify the camp.

Pull! Another club activity gaining popularity is skeet shooting while the mate is off taking a powder puff tour with the Jeep. Being active in a club is good insurance for having a good time.

A large encampment of off-roaders is a good opportunity to make new friends and swap off-road lore.

Sandhill climbing is one of the highly organized, fiercely competitive events sponsored by off-road clubs.

Shifting a four-speed transmission and a two-speed transfer case while trying to pick the easy way up a long sandhill sure can take your mind off the problems of the rest of the world.

Never go out in the boonies—or even to the grocery store—without your battery jumper cables! This owner pop-riveted a surplus strap to the fender and lashed the cables where they are ready for use.

FAMILY FUN

Family camping and hiking centering around an off-road rig is high on the list of things to do with your new pride and joy. Getting away from the telephone and doorbell for a long weekend adds real zest to family life. Strange things happen. Kids even do some chores without being told three times if they know their going camping depends on it.

A youngster learning how to drive can gain a new perspective on vehicles and what they can and cannot do, if he is given a chance behind the wheel.

If you live where travel in the winter is limited due to snow and ice on the road, a 4WD rig can mean new freedom—along with a chance to help your friends and neighbors.

You don't need an excuse to have an off-road vehicle. There are a lot of good solid reasons why one vehicle in the family should have off-road capability.

Plymouth Trail Duster shore looks purty in this publicity shot. Wet grass or a light covering of frost and a little wheel-spin and that truck could slide back in the water and scare all the fishes away.

This is fun! Just make sure you know the difference between 10 feet of water and 10 inches of water *before* you enter the stream.

This Hickey-prepared truck is loaded for bear. Four-wheel drive and the great hidden winch trick get you back where the big fish jump.

Youngsters love the freedom of off-road—gives 'em a change of pace from yelling parents.

Teach a kid to drive—off-road. In this event a young one has a go at the turtle race—slowest time wins. Just make sure the wheels never stop turning.

This is what it's all about—watching the sunset from the top of a dune.

You can have a lot of fun off-road with most any kind of vehicle—just don't push a vehicle to the limit if it really wasn't made for the rough stuff.

Youngsters out in the open never can understand why grownups like to sleep in—these two are keeping track of a rabbit feeding.

Nothing like rolling out of the sleeping bag and starting breakfast six inches away. In time you'll learn to put the coffee and water in the pot the night before and generally get things squared away so that first meal of the day goes together with a minimum of trouble.

OFF-ROAD DRIVING

As is the case with other skills acquired in life, driving off-road correctly and smoothly takes a lot of practice past the pages of a book. Here we can only outline the fundamentals. A good off-road driver develops a sixth sense about that ever-changing link between ground and vehicle. Knowing just what to do and when to do it with a vehicle off-road means you can take a far inferior vehicle into terrain a lesser driver could not negotiate with a better vehicle. Think about it—a very good driver and a so-so vehicle can go places a bad driver and trick vehicle can't go. We're not saying a good driver will never get hung up or stuck—but a bad driver will get stuck and hung up in places the good driver would either avoid or negotiate successfully. Be smooth and *think*. Make certain there's a living connection between brain and foot.

HIGH-CENTER

High-center occurs when your vehicle with ten inches of clearance between differential and ground comes to rest on a 14-inch-diameter log. High-centering can occur on an old fire trail or logging road where the track section of the road has eroded, leaving the center section high and dry. A dry wash sprinkled with bushel-basket-size rocks can become "home" for an hour or so while you get off of a high-centered position. Crossing a ridge or embankment squarely can hang up a vehicle. This last predicament can usually be avoided if the embankment or ridge is approached at an angle of about 45 degrees instead of at 90 degrees. The other situations require the driver to have a sixth sense about the terrain and the vehicle. For instance, if a high-centering situation arises on a logging road, stop far short of getting hung up. Can you easily move off the trail and work your way through the brush and trees to a more solid section of the trail? Can you do five minutes' shovel work and make the road passable with no danger or getting hung up? The Fearless Fred approach is to back up ten yards, get a running start and pray that by charging hard enough, momentum and a glass-smooth skid plate will skate the vehicle safely to solid footing. In many cases this will work. In those cases where it doesn't, count on spending some productive minutes (or hours) with a shovel. The charge and pray approach is full of surprises. For that reason you should look the situation over *very* carefully beforehand. We charged and prayed one afternoon and stopped about ¾ of the way to safe footing. The vehicle didn't really slow down and then stop—it stopped like we'd come to the end of an anchor chain. After some digging and a lot of cussin' we backed up. Seems there was a cedar stump about eight inches in diameter fully hidden beneath the soft earth. The skid plate found the stump. Had we used our noodle *before* charging we could have seen the roots trailing off from the stump and logically assumed there was a hunk of tree hidden in that mound of earth.

Sometimes a vehicle can be backed off a high-center situation—but don't count on it. If you high-center in snow and know there is solid footing underneath—maybe even a paved road—get out and rock the vehicle from side to side. This can compact the snow holding the wheels off the ground. Heat from the drive train will also melt the snow and may let the vehicle settle. If you try to back off a high-center, do it just as slowly and easily as you possibly can. A partner can stand ready with a board, rocks or whatever to feed under a spinning tire and possibly give you footing needed to back on out. Again, don't count on it! The solid plan for getting un-high-centered is to go to work with shovel and jack. Lift the vehicle just as high as practical and build up the footing under one wheel at a time until you can drive out.

Halfway through the shoveling and jacking exercise you'll probably say to yourself or your partner, "Well, I don't think we'll make it, but let's try anyway." So you try and fail and now the tires have clawed away what little footing you had put in place. Now you start over. Remember this: When you have trouble off-road, whether it be getting stuck, high-centered or breaking a component; do the very best job on it you can the first time. Save yourself time and countless headaches by doing it right the *first* time.

This is even touchier than it looks. Balance in this situation was so tricky—any driver movement moved the Bronco to the point of laying it on its side. Reason for this . . . .

. . . . was this hole hidden in the grass! This jewel was roughly four feet wide by three feet deep. Nice. One more reason to do a little walking where you plan to drive.

Notice hole was completely hidden from the driver by brush growing out of it. Always expect the unexpected when you start putting wheels where you can't see. When this Bronco dropped a front wheel in a hidden hole, opposite rear wheel lifted off the ground and vehicle nearly tipped over.

Even with a little help in getting the rear axle back on the ground, this four-wheeler could not get out of the hole alone. Notice front tire is jammed into the fender.

WHEEL-SPINNING AND HILL-CLAWING

As we've already pointed out there are times when a carefully planned and executed "charge" will prevent your getting stuck. But like the judge said, "There's a time and place for everything." Spinning the tires wildly and showering the landscape with rock and debris at every opportunity is just plain bad driving. John Q. Klutz may impress his wife and kids with his driving technique, but what are they going to think when you just pick your way up the hill at about one quarter of Klutz's speed with no wheel-spinning and just a trace of dust?

There's a hidden danger to the Klutz approach to a hill. Let's say it is *really* a bad hill, I mean a lunch-eater. There are no tracks around and Klutz rightly assumes the hill has never been conquered. He backs up and charges. By now all of the blood has drained from his brain to his right foot and the vehicle is on its way. Thirty feet from the top, the engine dies. The hard charge over the rough terrain flooded the engine. As the vehicle comes to an abrupt halt, Klutz slams on the brakes. His plan is to restart the engine, back down the hill and start over. No way. We said this is a bad hill—really! Although the brakes keep the wheels from turning, the vehicle starts to slide downhill. Klutz whirls around in the seat and gets ready to steer downhill. No way. The weight of the vehicle is now primarily on the rear axle, coupled with the fact that wheels that don't turn also don't steer very well. The vehicle starts to turn sideways and all Klutz can see out the side window is ground. Now in a 100% panic he backs off the brake pedal —maybe with a little more momentum the vehicle can be straightened out. No way. With all of the expensive sounds that accompany a roll over—glass breaking and rocks scraping the sheet metal—Klutz and vehicle slide sideways down the hill. Unhurt, but three beers later the blood has drained from his foot to his jaw muscles and he is cursing: (A) the vehicle, (B) the tires, (C) the dumb carburetor or (D) all of the above.

If you remember nothing else from this book, remember this: There *are* hills which *NO* vehicle can climb.

We can outline the basic "do's and don'ts" of hill climbing here, but only practice will give you the confidence needed to "try the big mutha."

Too much throttle at the wrong time can break a wheel loose. Don't be ashamed of taking another cut at a hill until you get the feel for gear and traction. This particular Jeep took five tries before getting over the top. Experience counts a bunch in a situation like this.

Sometimes you just have to back up and take a mighty run at a hill to get over. Hitting an unexpected rock or hole can cause a component to fail. Proving you are a hot dog can lead to a deflated billfold.

Pick your trail or line of travel before starting. Stay away from big rocks, trees, sharp drop-offs and anything that looks soft. In other words, pick the easy way up. Climbing the hill is enough of an accomplishment. Don't try to make it even more difficult. Lash everything down and check all seat belts. If you've got a stick shift, let the clutch out and go. Don't try to make an automatic transmission out of a clutch—*that's bad driving.* Set a steady pace and stay on the power. If you break traction and the vehicle starts slowing down, don't give it more gas because this will make the tires spin even more violently. Back off the throttle to allow the tires a chance to grip the terrain—not tear it up. Despite your best efforts to keep moving forward, the vehicle comes to a halt before you get to the top of the hill. Don't panic. Apply the brakes and clutch and immediately shift to reverse. *Let the clutch out.* Start backing down the hill *with the clutch engaged.* Don't try anything tricky like turning around or finding a new path on the side of the hill. Keep in mind if the brakes are locked, the front wheels won't steer. So stop short of a locked-brake situation.

You can safely drive down a hill far too steep to climb. Generally the same principles apply. Pick the straightest path you can. Let the clutch out and keep it out. Always stay on the rolling side of having your brakes completely locked up. Just as we advocated backing off the throttle when breaking traction going uphill, we now suggest you back off the brakes when starting to slide downhill. This is against all of your driving instincts but if you are to become a skillful off-roader you must convince yourself that backing off the brakes and keeping the clutch fully engaged is the right way to go downhill. Always be alert to the brakes locking up. Listen for the sound of a wheel sliding instead of turning. When you hear that, get off the brakes until the wheels are rolling again.

Many experienced drivers dig in on purpose in this situation to wait until the dust clears and then back down. Keep in mind there are some hills you just can't climb—and this was one of them.

Between the Blazer and the background is 1,500 feet of unforgiving Mexican terrain. It is wise to know your ability as a driver and mechanic before playing King of the Mountain.

The other side of the little hill is steep enough to pull the left rear tire off the ground on this CJ5 and anyone with a winch hanging off the end of a bumper dug the winch in plenty hard—and that can get expensive.

This one was tricky. Hill required a real head of steam to get up, direction of travel was directly in the sun, hill broke off sharply at the top. Here a driver has crested the hill, gulped, slammed on the brakes locking them up. The combination lifted a rear wheel off the ground, killed the engine which in turn cancelled the power steering. Fun, huh?

Going down can get even trickier than going up at times . . . get it into a low gear, four-wheel drive and keep your foot off the clutch.

SIDEHILLS AND HOW TO KEEP THE SHEET METAL INTACT

Wondering why in the world a safe, sane, prudent driver would need a rollbar in an off-road vehicle quickly changes to wondering if the bar is strong enough once you get a vehicle sideways on the side of a hill. Nothing will make your throat dry, your knuckles white and put your sphincter into the pucker mode quite as fast as getting sideways on a hill. Being on the high side of the vehicle is bad but being on the downhill side can make a stevedore stop cursing long enough to start praying.

If you are a novice off-roader, you will think the hill is getting a lot steeper as you go up. When you are an old hand at getting unstuck and climbing hills you will think the hill is not getting any steeper when it actually is. A roll-over is scary. It can be very expensive. A collapsing roof, shattering glass and whatnot can hurt plenty and sometimes kill. Getting sideways on a hill commands respect.

First of all you should know there are some neat little devices which will tell you how steep the hill actually is while you are driving it. They are all inexpensive and sold at most off-road supply stores. The Grade and Tilt Indicator by Trueline shows both grade of hill *and* side tilt in degrees. The Tilt-O-Meter gives degrees as well as percent of grade. The Lev-O-Gage shows the hill in degrees only. Any of the three are under 10 bucks and all of them tell you what you want to know. Install them per instructions—vehicle dead level, etc.—and then follow the manufacturer's advice on how to calculate the turnover angle of your vehicle. If you figure the turnover angle to be 29 degrees, I'd mark the indicator with tape at about 27 degrees and keep an eye peeled on the instrument while chugging around the side of a hill. Just keep in mind the indicators—any of them—are just that— they indicate. That means you have to exercise some judgment. Twenty-seven degrees can go to 30 degrees pretty quickly if a wheel on the high side encounters a nice size rock.

Keep a nice steady pace when driving a sidehill. This is one place to resist stabbing the gas. You must keep in mind the load is on the downhill side. The downhill wheels are doing the driving. If you stab it and she sinks, the ragged edge could turn into ragged sheet metal. When the screaming from the passengers gets to you, get out of the

This is a plenty steep hill. The driver hit the brakes too hard, locked up the wheels and now the rear end is starting to come around. Keep it pointing straight downhill and moving slowly. Wheels must be turning to be steered.

situation by turning downhill. Guys failing to turn downhill use up rollbars.

Every hill is different and each demands a different feel. Be prudent.

Sidesloping is a cat of a different color. In sidesloping you use the centrifugal force of the vehicle to hold you against the side of a hill the vehicle could not ordinarily climb. This is great fun and rather spectacular in a great bowl of sand. A vehicle will drive into the bowl, head for the bottom and then slowly start building up speed by running around the inside of the bowl. While building up speed, the vehicle is also brought up to the upper edge of the bowl. Because of the speeds needed to achieve the result don't even think of doing this in anything other than sand. Make sure everyone understands the rules of this game before playing. All vehicles had better be moving in the same direction!

This is fun. But work up to high-speed side-sloping gradually by getting a feel for the vehicle and the sand on smaller dunes. If things feel shaky, point it downhill and stand on the gas.

If you invest in any sort of device to let you know how steep the hill is—put it where you can read it in a hurry. This Lev-O-Gage is in a good location.

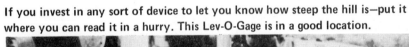

Vehicle construction, weight, center of gravity, speed and terrain are just some of the factors that determine when you roll over. When the Lev-O-Gage indicates close to 30 degrees, I find an excuse to turn down hill and get out of the situation.

HOW STEEP WAS THAT HILL AGAIN?

Off-roaders are always bragging about that steep hill they climbed when no one else could, and making great statements about how steep the grade was. "You wouldn't have believed it." Maybe you shouldn't! Listen carefully to these claims because *two* terms are used to express how *bad* the hill was: (1) percentage of grade or (2) number of degrees to the slope. Many times the storytellers get percent and degrees all mixed up . . . even interchanging them without realizing they aren't supposed to do that.

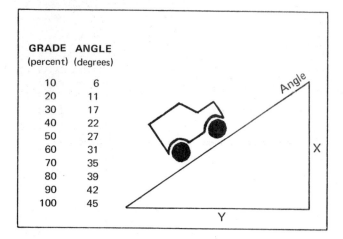

GRADE (percent)	ANGLE (degrees)
10	6
20	11
30	17
40	22
50	27
60	31
70	35
80	39
90	42
100	45

If X is 20 feet and Y is 20 feet, the *grade* is 20/20 = 1.00 = 100% grade. The *angle* is 45 degrees. If X is 30 feet and Y is 50 feet, the grade is 30/50 = 0.60 = 60%. The angle is 31 degrees. If your off-roading friends start transposing terms or figures around without giving this some thought, you'll be expressing percentage of grade figures describing hills which just can't be negotiated from a standstill . . . unless you approach them from the top to go *downhill*.

Those who are not experienced always estimate the grade to be larger than it actually is. Virtually all boondocking is done on grades of less than 60%—except for severe competition hill climbs.

Coincidentally, grade percentage is mathematically equal to the minimum coefficient of friction required to traverse the grade with pure friction—which means no running start. Those who speak of traversing a 100% grade are talking about achieving a coefficient of friction of 1.0. This is impossible to achieve in dirt and sand without paddle-wheel tires and/or momentum— a running start. The true gradability of a vehicle is measured by its ability to stop and start again on a given slope.

GRAB A LOWER GEAR

With the silky-smooth automatic transmissions in the cars we drive back and forth to work, the connection between engine and rear axle often seems to be somewhere in the vapors. The engine loafs along, there is no vibration and we rarely if ever depend on the transmission to help us slow down. Don't carry this thinking with you out in the boonies. We could almost make a blanket rule here to the effect that when in doubt—grab a lower gear, even with an automatic. Low gear—KEEP YOUR FOOT OFF THE CLUTCH—will allow you to crawl along nice and easy. This is easy on your equipment and allows you to concentrate on where all of the wheels are and where they are going. Even a puny little four-banger engine provides an immense amount of braking power if you will just let it by getting that gear box down to the lowest gear. When going uphill or crawling through sand, mud or snow, lower gears keep the engine from lugging. Let the engine run free. Don't punish it!

All of this discussion about brakes, gearing and keeping the clutch engaged applies equally to two- and four-wheel-drive vehicles. If your vehicle is equipped with an automatic transmission, you're home free in the clutch department. You should drop to a lower gear in the automatic just as soon— if not sooner—with the automatic than with the stick-shift. Using a lower gear in an automatic increases the fluid flow between cooler and trans and prevents excessive heat buildup in the automatic. Excessively hot oil shortens the life of seals and clutch material in an automatic—drop to a lower gear and fight the problem. I'm assuming you have an auxiliary cooler for the transmission.

ROCKS: LARGE HARD ONES

If you are driving over rock(s) you might be inclined to hit it "just kinda on the edge." Don't be inclined. If you know you are going to hit a rock—at slow speed or fast—hit it *squarely* with the tread of the tire. The tread area of a modern tire can take tremendous punishment but the tire sidewall and wheel rim can fail instantly. We don't mean to imply you should go around looking for rocks to drive over but if you have a choice between hitting it squarely, letting it high-center you or glance off the sidewall, hit it squarely.

If you are picking your way through rocks with a stick-shift vehicle, put it in low or low-low

Work that tire pressure down until you get this kind of bulge in the sidewall. Run it easy and the tires and vehicle will last a long time.

Only fifty more feet to the "freeway." This kind of running is plenty rough on tires, wheels and body panels. Stay a dozen yards or so away from the other vehicle when running this stuff. Someone may need to back up and take another cut at a section. The following vehicle might not find it so easy to get out of the way.

Slow, slow, slow and if a big mean one looks like it wants to eat a skid plate, don't be ashamed to move it. Make the passenger earn his keep by keeping you posted on what you can't see.

You're not after momentum in this situation. Stop to look at the next ten feet. Decide where you plan to put the tires for maximum traction and minimum risk of damage to the vehicle.

Low gear, low range and if you have an automatic trans so much the better for a slow, steady pull. If a canyon is new to you, keep an eye open for turnaround areas—backing out in this terrain is only so much fun.

This stuff messes up mag wheels something fierce! Even the amateur can move around in this terrain with a good 4WD—keep your foot off the clutch and pick your moves carefully.

4WD, get off the clutch and creep. Let the gears not only take you up the rocks but also take you down by using the engine's compression as a brake. One of the most difficult things for a novice off-roader to learn in a stick-shift vehicle is to keep from depressing the clutch at every opportunity. So you kill the engine once in a while. So restart it, get moving and *keep your fat foot off the clutch.*

With an automatic transmission things work a little different coming off a big rock. The automatic will let you creep up the rock nice and slow, but when the tire starts coming down it will do so in a hurry. The automatic is simply not as good as a stick shift tranny when used as a brake. There is certainly no problem in driving rocks with an automatic—just keep the left foot touching the brake pedal and ready for use when coming down a rock.

If you are picking your way down a wash littered with basketball-size stuff that moves around on you as you drive from one rock to another, make a passenger earn his beer by getting

out and guiding you from rock to rock. This can save a lot of time and sometimes equipment.

Making U-turns in a sheer-sided box canyon littered with "big uns" is easier said than done. Before getting all of the way in there, keep in mind you want to come out. Backing out is even less fun than trying to turn around. If the terrain is all new to you, consider walking it first or getting the passenger to do it for you. Like the rest of off-road driving, rock work takes practice and confidence—confidence in the vehicle and in your driving ability.

A skillful driver can pick his way over rocks at crawling speed to the delight of those awaiting their turn at the fun. The secret is to know where all of the wheels are and where they are all going to be in the next several feet. Having one wheel completely off the ground by six inches is of no concern in one location but could spell certain high-centering in another. Only hours of practice will give you a feeling of confidence about your vehicle and your ability as a driver.

SAND

As you are bound to find out on your own, there is sand and *there is sand*. How you drive in it—on it?—depends greatly on the sand and on the vehicle. First, let's look at sand. Moist or wet sand like that on or near the beach may be damp just on the surface—or it may be wet and hard-packed. If it is the latter, then driving on this hard-packed surface won't be much different than running down a paved street. If the moisture is a mere crust over a dry-sand base, then you might as well be driving on dry sand. If the moisture extends only an inch or so, the weight of the vehicle will break the tires through the crust. In a case such as this, inflation pressure should be adjusted for dry-sand running. The moist sand we've encountered packs much like snow, has a firm base and offers no real problem for either two- or four-wheel-drive vehicles. Dry sand is a different matter *entirely*.

Dry sand is far more complicated to negotiate successfully than wet sand. Let us assume for the moment you do not have an 1800-pound, 350-horsepower, four-wheel-drive vehicle with 12-inch-wide wheels and $375 worth of the latest sand tires. If you had all of this, you wouldn't have any trouble driving in sand! Let's say you've got a 10-year-old six-cylinder, one-wheel drive—no limited-slip—pickup and you are primarily concerned with not getting stuck while hauling a couple of dirt bikes back into the desert. That's where it's really at—not getting stuck! Never mind about fuel-burning, 200 mph, double-throw-down sand drag-sters. Not getting stuck means a cold beer while sitting on the tailgate—instead of an hour-long shovelling session.

There are a couple of very obvious "secrets" to driving in sand. Time and again we've violated these secrets—and gotten stuck. Our usual lame excuse, "I really didn't think I'd get stuck," doesn't hold much water—or help—when you are stuck. *Maintain momentum!* Eyeball the terrain from *solid* ground. Figure out where you want to go and the best way to get there without getting stuck. Avoid sharp turns and anything which might require braking.

Be dune-savvy before getting in over your head. Portion of the dune in the shadow is super loose and very steep. Lighter part generally consists of gentle slopes and is rather well packed. Just keep it in mind when breaking over the edge.

If you're careful you can take a four-wheel drive vehicle down a grade as steep as sand will stack. Just keep in mind that getting the vehicle sideways is very hazardous to your health. If rear end begins to swing around, straighten vehicle by applying a little throttle.

This is the deep Mexican silt you've probably heard a lot about. Don't run in this stuff any faster than you have to; there can be holes in it large enough to break an axle or frame if vehicle speed is up. You can't see 'em until it's too late.

In a way this says it all for constant attention to maintenance. That dust will work into places you didn't even know there were places. Take care of your vehicle and it will most likely take care of you in situations like this.

This is an aggressive tread tire chewing up the silt with a lot of drama but not much forward movement. Durned if I wouldn't find something a little harder to drive on.

Back up, get a running start and maintain momentum. Whether you are on a little-used, sandy back road or you are truly off-road negotiating some dunes, drive heads up, figure out where you are going and maintain momentum.

With momentum, a 5000-pound pickup with one-wheel drive and 35 pounds' pressure in the tires can cross a sandy wash that from a standing start would otherwise take half the tire pressure, twice the tread area and four-wheel drive. Once the vehicle stops moving *forward* and starts moving *downward*, consider yourself stuck and *GET OFF THE GAS*.

Whether you have two-wheel-drive or four-wheel-drive, consider the following *before* you back out of the driveway. Shove a good pair of work gloves in the glove compartment. Throw a strong shovel in the bed of the truck. Unless you are a glutton for punishment, bypass the folding GI-type fox-hole digger. Select a shovel you can handle with muscle. If you've got room for a contractor's shovel with a long handle, haul it along— they don't rattle any more than a short shovel. If you get stuck—and it's just a matter of time—don't expect the guy in the trick four-wheeler to pull you out with his tow strap. Why should he carry a tow strap or a shovel? Chances are he'd pull you out though if *you* had a strap.

If you carry a double-handful of newspapers in your vehicle you can stuff them under the tires and drive up on top again. It's worth trying anytime it looks like you have a massive shovelling job ahead of you. You can put the newspapers

Hill climbing contests have become very competitve and have produced some rather specialized 4WD equipment over the past several years. Tire technology, keenly tuned engines and driver savvy are all part of the competitve fun.

Paddle-tread sand tire is typical of speciality tires available for specific terrain. These tires are used by those who drag race or hill climb in sand.

Angle into a ditch or wash; don't attack it at 90 degrees as the driver of this Bronco did. Bumper digs in, rear wheels unload and front ones tend to dig a hole, skid plate hangs up on the edge of the entrance bank. Bad news!

Running fast enough in the rough to get the axles off the ground is part of the game in off-road racing—just make sure you have the heavy-duty suspension pieces to cope with this sort of loading, otherwise you'll be walking home as a sadder but wiser off-roader.

Another tactic to avoid. Driver was going very fast, saw gully too late and slammed on the brakes. All wheels are locked-up and suspension is in a bind from the braking torque. Suspension should be relaxed when bumps or ruts are hit. This is very hard on all suspension components.

under the seat, under your tool box or wherever to keep them from blowing away or getting in the way. Incidentally, they have to be dry to work for this purpose.

Being stuck in sand without a shovel, with one-wheel drive, no other vehicle in sight and no promise of one before the sun sets is very unfunny. You might not laugh about it for days—maybe even weeks. Let's say you are faced with this situation—what do you do? First off, get your head on straight and do the very best job of getting unstuck you can the first time around. If you don't, the vehicle will only go deeper. With no shovel, moving enough sand to unstick a one-wheel drive passenger car takes a very long time—like an entire day. Very unfunny—especially when you have your family with you.

The plan is to lower pressure on all driving tires. Let the air out until you get a nice fat bulge on the sidewall. Scoop out enough sand with your hands to get a clear view of the sidewall. While you are down on all fours getting dirty, take a look at the underside of the vehicle. If it is hung up on any obstacle or looks like it might get that way when you start moving again figure out how to get the obstacle out of there. If it's all free and clear underneath, jack up both rear wheels one at a time. You've probably dug a nice hole in the sand with a spinning tire. That hole must be filled up. In fact, you can make a nice little mound there.

Use rocks—big ones, wood, newspaper, boards, brush or anything else around to go between tire and sand. Chances are pretty good you have everything you need in the car. Use the floor mats or pull the rubber mat out of the trunk. If you have to walk a hundred yards to bring back some branches or rocks—start walking. Do it right the first time. Get both rear wheels on firm footing. Make the approach to the front and rear of the tires as smooth as possible. Do this around all four tires—not just the rears. Get all of the weight out of the vehicle you possibly can. Now get in and drive out slowly. If you drive off the edge of the mat or board or whatever and promptly get stuck again, you'll have to start all over again with the same process. Cheer up; you are making progress. After all you've gotten unstuck once.

We fully realize the misery of this situation but there ain't no easy way to get unstuck without the proper hardware or outside help.

As soon as you stop moving forward, get out and provide gentle entry and exit ramps for the rear tires. Lower the tire pressure and try again.

Brush, limbs, rocks and even small logs can be used effectively to provide traction in soft terrain. Do the best job you can the first time around.

27

This Land Rover was crossing a riverbed when the water was considerably deeper than shown here. Driver waded to shore, then came back for the digging out days later. This can be very unfunny when you're miles from nowhere . . . .

. . . . but in this case there was a paved street—complete with bridge—within rock-throwing distance which sort of makes you wonder what he was doing down in the river bed. Hmmmmm?

Never underestimate sand. I have seen the best prepared, most expensive 4WD off-road race cars ever built to conquer Baja stuck right up to the differential covers in sand. High-flotation tires, low pressure and 4WD help a lot but don't think the combination can't be stuck.

I'll tell you a bit about jacks later on in the book. Buy the right kind and carry it whenever you go off-road. And remember that a long plank can be your salvation when it comes to getting unstuck.

SOAKED SAND OR QUICKSAND

Being a country bumpkin brought up in the land of the cacti and horny toad I'm not sure I know what quicksand is. As I recall I saw a lot of it in those old B-grade movies on Saturday afternoon where I nearly went blind sitting on the front row. Seems people were always sinking in this great area of oatmeal placed in the middle of their jungle path. The dictionary nails it down pretty good though—a deep mass of loose sand mixed with water into which heavy objects sink. Just like the movies.

I've encountered some of this stuff in Baja in the tidewater area adjacent to a beach. The sand was soaked with water—a far cry from just

being wet sand. Due to the location—near the ocean, and some just-under-the-surface water table, the sand never dried out to the point it could be called wet. No sir, it was soaked sand—or quicksand. It took me about 15 seconds in a 1300-pound Volkswagen to go from 40 mph to come to a complete stop on the floorpan. It took close to an hour for two 4WD vehicles to get that VW out of that mess. I can tell you no jack could be used in that bog. No traction mat could have helped. Any hole created by a shovel was quickly filled with water which smelled like the back end of a fish cannery.

About all I can tell you about soaked sand/quicksand is avoid it. If you do encounter it, go for help—a lot of help.

I understand a similar situation exists in Alaska in certain low areas when things start to thaw out. The word is simple—stay out of there.

DON'T BE AN IDIOT

A $10,000 4WD with every option and accessory known to man *is not invincible.* By now I am fully convinced anything one man is smart enough to build, another man and nature can either stick or break. One klutz can get so buried that a heads-up guy with a 4WD and winch can't get it unstuck.

There are times when a hard charge will get you through mud or water where you would get stuck otherwise. Don't make a practice of this though. When all of this weight comes back down, spindles can bend, axle tubes sag and frames go south. These repairs don't come cheap—on anything.

Sticky mud indicates a high clay content. It is very, very slippery. Keep a slow and steady speed when running this gumbo or you'll be off the road and into the ditch in short order.

Guaranteed to make a female passenger scream—and the driver groan when the engine starts to miss. Skip this kind of fun unless you have a waterproof ignition.

Don't try this with just any LUV! Jumping most any truck at speed is bound to break or bend something unless special work has been done to beef up the suspension.

If the trail is washed out, the trail is washed out. Two bucks worth of cheap whisky and a mad charge most always creates a problem—not a solution. Every vehicle we've ever driven was equipped with a reverse gear. If you just have to prove something—try proving you know how to find reverse once in a while. Get the point?

HIGHWAY DRIVING IN THE WET

You might think it more than just a little odd that we would include anything in this volume about driving on the highway—even a wet one. You have to be in trouble on wet pavement in an off-road rig to get a true appreciation of what this is all about. Hopefully we'll give you some appreciation so you won't have to experience the it's-all-over-now feeling.

Chances are any 4WD rig you're apt to drive weighs as much or more and has a higher center of gravity than whatever you normally drive on the highway. The wheelbase is probably shorter and due to gear you're carrying and heater/defroster design, visibility is not as good. Starting to get the picture?

The plan is to cool it. A brown or green Jeep with a tan top spotted here and there with mud can be pretty difficult to see when visibility drops

and colors start blending with grey. Turn on your lights, even in the daytime. City slickers ought to do this too. Sure makes a vehicle easier to see. Fog on the inside of windows has a way of sneaking up on you and covering all of the glass. Don't let it. Turn on the windshield blower at the first sign of fog and crack the side glass to eliminate fog on the back and side windows. All of this may sound like telling someone snow is cold. But, with a rig full of kids and you trying to read a map while driving, it's easy to overlook the obvious! Visibility is of prime concern in any type of wet-weather driving.

Off-road rigs with big fat tires are prime candidates for hydroplaning. This interesting and very hazardous phenomenon occurs when the tires lose contact with the road surface and actually ride on a layer of water. If the road is completely covered with water ¼-inch or more deep and you're moving more than 35 miles an hour, you could be in trouble. Steering and stopping control can be non-existent when the tires are hydroplaning. Only one driver needs to get in trouble and a long string of cars can follow. The plan is to put plenty of distance between you and the next vehicle. Regardless of whether you are going or coming from an outing, remember that it is far better to be John Doe, late—than the late John Doe.

DRIVING IN THE SNOW

Regardless of how much you paid for your rig—whether 2WD or 4WD, regardless of trick tires and chains, just figure you are going to get stuck in the snow when you go out for a wintry cruise. This much you should *assume.* Now you can prepare for the run and have fun. You won't be able to keep up with snowmobiles—but you can go pretty far.

The key to forward progress in the snow is called *momentum.* Get moving and *keep moving.* Select one of the lower gears to allow the engine to work comfortably in the power range without screaming along at high RPM. You may have to experiment with low-range/second-gear and with high-range/second-gear if you have a four-wheeler. Just which gear is the right one depends on engine, gearing, tires, depth of snow, how fast you want to travel, etc. The point is to select the gear that feels comfortable to you and the vehicle and stay in it. Move steadily. Slipping and sliding just means you

One vehicle hangs back while the other checks out part of the spring thaw. Muddy water sure looks cold to me. Photo courtesy of Jim Hanna.

are not making progress and could be headed for trouble.

Limit your snow driving to back roads or terrain you are very familiar with. Snow has a neat way of drifting around and hiding items like a three-foot hole or a frozen creek. More than one four-wheeler has had to hike out and leave his rig stuck until the snow melted or he could talk someone into pulling him out.

Drive the crown of the road. Stay away from ditches. Take the high side on a banked road. Don't just slam on the brakes; make sure you can get moving again from wherever you stop. Pick a bare place on the road or at the top of a rise. Do more than just a little thinking before starting a downhill charge in fresh snow.

If you are plowing through deep drifts, stop every mile or so and open the hood. Snow has a way of packing up and it can create some problems like melting and shorting out wiring. After a while you'll be able to tell how you are doing not only by the progress you are making but by the sounds

For really tough going in snow and mud you should put chains on all four wheels, but if you only have one set—put them on the front. Photo courtesy of Jim Hanna.

the snow makes against the vehicle. If you are running through the deep stuff listen or "feel" for anything that might tell you the wheels are breaking through but the frame is not—which could lead to a high-centered situation. This is the sort of thing that comes with experience so you might as well start working on it.

Never set a parking brake in freezing weather—it might just stay that way when water in and around the cable freezes. If you are headed uphill and start slipping, turn the wheels—first to the left and then to the right as you continue to apply the power. This helps give you a new bite up front. This works pretty good with 4WD—but is of no help to the 2WD vehicle. Drive down a hill; never coast down. Make slow, deliberate moves on ice. If you are driving on an ice and snow covered road, remember snow has a great deal of resistance and will require some amount of throttle to get through. Ice, on the other hand, offers little resistance. If you are driving from a drift onto a sheet of ice on an asphalt or concrete road; get off the power in a hurry. When driving on ice, don't attempt the impossible. If you don't have studded tires or chains, ice on a road can just be impossible for the normal vehicle—even 4WD—to negotiate.

Give even more thought to your snow driving when the sun has been out for several days and melting is obviously under way. If you are on a road that hugs the side of a southward facing slope

the road could give way in a mud slide or you could be surprised by falling into a deep crack cut in the mud by running water under the snow.

When you are running through slush in freezing temperatures, check under the vehicle for ice buildup. It can put a steering arm or tie rod in a bind when the buildup is severe.

If you don't have a winch, pack a flat-necked shovel to get between the vehicle and a low spot. Also bring along an ax. With an ax you can cut enough brush and small trees to get under the tires if you get stuck—so pack one for a run in the snow if you don't have a winch.

One closing thought on all of this just before you slam the door and take mama and the kiddos for a ride in the snow. If you got stuck up there in the afternoon and couldn't get help—do you have enough warm clothing, sandwiches and hot chocolate to keep everyone comfortable until tomorrow noon? Give it some thought. This sort of thing can lead to terrible discomforts and outright sorrow if you haven't kept your head straight about the possible dangers and problems you could get into.

RUST CITY AND GOODBYE JEEP

From time to time when I camp out on the beach I see guys getting into the shallow part of the surf with a vehicle—plowing along in six to ten inches of water. This makes a nifty sight and brings forth a lot of screams—delight, panic, disgust, I dunno—from the occupants getting sprayed.

I can't get excited about running the ocean for two reasons. Salt water rusts the sheet metal like you can't believe; it causes electrical problems, shorts out the ignition and generally corrodes everything but solid oak. That kind of misery I don't need. If the vehicle stalls in the water from a drenched ignition you can expect the surf to slowly but surely start taking sand out from under those SuperWide-TractionExpensive Tires mounted on GenuineMag-TypeRacer Wheels and sink that mutha right up to the floorboard while you are trying to dry out the ignition and run for help at the same time. This is funny? You may never *start* laughing.

If you do get into the surf by accident or design and want to get the salt off the underside, place a sprinkler hose under the vehicle as soon as you get home and let it run for several hours. If you do get in the surf and get stuck, find help fast; your chances of making it out by yourself are just about zero or less.

TOWING AND PUSHING

Sooner or later you'll be in an off-road situation where one vehicle will be needed to get another moving again. Maybe one vehicle refuses to fire or maybe it is stuck and the traction and power offered by another vehicle is needed. There's rarely a problem with one vehicle assisting another—unless someone gets in the act who does not think or there is a mix-up on what is to be done.

Unless the terrain is very flat and smooth—such as a well packed beach, pushing is an absolute bummer·off-road. Front and rear sheet metal and bumpers can get ruined and you can lock two vehicles together when pushing. If one vehicle is stuck, another one pushing will probably get stuck. The only thing worse than having one vehicle stuck is having two of them locked together—*both* stuck. Don't push—there's got to be a better way.

There are several varieties of tow strap around —and they are the hot tip for towing. Some are rated at 10,000 pounds and you'll need that strength if you've got a tough job to do. Attach the ends of the tow strap to some part of the chassis—NOT THE SUSPENSION! If there is no easy place to hook the strap and it must be wrapped about something for an anchoring point, make sure the strap will not be severed by a sharp metal edge. A nylon tow strap allows the vehicle doing the towing to get in motion. This multiplies the pulling

force by as much as three times that which could be generated from a dead stop. The stretch of the strap absorbs the major portion of all that jolting shock load.

A chain is heavy and hard to carry and putting a tow cable in most vehicles is also very unfunny. Don't be a hardhead, tow with a strap designed for the purpose.

Both drivers should talk the situation over. Make durn sure you know what *he* is going to do and have it planted in your mind what *you* are going to do. Regardless of which vehicle you are in take a look at which way the front wheels on your vehicle are turned. Do you want them turned? For minimum resistance to the terrain, you don't. But in some situations it might be advantageous to have them turned. Feeling where the wheels are pointing is next to impossible when you are really stuck. The towed vehicle should be placed for maximum tractive effort and safety. If at all possible, tow with the front of the vehicle. This way the driver of the towing vehicle can have a clear view of the situation instead of trying to turn around in the seat, or hang halfway out a door and still not have a good view of it all.

I don't particularly like to have anyone in the vehicle when I'm doing any towing or being towed. Concentrate on the situation—I ain't interested in some six-year old's assessment of the trouble or some four-year old's request to go to the bathroom. Sometimes, weight is needed to gain traction and you'll have to ask for the help— but remind them they are there to add weight— not quarterbacking.

Vehicles involved in towing don't always go straight as a string and for this reason all spectators should be moved back—way back.

If you are towing someone out of a stuck situation at night and there are several vehicles around, experiment with using the lights from other vehicles to illuminate the area instead of having headlights from the two vehicles involved shining directly in the drivers' eyes. If this is not possible, try just turning on some parking lights. Decide all of this before starting the tow. Talk it over. Plan your moves.

Are you going to be able to accomplish your objective in one tow? Talk it over. Maybe the plan is to straighten the towed vehicle with one yank, relocate the towing vehicle and pull again to do the unsticking. Is there a danger the vehicle being yanked out will overtake the towing vehicle? Talk it over. Figure out where you want to go and what the problems are in getting there. A stuck vehicle being towed should be fired up and put in gear to help the towing vehicle get out of the situation. A small application of power will do nicely; a shower of rocks and mud usually helps to make a bad situation worse.

Towing a vehicle to get it started is a shaky situation at best. Put as much distance between the two vehicles as possible by using extra straps, ropes or chains. Because you can't start a modern automatic transmissioned vehicle by towing, you'll be dealing with stick-shift vehicles for this. The driver of the towed vehicle will have to let out the clutch and work the throttle to get his beast fired off, then will have to keep from running over the guy that got him started. Don't slam on the brakes of the towed vehicle either or the slack in the strap will disappear and the towing vehicle will come to a very abrupt halt. Once the towed vehicle comes to life, blow the horn. At this point the towing vehicle can start to slow—but not brake. This gives both drivers a chance to reduce speed gradually.

For towing to get started, start with the strap tight, for towing to get unstuck start with the strap just barely touching the ground. Towing to get started seems awful ridiculous to me because I always carry jumper cables to eliminate all the hoorah of getting a dead engine lighted off again.

DRIVING TO PROTECT THE ENVIRONMENT

Without getting into all of the how's and why's of the closure of Federal land areas for recreation, the fact remains that vast areas of land are already closed—and more of this is on the way. We feel strongly that all off-roaders should do their part in protecting land still open. To do this takes just a little common sense and very little effort. Lower the tire pressure to provide more of a footprint and thus keep the tracks as shallow as possible. Don't choose the most aggressive tread design in the store. A mild tread and radial construction can provide far more traction than a stiff, aggressive tread design. This combination is not nearly so destructive of the environment, and if you must drive over a small bush, chances are that in a few hours it will spring back and leave little, if any, evidence of your passing. But, if you drive back over the same bush in the opposite direction, chances are very good you will break the bush— which means evidence for years that you were there and didn't care enough to travel a different route. In a wooded area work still harder to drive around small trees and bushes. We know you can knock down the sapling. We can accept that. You don't have to prove established laws of physics to us or anyone else.

Don't go cutting across the middle of a mud flat just to leave tracks. This evidence will remain for years. Why break through the thin desert crust where all can see—including Federal employees checking for such things—when you can drive down a dry wash to reach the same destination?

Doesn't it make sense not to drive across a grassy meadow in the spring? These tracks will appear as an ugly scar until mid-fall. If you want to drive the meadow, do it in the winter—preferably on a blanket of snow.

Trash is becoming an overwhelming environmental problem. The rule here is very simple. IF YOU HAUL IT IN; YOU HAUL IT OUT! To that slogan I would add—ALL OF IT. A hundred years from now mankind will be tripping over the pull tops from aluminum drink cans. Put every scrap of everything in plastic garbage bags and haul it out to the nearest roadside garbage can.

Last but not least—if you have four-wheel drive in your vehicle—use it! Spread the driving force out to four wheels instead of two. Using the front differential does not "hurt it"—if it did we would not have constant four-wheel drive. Four driving wheels leave a lot less impact on the environment than two if those two have to spin and claw and sink down to maintain forward momentum. THINK!

OFF THE ROAD FOR FUN—IN SAFETY

As every camper, Jeeper or woodsman will tell you, there's plenty out there for everyone to enjoy—but first you've got to get there and get back before the real enjoyment soaks in. The inexperienced can get into a lot of trouble—with or without a vehicle—out away from civilization. If you are in the category of the inexperienced, admit it, start learning and begin having fun.

Thought-out, deliberate action coupled with common sense is a very hard combination to beat. Start working on it. For instance, you should know that the vehicle is in excellent mechanical condition before ever leaving home. You should have checked all tires for cuts, gouges or sticks imbedded in the rubber. The battery should be fully charged and the terminals free from corrosion. A small, home-type battery charger is a wise investment and can save a lot of grief. Do you have enough gasoline to take you where you want to go and get back? You'd be surprised at the number of people who run out of gasoline in the middle of nowhere. On the first several outings, whether long or short, keep careful tabs on distance traveled and gas consumed.

As you drive, try to file away small bits of information you may need later. Did you just pass an old campsite? An excellent place to look for a coat hanger or other wire to be used for making repairs! Need a tin can or block of wood? How far back? This can save time and a lot of thrashing around.

Think about creature comforts inside your off-road car. Would a grab bar across the dash be helpful to a passenger? Should the lower edge of the dash be padded? Should the seats be shoved further to the rear? All of this may seem trivial, but when you start banging a knee against a hard steel door and know you have four hundred more miles to go you'll not think it trivial. Seat belts are a must, and not just for the normal safety reasons. They keep you in the seat instead of bouncing and banging around constantly. Buckle 'em up and leave them tight.

If children are to be riding off the road with you, give special thought to their needs. If they are unhappy with the situation, you can bet that you'll be doubly unhappy. Naturally, they like to see what's going on, so make sure they can see where you're taking them. Children should be

As pickups become increasingly popular more attention is being paid to useful accessories—like this double roll bar, extra gas tank and a close fitting tarp which protects gear without bolting on a camper shell.

The owner of this early military Jeep not only constructed a well designed roll cage, but also gave himself the added margin of thick, closed-cell padding over the entire structure.

strapped into place. Figure out where they would go or what will happen if you suddenly slam on the brakes or have to whip sharply to either side. Foam rubber padding in the area of the rear side window of vans or other two-seat trucks might be indicated here.

The prudent move, whether you are experienced or not is to go off the road with another vehicle. This just makes good sense. Four men can move a truck when two men can't budge it. Parts can be borrowed from one vehicle to help another along. The combinations are endless. By sticking with another vehicle, the prospects of having serious trouble are practically nil.

There is one danger, or potential danger, in going off the road with another vehicle. If the driver of the other vehicle is experienced and you are not, you can get into trouble by attempting to keep up. Cool it. When you overextend your-self, the possibilities of a wreck or component breakage reaches a certainty very quickly. Never drive further than you can see. Those who cheat and violate this little rule have to pay for it sooner or later. If you once drive further than you can see—"over your head"—as the saying goes, it only encourages you to do more and more of it. Sooner or later there will be a rock, tree, gully or whatever right where it should not be.

Never be ashamed to stop, get out and walk over a particularly tricky area. You can "feel" out the terrain. Perhaps you can move a rock here or there or check to see if there is a huge hole or rock on the far side of the bush that you had planned to edge around. While you are out of your vehicle, walk around it. Is a tire low? Have you bent a rim? Is a fender torn and will it cut a tire? A small problem now can be a very big problem a little later on.

Commercial air-conditioning insulation can be slit and slipped right over the roll bar tubing to give your noggin' extra protection when the road gets rough and the seat belt is not as tight as it should be. This is called closed-cell insulation—sold under the trade name of Rubatex, Armaflex and Aerotube.

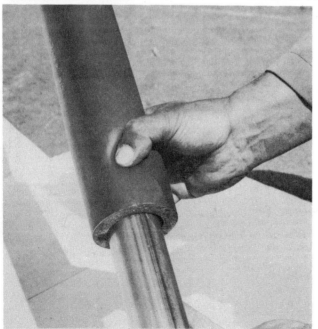

If junior goes along on a short trip in the outback, make sure he is safe and comfortable. Drive extra careful though; if you jerk him around, he can get mighty scared and in turn spoil your fun.

If you take youngsters with you off-road, give more than just passing thought to their comfort and safety. By putting a baby up front like this, mommie can extend a reassuring hand when the riding starts moving his head around.

Running a door strap *and* seat belt is a good idea in a wide open vehicle like this. Bet that rollbar on the knee can smart though.

This rollbar features a plate between the two main bars—a sound plan if you do a lot of sand running. That plate can keep a vehicle from burying in the sand when it gets upside down.

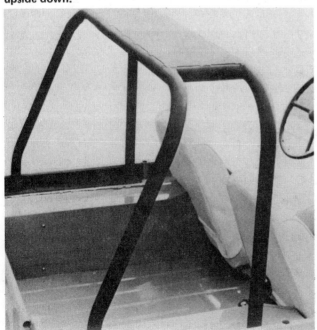

Hauling motorcycles in the back of a pickup off the beaten path can be a scene. Bikes, gas cans, and coolers have a way of beating themselves to death without the proper tie down. Here's a step in the right direction—a rollbar incorporating wheel chocks for three bikes. Sure makes life easier . . . on you and the bikes.

If you spend a lot of time behind the wheel of your rig, you'll appreciate a padded steering wheel—but unless you have power steering don't buy one any smaller in diameter than the stock one.

Some good ideas here. That's a nice out-of-the-way mounting point for the whip antenna. The bumper and gas can rack is sanitary but best of all is that tall, full roll cage.

This console/mini-seat accessory might interest you if you have a bucket-seat arrangement in your present rig. Back folds up or down for arm rest or seat when you have more than one front-seat passenger.

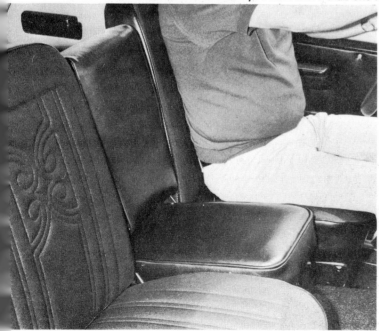

When camping it just makes good sense to place all of the gasoline a considerable distance away from the camp and/or campfire.

With idiots standing around flipping cigarette butts—an overfilled gas tank can provide more excitement than you ever wanted out of life.

A fire extinguisher in the middle of the desert seems pretty silly until you start trying to figure out what you would use to put out a gasoline fire. Mount one in the vehicle and check it frequently to see that it is fully charged.

Failure to tighten lug nuts and keep them that way can mean wheel failure in short order. Notice how the lug nut holes are ovaled. The center has fractured in two places.

If you spend a lot of time driving in desert areas, you would probably appreciate having less glare in your eyes. Painting big hoods flat black has been racing practice for many years. More and more off-roaders are doing this to reduce eye strain. Another lo-buck good idea.

While all of this may be necessary, it should be kept in mind that hardware has a non-funny way of hurting you should the vehicle be involved in a mishap. Cinched-down seat belts and shoulder harnesses must become a way of life if you're serious about remaining in the game.

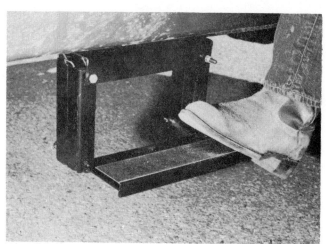

Hickey and other suppliers sell this swing-away step to fit most off-road vehicles. If you are short, have a tall vehicle or a wife who complains about getting in and out, this could be the answer. Regardless—that anti-skid strip attached to the door sill can prevent many a nasty slip.

A shoulder harness used off-road has a way of moving from side to side and chafing the neck. This can become quite painful over a period of time. Here is a neat way of containing the harness strap. Attachment is a grade 8 bolt through a Heim-type joint bolted to the chassis.

Handy mounting for trenching shovel and jack on inside front fender of Dodge Power Wagon. Put space to use under that high hood!

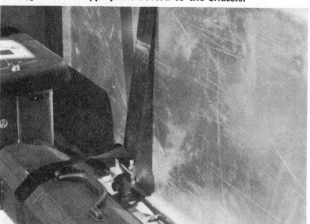

Dick Cepek sells this handy little drill that works off 12 volts. How strong is it? Hang the drill up in metal and the drill motor will twist out of your hand—it's that good.

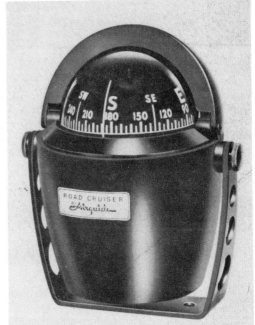

I used to laugh at guys that ran a big old compass on the top of the dash. Course that was before I lost my sense of direction in Death Valley. A compass would have saved me a couple of heartbeats and quite a few miles. I have one now.

One way to fight this is to join a club and prove to the land owners or Feds that you are really worthy of going off-road. The wrong way to fight it is to steal the sign and drive on—next year you'll see a fence here for sure.

. . . yes, and please make up for the idiot who can't read this sign.

AFTER THE TRIP

Part of preparing for the next trip is cleaning off your vehicle and inspecting it thoroughly *immediately* after returning from an off-road trip. The dollar or so you spend at the local quarter car wash is very low-cost insurance. For one thing you get to deposit all of the big clods of dirt and mud on someone else's property instead of your own driveway. Then by the time you get home, the running gear will be dry enough for you to slide under and start inspecting. Are all cotter keys in place? Did you bend a tie rod? Are all bolts tightly holding the steering box to the frame? Does a flexible brake line have a nasty nick in it? Is a steel brake line nearly pinched through? While you are under the vehicle, check the inside sidewall of all the tires—any cuts or blisters? Any oil dripping from the engine? Transmission? Transfer case? Rear axle? All rubber bushings still in the shocks? If you will make a list of all the things that need fixing while you are inspecting the vehicle, it is then just a routine matter to take care of the items one by one in your spare time until they are all taken care of and you are confident about going off-road.

Before heading off to the local "get yourself wet" car wash, pull your safety goggles off the workshop bench. Soap and water bouncing off a wheel or inner fender panel can sting like blue blazes. If you don't have a pair of clear plastic goggles we'd suggest you get a pair at the local hardware store or discount house. These things are not all bad to have on when you are following a vehicle or two in dusty terrain.

Invest your quarters at the local do-it-yourself car wash. Use that high-pressure water with detergent to clean off all the suspension, drive train, etc., so you can figure out what needs attention or fixing before you go back after the deer you missed this trip. Wear safety goggles or glasses to keep the detergent out of your eyes. It stings!

DRIVE TRAIN

If you haven't kept up with automotive developments in the past several years or you are just plain new to vehicles in general, there are several things you should know before spending a lot of time and money modifying an engine to take you off-road.

The best all-around engine for off-road use is one which gives good gas mileage and produces gobs of smooth, low-end torque. The vast majority of aftermarket high-performance parts are not designed for this. With a little help from a sharp and interested parts man at a local dealership you can gather up most of the pieces for a very good engine—regardless of make of vehicle. Avoid trick stuff. Work towards a reasonable goal. Don't buy parts just because you "got a deal" or because Joe

Glotz says it works fine on the truck he races off-road. You want smooth, reliable low-end torque produced by parts that are easy to replace when the time comes.

Engines are far less efficient and for the most part—far less powerful now than they were in the late 1950's and early 1960's. As emission-control laws began tightening up, Detroit resorted to more and more modifications to ensure that the engines would pass the federal test schedule. As a result engines are now low on horsepower, idle roughly and guzzle huge amounts of gasoline. The effect all of this has had on the pollutant level in this country can be argued—will be argued—for many a day to come.

Although it takes a sharp man to do it, modi-

The current recreational/work off-road rigs are pretty rugged as you can see in this view of the Plymouth Trail Duster. Note leaf-spring front suspension and front disc brakes.

fications can be made to improve the horsepower and gas mileage these engines provide—and still meet the federal requirements. Basically, emission control engines perform quite badly because of a great number of interrelated factors built into the engine. Ignition timing is severely retarded with little or no advance until the vehicle is moving along smartly in high gear. Low compression is achieved by the use of dished pistons or large volume combustion chambers in the cylinder head. Camshafts are ground with strange overlap patterns that give the appearance—on paper—of being a racing cam—but they are installed in an engine that will never run fast enough for the camshaft to operate at peak efficiency. Carburetors are designed to idle the engine at a very high rpm, run lean at low speed or while operating in the primary circuit, then run rich in the secondary circuit. A portion of the exhaust is recirculated back into the intake system and the engines operate at higher temperatures than early ones. This is a general explanation of what has been done—specifics vary among the manufacturers.

Remedying the effects of all this is rather time-consuming, can be expensive and in some cases may be illegal. Time, expense and legality of the modifications must be weighed against the goal you've set for the engine. We can tell you rough and dirty what needs to be done to most emission control engines for sharp performance off-road but we can't advise you on costs, legality or make a judgment about your having the skills needed to perform the work. Do some thinking; do some research before tackling the project blindly.

Again—speaking in general terms—a number of things can be done to improve performance and mileage. Some of the modifications are minor; others are quite extensive. For maximum performance and mileage, the mechanical ignition advance curve should start coming in by about 1,000 rpm and be completely in by about 2,400 rpm. Ideally, vacuum-advance should be available in all gears in which the vehicle is being operated. Current production carburetors can be changed to richer jetting on the primary circuit and both mileage and performance will benefit. Normally, bringing the secondary circuit in somewhat sooner than production will also help in both areas. Don't be lured into installing a larger carburetor in hopes

that you'll increase performance and/or mileage— it just doesn't work that way. A larger carburetor kills low-end torque—not what you had in mind, exactly. In most all cases you'll be better off by working with the carb that came on the engine.

After ignition and carburetion are taken care of, you'll have to go to the larger wrenches to effect much of a change in engine performance. A short-duration, high-lift camshaft can help put the torque where you can best use it. The cam change should be accompanied by higher compression— different heads or pistons—for maximum effectiveness. Some of the later aftermarket intake manifolds are designed to increase low-end performance and give better gas mileage. The Edelbrock *Torker* and *Streetmaster* manifolds are two examples.

Doug Roe, who wrote the H. P. Book *Rochester Carburetors,* offers mileage kits for GM-type engines using Rochester Carburetors. The kits are advertised and sold under the name "Perfectune."

A different exhaust system—headers—might help at highway speeds but are of doubtful benefit at the lower off-road speeds. Any exhaust system changes should keep stock mufflers tucked up under the chassis to protect against damage.

As you can now see there is no simple, low-cost, ten-minute fix to turn a late emission-controlled engine into a rip snorter while keeping it reliable, legal and economical. Obviously the vast majority of us off-roaders won't get involved with modifying anything in the engine compartment of our rig—regardless of the course you choose, follow our warnings elsewhere in this book about taking care of your truck and keeping it in the best of tune.

AN ENGINE SWAP FOR YOUR OFF-ROAD RIG?

A good engine swap can upgrade your off-road vehicle and give you power to spare. On the other hand you should realize there is a lot more to an engine swap than meets the eye: A bad engine swap can give nothing but trouble. There are scores of combinations. Engines, transmissions and transfer cases can be juggled around to provide various levels of power, torque and gearing. The question remains—is an engine swap for you?

If you contemplate an engine swap we suggest you secure the catalogs of Novak Enterprises and Advance Adapters Inc. Each catalog costs $1, lists engine, transmission and transfer-case swap hardware along with suggestions on what to and what not to do. These catalogs plus an honest assessment of what you have to gain and lose in the swap is a starting point to getting you the answers needed *before* taking a torch to the existing engine mounts.

Nit-picking, time-consuming items you will have to face and conquer include moving batteries, rewiring and building an exhaust system. All sorts of fabrication problems can come up—moving the radiator or reshaping the firewall are just two examples.

If you contemplate doing the job yourself, make sure you have the necessary skills, knowledge, time and tools to do the job. You are the best judge of that—or you should be. Be honest with yourself—it pays off in the long run. On the other hand, if a shop does the job; make sure the shop is willing to take the time to do the job correctly and make certain you understand what the cost will be before taking the vehicle in and leaving it.

That under-powered but faithful flathead Jeep of yours might start overheating, twisting axles in two and develop strange—and expensive—transfer-case noises if you just bolt in a small-block Chevy. Consider the total package you'll wind up with—not just the parts.

AUTOMATIC TRANSMISSIONS

An automatic transmission in an off-road rig is the neatest thing since sliced bread and highly recommended if available for the vehicle of your choice. Power can be eased to the ground in mud or sand and the vehicle can be gotten out of sticky situations which bury stick-shift vehicles simply because the tires dig in instantly when the driver tries to ease the clutch out—but can't. We will concede an automatic puts more load on the brakes in a downhill situation where the engine would normally provide braking in low gear. This is far outweighed by your being able to ease over the roughest terrain and be very gentle to the entire vehicle by a smooth application of power. Protected by a skid plate, an automatic transmission will normally last as long as a stick-shift tranny. Ring and pinion and axle breakage is al-

A transmission oil cooler is a wise investment for a vehicle equipped with an automatic transmission. This may not be the best mounting location in the world but careful driving has kept brush and rocks from puncturing the cooler during several years of constant use.

most unheard of with an automatic due to the lack of jerk in the entire drive train . . . even though there's a jerk stabbing the throttle.

A worthwhile option for the automatic is a heavy duty oil cooler. Normally, automatic transmission fluid is cooled by routing it through a core in the lower tank of the radiator. More efficient cooling is obtained by directing the fluid to a small radiator mounted somewhere near the front of the vehicle in a stream of cool air, normally in front of the water radiator. Several firms manufacture quality kits—check Suppliers List—which are worthwhile additions to any vehicle with an automatic. Most manufacturers now offer an auxiliary transmission oil cooler as an option — something to keep in mind when ordering a new vehicle. You will be hard pressed to beat the price or the quality. Keeping the fluid temperature down in the neighborhood of 200 degrees greatly extends the life of an automatic. Without an auxiliary cooler, temperatures will soar to well over 300 degrees in slow desert going. For your own peace of mind, install a direct-reading—non-electrical—oil-temperature gauge onto your automatic—regardless of the type cooler employed.

Use low range in the transfer case as much as possible with an automatic when you are in slow going situations. Component strain is less and oil temperature is subsequently lower.

LOCKING HUBS

Locking—also called free-running or free-wheeling—hubs are probably the most popular accessories for four-wheel-drive vehicles. On some 4WDs, the hubs are standard. The hubs are manufactured and sold by several firms. Trade names include Power-Lock, Lockomatic and Dual-matic as a few examples. Without a set of hubs—one for each front wheel—front axles, ring and pinion gears and front drive shaft all rotate as the vehicle is being driven in two-wheel drive. When the locking hubs are unlocked or in the "free" position, none of this gear rotates and according to advertising—and those with a vested interest in selling hubs—this cuts down on front-end wear, tire wear, increases gas mileage and makes the vehicle easier to steer in two-wheel drive.

To engage four-wheel drive, the vehicle is stopped, a part of the exposed hub is rotated or otherwise manipulated to "lock" the hub to the axle. Then four-wheel drive is selected at the transfer case. When returning to two-wheel drive, the vehicle is stopped, hubs placed in the unlocked or "free" position and the transfer case is taken out of four-wheel drive.

If you run in rocks—and run hard—or run in water or mud and are sloppy about maintenance, hubs can give you trouble. Rocks can damage them and water or mud can jam them in either position. The hubs should not be blamed for either problem. Prudent driving in the rocks and regular maintenance will sidestep all of this.

Quite frankly, we can't tell the difference in gas mileage, ease of steering or tire wear with or without locking hubs. As to the argument about reducing wear of the running gear, we only opine that we simply can't remember the last time we wore out a ring and pinion or axle in the *rear* end of a four-wheeler and they stay in gear constantly. One experienced off-roader friend will not install hubs on the front of his Wagoneer which spends 75% of its miles on pavement. His argument that when he wants four-wheel drive, he wants it *right now*, holds more than just a little water.

You should know that thousands of sets of

Locking hubs are just downright useless unless you lock them when you put 'er in 4WD. Some hubs are a little stiff and require Vise-Grips or pliers to turn them in to place. Putting the vehicle in neutral and rocking it slightly will make them snap right in place most of the time.

Become familiar with the locking hub operation of a 4WD vehicle before you leave the dealer's lot. Several are offered and all are just a bit different. This particular hub is in the free-wheel F position. Arrow must align with dot near L to lock hub.

hubs are in service and that their usage is the rule and not the exception. Hubs do speed up adjusting the front brakes and they do allow faster and more accurate balancing of front tires and wheels.

Some locking hubs are easier than others to engage and disengage. Ideally, they can be manipulated with the twist of your fingers. If one or both of the hubs is balky, place the vehicle in neutral and rock it back and forth while attempting to rotate the hub until it locks—or unlocks. We have experienced units which could only be manipulated with a pair of pliers or vise-grips. Depending on the brand and the vehicle they're to go on, a set of hubs generally costs less than $75.

A TRANSFER CASE IT IS; MAGIC IT AIN'T

If you are new to off-roading, you may have a little trouble with the term *transfer case*—not in pronouncing it—just in getting a grasp as to what it is and does. The transfer case is another gear box attached to the rear of the regular transmission—be it stick-shift or automatic.

The transfer case sends some power to the rear wheels and some to the front wheels when 4WD is engaged. Several transfer-case designs are

For the uninitiated, this is a locking hub. This one is an International Harvester unit; others have a similar appearance with arrows and "LOCK," "UNLOCK" or "FREE" showing.

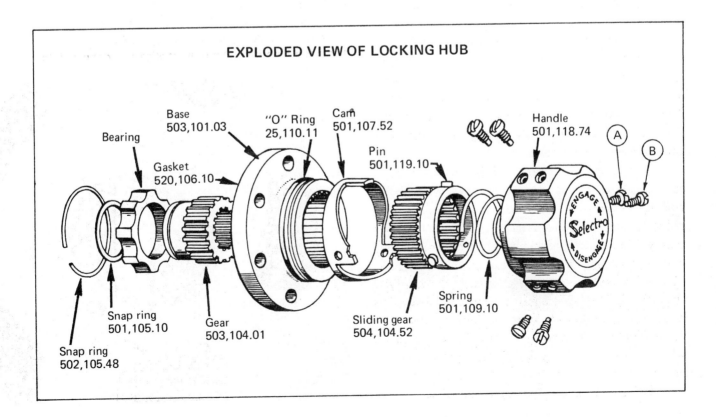

EXPLODED VIEW OF LOCKING HUB

Bearing

Base 503,101.03

Gasket 520,106.10

"O" Ring 25,110.11

Cam 501,107.52

Pin 501,119.10

Handle 501,118.74

(A) (B)

Snap ring 501,105.10

Gear 503,104.01

Sliding gear 504,104.52

Spring 501,109.10

Snap ring 502,105.48

found in the run-of-the-mill four-wheel-drive vehicles you will encounter if you do a lot of off-roading.

Older vehicles like military-vintage Jeeps and Dodge Power Wagons have all sorts of levers sprouting from the floor—enough to scare a novice out of trying to drive one. Actually, they are pretty simple. One lever is for the regular transmission. Another is used to engage the front axle; in other words, to get into four-wheel-drive. A third lever lets you select between the two speeds of the transfer case. Because this is the most complicated type of transfer case for the novice to drive, let's put one of the old military jobs through the weeds for a minute. Let's say you are sailing down the highway in third gear. The front-axle drive lever is in OUT. The transfer-case lever is in LOW. What all this means is that you are in two-wheel drive because the front-axle drive lever is in the OUT position, that is, meaning OUT of drive. You pull off the highway and start across a field. Things feel a little greasy underfoot due to a recent rain so you decide to stop playing Joe Hero and go to four-wheel drive. Depress the clutch, lift your foot off the accelerator pedal and pull the axle-drive lever back to IN. The transfer-case lever is

On some 4WD's, it is all too easy to engage the front axle and not know it. Youngsters have an uncanny knack for doing it. Many off-road accessory firms sell a small warning light mechanism. It lights when the axle is engaged. This is only for the old-style, i.e., non full-time 4WD.

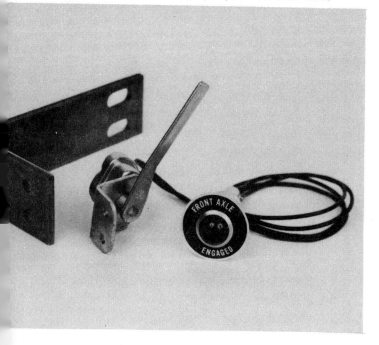

already in LOW so you can leave it there or shift to HIGH. Let's say you leave it in LOW. You are now in low-range, four-wheel drive and you can continue to shift the transmission in the normal manner without paying any attention to the transfer-case controls. Let's say you work up to third gear and you are sailing over the field at a goodly clip and it seems like the Jeep could go a lot faster, but it sounds like four rods are going to come sailing through the hood any minute. Time to shift to HIGH with the transfer-case control. You retain four-wheel drive, but can now go a lot faster. What you have lost is torque multiplication. If the mud begins to get deep and the engine starts to lug, even if you continue downshifting the transmission, it's time to go back to LOW at the transfer case. Reverse gear continues to function in either HIGH or LOW range, two- or four-wheel drive.

This may all sound pretty dumb and an over-simplification of things if you have been driving one of these vehicles since VJ day; if this is pretty new to you and you've never had the experience of sorting out all the "trees" on the way up a sand dune, hopefully this will be of some help.

The most common—in terms of numbers—transfer case you are likely to run across lumps all of transfer case *and* axle controls into one lever. Let's say you got a pay raise and decide to surprise the little woman with the purchase of a used Wagoneer you've been eyeing on a used-car lot for several days. Your new purchase is equipped with a three-speed manual transmission and four-wheel drive. The transmission control is known as *three on the tree,* meaning it is controlled by a lever on the steering column. One shift lever sprouts from the floor. This one lever controls in or out of four-wheel drive and also controls your selection of high or low range.

Let's say you decide to surprise the wife and kids with the Wagoneer by pulling off the highway and running across the field to the house. You work it just like you did the old military—into the field, clutch it, grab the one floor-mounted lever, find four-wheel drive high, downshift the transmission to second gear and start across the field. The Wagoneer slows down—slower—"what the devil is wrong with this thing?"—slower, slower, down to low gear, down to low range—"what the devil . . . " STUCK!!!

Sorry about that friend. Maybe we can get you out, and maybe you'll have to dig. Seems your pride and joy is equipped with locking hubs. You never even thought about that. When you went through all the motions of shifting the transfer case, all you did was get the transfer case front driveshaft and front axles in motion—but not the hubs. If you've got locking hubs and they are unlocked, you are still in two-wheel drive. You can shift all day and will still be in two-wheel drive.

Remember: First engage the hubs, then get into four-wheel drive. Failure to do so will result in a violation of Stuckk's Law!

Over the years there has been a lot of talk and a lot of work done on the subject of fulltime four-wheel drive. There were a lot of problems to solve. The gear-driven transfer case creates a lot of noise—so much so that the noise level is downright uncomfortable to live with at highway speeds. Secondly, four driving wheels create some weird handling problems at speed on the pavement. Tire wear is accelerated and there is a problem called "drive-train windup" caused by front and rear wheels traveling through different distances. The Warner Gear division of Borg Warner came up with a trick chain to be used in four-wheel-drive transfer cases and it solved the problems—to the extent that the Hy-Vo chain is now used in all production fulltime four-wheel drive systems.

FULLTIME FOUR-WHEEL DRIVE

A relatively new development for off-road equipment is called the *fulltime four-wheel-drive system.* Chevrolet introduced it on the 1973 Blazer, GMC on the 1973 Jimmy, Jeep made a similar move with Jeep trucks and their Wagoneer. This hardware's popularity is spreading. In 1974 Chrysler offered fulltime four-wheel drive on some of their vehicles and it will spread to other makes in short order. Although full-time 4WD systems have been around for years, only an occasional development or "testbed" for the hardware was seen in the off-road picture. Thus, a lot of old-time off-roaders are trying to figure out just what it all means and how it works.

The simple way to explain this "new" system is to compare it with the "old" 4WD system. In the typical 4WD system the vehicle is driven in two-wheel drive until it is taken off-road. Once

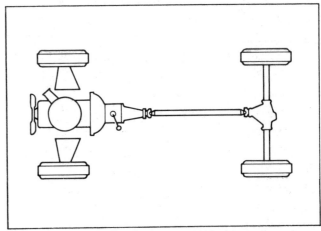

Conventional 2WD (2x4) has rear wheels driven through a conventional differential. Maximum traction available is limited by rear wheel having least traction. Maximum traction = 2 times traction value of wheel having least traction.

Conventional 4WD (4x4) has 4 wheels driven through conventional differentials in front and rear axles. Transfer case allows vehicle to be driven through rear wheels only, or all 4 wheels driving. Must engage front axle by shifting transfer case into 4 HI or 4 LO. Maximum traction of either axle is limited by wheel having least traction. Example—if one front and one rear wheel slip with no traction—the vehicle is immobile. Caution: Vehicle should not be driven on smooth, hard surface roads for extended periods in 4-wheel drive—no differential action between front and rear axles—excessive tire wear or possible mechanical failure.

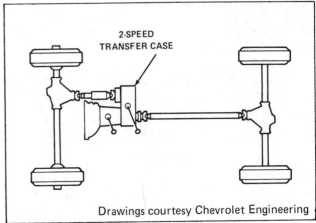

Drawings courtesy Chevrolet Engineering

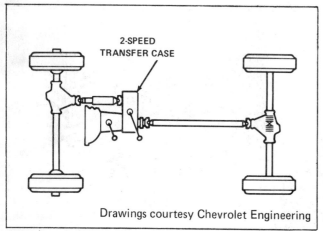

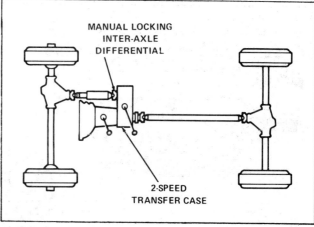

Drawings courtesy Chevrolet Engineering

Conventional 4WD with limited-slip or locking differential rear axle provides maximum traction. This combination gives best overall vehicle control for the average weekend sportsman or casual off-road driver. Adding a limited-slip differential to the front axle is o.k. for special uses such as snow plowing or special tow-vehicle use. This is not recommended for average drivers because it requires driving expertise to cope with poor controlability on slippery roads and poor steering qualities.

FULL TIME means 4-wheel drive at ALL times. Inter-axle differential permits speed variations between front and rear axles. Engaging manual lock in differential stops differential action between axles. Note: Manual lock to be used only when wheel traction is poor, i.e., loose sand, snow, mud. The main feature is that you can run on or off the highway without stopping to engage the front axle or to lock the front hubs. Conventional differentials are used in both axles, so the tractability under adverse conditions is just like a conventional 4WD.

off-road where more traction is needed, the transfer case is used to engage 4WD and power is also transmitted to the front axle. This 4WD is obviously a *part-time* system. In the new *full-time* 4WD units, there is no provision for disengaging the front axle. The front axle is engaged on or off the highway. As a result, acceleration and cornering power is increased on pavement. Off-road there is never any concern about whether you should be in 4WD. You're already there.

The first production off-road vehicle with full-time four-wheel drive for the consumer market was the 1970 British Range-Rover. This vehicle was equipped with an open differential—as opposed to limited-slip—in the transfer case, but there was provision for locking the front axle to the rear so they would rotate at the same speed.

The optional full-time four-wheel-drive system offered for 1973 and later Blazers and Jimmy has at its heart a transfer case made by Chrysler and called *New Process.* New Process Gear is a Chrysler gearbox-building division. It builds

Full-time 4WD with a limited-slip or locking differential in the rear axle provides all of the versatility of full-time 4WD plus the same tractive ability as a conventional 4WD with limited slip in the rear axle. Limited slip in the front axle offers the same advantages and problems as similarly equipped conventional 4WD.

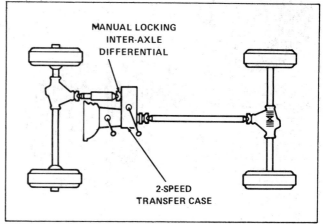

Shift pattern for the New Process constant 4WD transfer case found on Blazer, Ramcharger and Trail Duster is simple and self-explanatory. Both Loc positions mean front and rear wheels are rotating at same speed—for slippery stuff only.

Drawing of Quadra-Trac drive gear from Jeep shows advantages of full-time 4WD systems.

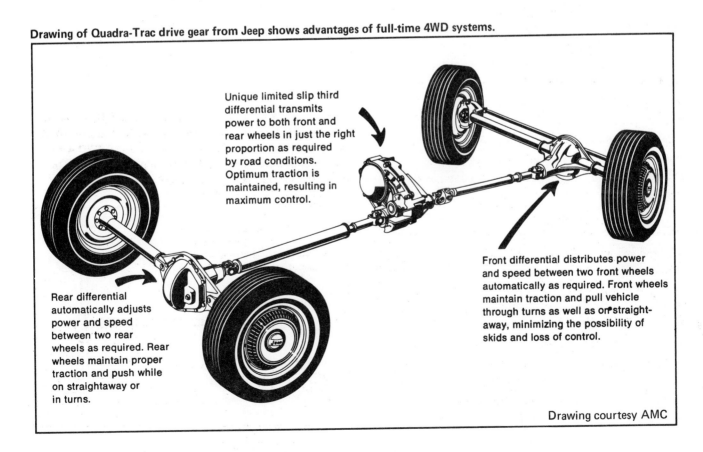

Unique limited slip third differential transmits power to both front and rear wheels in just the right proportion as required by road conditions. Optimum traction is maintained, resulting in maximum control.

Front differential distributes power and speed between two front wheels automatically as required. Front wheels maintain traction and pull vehicle through turns as well as on straight-away, minimizing the possibility of skids and loss of control.

Rear differential automatically adjusts power and speed between two rear wheels as required. Rear wheels maintain proper traction and push while on straightaway or in turns.

Drawing courtesy AMC

gearboxes for a wide variety of machinery outside of the parent corporation. The New Process full-time four-wheel-drive transfer case simply bolts to the rear of the GM Turbo Hydramatic. A drive-shaft extends from each end of the transfer case to feed power to both axles. A heavy chain feeds power directly from the transmission to the front prop shaft in the transfer case. Thus the front axle is always driving at gearbox speed. Between the drive chain and the rear driveshaft there is a differential mechanism. Thus, depending on traction conditions, the rear axle may or may not be driven the same speed as the front axle. There are no locking hubs on the front axle because the axle is constantly driven. Much like the Range Rover, there is provision to lock the two axles together to rotate at the same speed for traversing less-than-ideal terrain.

The other currently available fulltime four-wheel-drive system is Jeep's Quadra-Trac. Although the hardware is completely different from that found in the Blazer, the basic difference lies in a differential located in the transfer case. Jeep uses a limited slip incorporating an unloading cone. Internal friction increases as traction at the wheel decreases. This feeds power to the drive-shafts proportionally to what each will accept without breaking traction. This is called torque-biasing because power is biased in favor of the wheels able to accept it without going into full slip. The driveshafts can be locked together or the biasing mechanism locked out. Additionally,

TYPICAL GRADEABILITY — 2-WHEEL DRIVE VEHICLE

WT. = 5800 LBS.
3200 LBS. REAR
2600 LBS. FRONT
24" C.G.

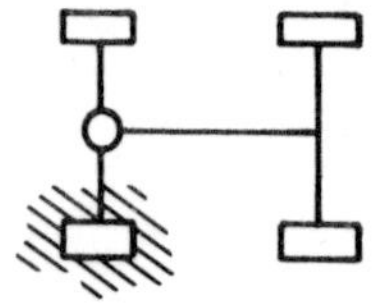

ONE REAR WHEEL ON SLIPPERY SURFACE

	ICE—SNOW F = 0.15	WET PAVEMENT—MUD F = 0.35
OPEN DIFFERENTIAL	4.5%	14%
LIMITED SLIP DIFFERENTIAL NO PRELOAD	7.6%	23.5%
LIMITED SLIP DIFFERENTIAL PRELOADED	9.4%	25.5%
AUTOMATIC LOCKING DIFFERENTIAL	26.3%	31.3%

NOTE: MUD AND SNOW MAY PILE UP IN FRONT OF WHEELS TO CAUSE GREATER OBSTACLE THAN ABOVE FIGURES INDICATE.

Drawings courtesy Chevrolet Engineering

Quadra-Trac can be ordered with or without low range because this housing and set of gears just bolts on the back of the existing transfer case.

The future of full-time four-wheel drive? Bright! Watch for the current crop of transfer cases to be phased out as more manufacturers incorporate full-time transfer cases in their designs.

Currently, if you want full-time four-wheel drive and don't have it, about the only thing we can suggest is buy a new vehicle with the device already installed. With enough work, either the Jeep or Blazer transfer case and driveshafts could be adapted to another vehicle, but that would strictly be a one-off proposition at more expense than I can even calculate.

Front differential shield by Drive-Gard can save this component and its U-joint from expensive damage when you're traveling through rocky country.

TYPICAL GRADEABILITY — 4-WHEEL DRIVE VEHICLE

WT. = 5800 LBS.
3200 LBS. REAR
2600 LBS. FRONT
24" C.G.

	ONE FRONT — ONE REAR WHEEL ON SLIPPERY SURFACE		ONE REAR WHEEL ON SLIPPERY PAVEMENT	
	ICE—SNOW F = 0.35	WET PAVEMENT—MUD F = 0.35	ICE—SNOW F = 0.15	WET PAVEMENT—MUD F = 0.35
2-WHEEL DRIVE	4.5%	14%	4.5%	14%
BASE FULL TIME 4-WHEEL DRIVE	9%	29%	9%	29%
INTER-AXLE LIMITED SLIP DIFF. FULL TIME 4-WHEEL DRIVE	10%	30%	16%	60%
INTER-AXLE LOCKED DIFF. 4-WHEEL DRIVE	10%	30%	55%	64%
INTER-AXLE LOCKED DIFF. 4-WHEEL DRIVE WITH REAR AXLE LOCKED DIFF.	32%	48%	76%	81%

NOTE: MUD AND SNOW MAY PILE UP IN FRONT OF WHEELS TO CAUSE GREATER OBSTACLE THAN ABOVE FIGURES INDICATE.

Drawings courtesy Chevrolet Engineering

TYPICAL TRACTIVE CAPABILITY
WITH 4-WHEEL DRIVE

DRAWBAR COMPARISON – 4-WHEEL DRIVE

	TYPE – INTER AXLE DIFFERENTIAL	ONE FRONT WHEEL ON ICE LBS.	ONE REAR WHEEL ON ICE LBS.	ONE FRONT AND ONE REAR WHEEL ON ICE LBS.
1.	CONVENTIONAL – UNLOCK	2,400	200	200
2.	CONVENTIONAL – LOCKED	2,600	2,600	400
3.	LIMITED SLIP DIFFERENTIAL – FULL TIME	700	960	400
4.	OPEN DIFFERENTIAL – FULL TIME	400	400	400
5.	OPEN DIFFERENTIAL – LOCKED	2,600	2,600	400

WITH REAR AXLE LOCKING DIFFERENTIAL

1.	CONVENTIONAL – UNLOCKED	2,400	1,300	1,300
2.	CONVENTIONAL – LOCKED	2,600	3,700	1,500
3.	LIMITED SLIP DIFFERENTIAL – FULL TIME	700	3,700	700
4.	OPEN DIFFERENTIAL – FULL TIME	400	2,600	400
5.	OPEN DIFFERENTIAL – LOCKED	2,600	3,700	1,500

BASED ON: 1,200 LBS./WHEEL HIGH TRACTION
100 LBS./WHEEL ON ICE

Table courtesy Chevrolet Engineering

Warner constant 4WD gearbox used in Jeep Quadra-Trac differs from NPG box in that torque-biasing differential limited-slip is included. This drawing shows optional 2.57:1 low ratio range unit.

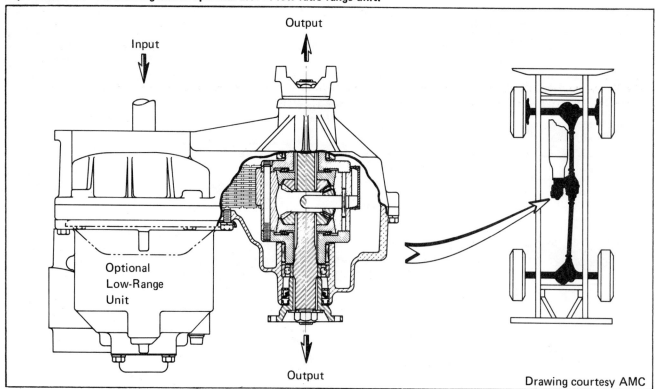

Input

Output

Optional Low-Range Unit

Output

Drawing courtesy AMC

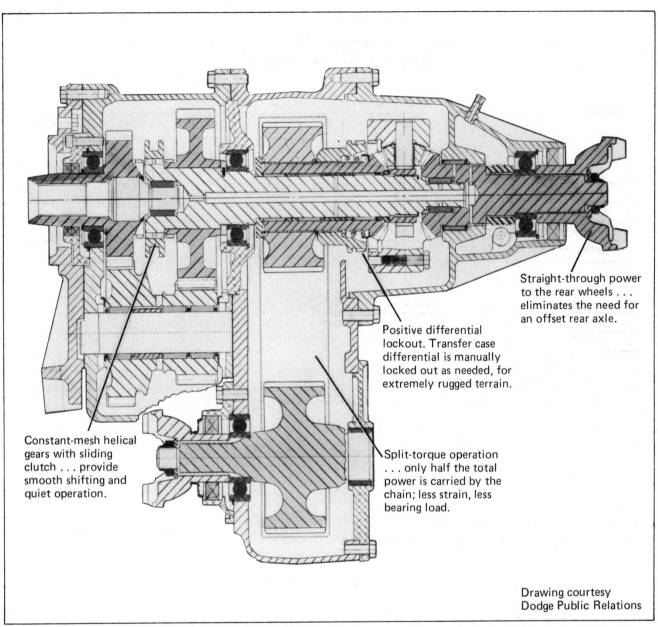

Constant-mesh helical gears with sliding clutch . . . provide smooth shifting and quiet operation.

Positive differential lockout. Transfer case differential is manually locked out as needed, for extremely rugged terrain.

Straight-through power to the rear wheels . . . eliminates the need for an offset rear axle.

Split-torque operation . . . only half the total power is carried by the chain; less strain, less bearing load.

Drawing courtesy Dodge Public Relations

NPG full-time transfer case also used the Borg Warner Hy-Vo chain, but note difference in design and the lack of limited-slip within the transfer case. This is used on Plymouth off-road equipment.

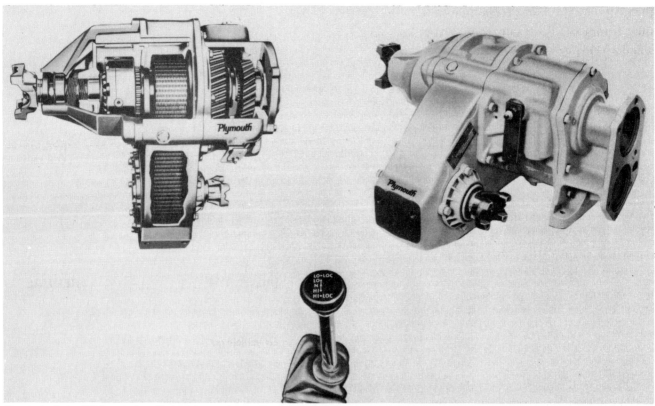

Control of the NPG unit handled with one lever clearly marked for transfer case positions.

Late-model Dodge practice is to "float" the transfer case without support. This leads to all sorts of grinding and thumping noises—most of which can be eliminated by something like this transfer-case strut rod. This is another Hickey Enterprises item; if you make you own, don't use flat strap because it will flex under load.

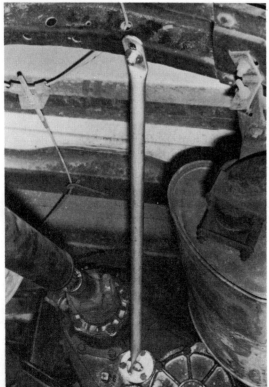

HOW A DIFFERENTIAL WORKS

In the conventional bevel-gear differential power from the propeller shaft enters the axle assembly through the drive pinion, passes to the ring gear and differential cases, is transferred by the cases through the differential spider to the differential pinions, goes from the pinions to the side gears, and is delivered by the side gears to the axle shafts. Each bevel pinion functions as a balance lever between the two side gears. Thus, any torque impressed on the differential cases is always divided equally between the two side gears, dividing output torque equally between the two axle shafts and wheels. Torque equalization is maintained regardless of whether the vehicle travels a route that is straight, curved, rough, or flat. During straight-ahead travel on flat surfaces the whole differential assembly revolves as a unit;

the differential pinions remaining stationary on their trunnions. Both side gears turn at the same angular velocity and both road wheels revolve at the same speed.

If you are still with us on this "hip-bone-connected-to-the-thigh-bone" routine, we'll go into what happens when on curves and uneven surfaces. When this happens, the differential pinions revolve on their trunnions. One wheel speeds up and the other slows down an equal amount, maintaining equal torque distribution to the axles. The change in speed of the two wheels will always be such that their average speed equals the speed of the differential case assembly.

Wide variations in tractive effort can exist at each driving wheel of a vehicle. If the tractive effort that can be developed by the two wheels is unequal, the total tractive effort available for vehicle propulsion will be twice that available at the wheel having the least traction—which can be two times nothing!—because the conventional differential always divides torque equally between the two wheels.

When one wheel rests on ice while the other is on dry pavement, a relatively low wheel torque will cause the wheel on ice to spin. This same low torque will be all that is available at the wheel on dry pavement, and will probably be insufficient to move the vehicle. That means you are stuck, Herm. This is the big disadvantage to a conventional bevel-gear differential.

LIMITED-SLIP DIFFERENTIAL

We've lived with limited-slip differentials in passenger cars, pickups and 4WD's for so long they're now taken for granted by many drivers. They shouldn't be. Basically, a limited-slip differential feeds power to both wheels on the axle assembly even though one loses traction. And, the differential action is retained when the vehicle turns a corner. These limited-slip devices are available as a factory-installed option on all domestic pickups and all 4WD rigs I know about. If you are buying a vehicle for even occasional off-road use, we highly recommend a limited-slip device in the rear axle. The devices are durable, reasonable in cost—about $50 when installed by the factory—and with one exception require no special maintenance. The exception is that differentials containing a limited-slip unit require special limited-slip lubricant. Do not pour regular

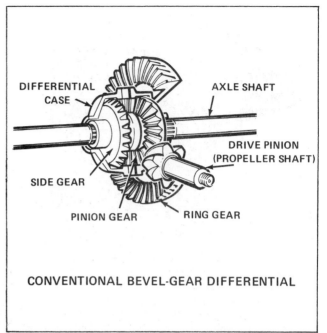

CONVENTIONAL BEVEL-GEAR DIFFERENTIAL

Help your vehicle go with a limited-slip differential. A limited-slip differential is basically a conventional differential in which the amount of slipping of either wheel is controlled. The control method is usually torque limited clutching plates or mechanism that allows one wheel to turn faster than the other whenever the pre-determined torque value of the clutch is exceeded, i.e., vehicle cornering. When the traction of one wheel approaches "0" that wheel will not spin free because of the preset clutching torque load, thus the other wheel having traction will drive up to its traction limit.

Drawings courtesy Chevrolet Engineering

What makes your vehicle go? This is a comparature traction diagram for a conventional differential showing the ideal situation where both tires have equal traction.

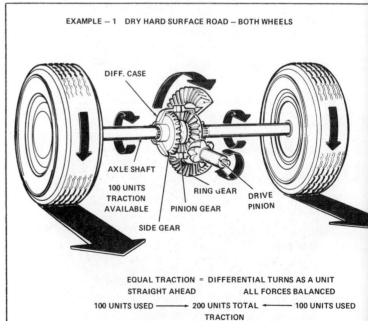

EXAMPLE — 1 DRY HARD SURFACE ROAD — BOTH WHEELS

EQUAL TRACTION = DIFFERENTIAL TURNS AS A UNIT
STRAIGHT AHEAD   ALL FORCES BALANCED
100 UNITS USED ——→ 200 UNITS TOTAL ←—— 100 UNITS USED
TRACTION

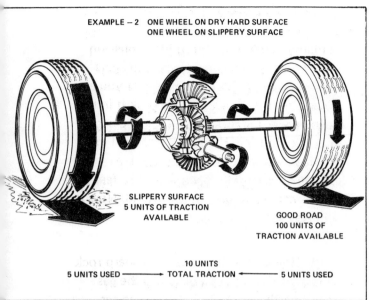

EXAMPLE – 2   ONE WHEEL ON DRY HARD SURFACE
ONE WHEEL ON SLIPPERY SURFACE

SLIPPERY SURFACE
5 UNITS OF TRACTION
AVAILABLE

GOOD ROAD
100 UNITS OF
TRACTION AVAILABLE

10 UNITS
5 UNITS USED ⟶ TOTAL TRACTION ⟵ 5 UNITS USED

When your vehicle with conventional differential won't go, here's why if one wheel is on a slippery surface. Differential says, "If you only give me 5 units of traction from the slippery surface, I'll throw away 95 of 100 units of good-road traction so you get equal pull at both wheels, which won't be much, and maybe not any!"

Drawings courtesy Chevrolet Engineering

Help your vehicle get through the tough spots with a limited-slip differential. A limited-slip differential is basically a conventional differential in which the amount of slipping of either wheel is controlled. The control method is usually torque-limited clutching plates or a mechanism that allows one wheel to turn faster than the other whenever the predetermined torque value of the clutch is exceeded, i.e., vehicle cornering. When the traction of one wheel approaches "0", that wheel will not spin free because of the preset clutching torque load, thus the other wheel having traction will drive up to its traction limit.

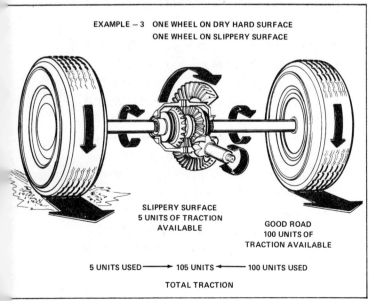

EXAMPLE – 3   ONE WHEEL ON DRY HARD SURFACE
ONE WHEEL ON SLIPPERY SURFACE

SLIPPERY SURFACE
5 UNITS OF TRACTION
AVAILABLE

GOOD ROAD
100 UNITS OF
TRACTION AVAILABLE

5 UNITS USED ⟶ 105 UNITS ⟵ 100 UNITS USED
TOTAL TRACTION

gear lube in a limited-slip rear end! The unit will clack, chatter, grab and generally make your life miserable until the unit is drained and the fluid is replaced. Don't let any lop-eared kid in a service station put even a little bit of regular rear end lube in a limited-slip differential. GM dealers sell a quality limited-slip lube—Positraction lube—as part number 105022. They also have an additive which is very effective for turning a noisy limited slip into a quiet one; ask for 1050428. Ford had both an additive and a lube, but combined the two products in part number C9AZ19580A.

None of the 4WD vehicles currently being sold are offered with a limited-slip differential in the front axle. However, many dealers are eager to install one for you because the limited-slip hardware from the rear bolts right into the front differential on some vehicles. Their sales pitch can be convincing: "If you have a limited-slip rear end in a 4WD vehicle, you actually have only three-wheel drive and for X dollars more, you can have 'true' four-wheel drive."

The argument sounds very logical—and is. But the dealers probably don't bother to mention that limited-slip in the front end makes the vehicle harder to steer. If you are rat racing around at some speed in rough terrain the limited slip can steer you into trouble as it "hunts" for solid footing. We've driven a Jeepster with limited-slip front and rear the length of Baja. The vehicle also had power steering so we didn't have to have arms like Popeye for the job. Did the front limited-slip get us into trouble? No. But it didn't get us out of any trouble either, because when we high-centered, nothing short of the power to part the Red Sea would have helped.

What we've had to say here about limited-slip differentials should not be confused with the "new boy on the street" called constant four-wheel drive as offered on a number of 4WD vehicles. This is discussed separately.

Is there an exception to our advice of not installing limited-slip in the front end? Yes. We talked to a Montana rancher who said he wouldn't be without it. Nine months of the year he slogs through mud, snow, and brush or slick grass. The vehicle stays on the ranch and almost never sees a good dirt road—much less pavement. Driving is slow and rough. In a workhorse situation the front limited-slip would be money well spent.

It must be kept in mind that all clutch-operated differentials are a compromise and are marginal in performance in really rough going. For all-out performance, a locking differential such as that produced by Detroit Automotive Products—Detroit Locker—are far more effective than a cluth-type differential.

In a SAE paper entitled *Arctic Operations With The Twister Testbed*, William R. Janowski—formerly with the Ground Vehicle Systems, Lockheed Missiles and Space Co., and now President of DataMotive—made the following comments on clutch and locking diffcrentials.

"The Power train of the Twister testbed was fitted with clutch-type, limited-slip differentials in the No. 1 and 3 axle gearboxes. Positive-locking —Detroit Locker type—assemblies were fitted in the No. 2 and 4 axle gearboxes. Throughout the trip—800 miles of Arctic off-road operation—operation of the two types of units was observed and compared. The clutch-type units were unsatisfactory because of occasional wheel spin-out when off the ground and wheel stoppage on the ground under low-traction conditions. The positive-locking differential appeared to pull far more evenly although some 'ratcheting' of the tires was noted. The wheels on the axles with these differentials were not observed to spin free or be independent of the opposite wheel. An effective-limited slip differential is mandatory for snow operations, and having positive-locking differentials in all the gearboxes—except possibly the steering axle—would have improved the overall vehicle performance on steep grades and in deep snow."

Running a positive-locking differential in the Arctic is one thing—running one on and off-road is something else. The Detroit Locker manufactured for some vehicles should probably be avoided unless you stay off-road in really rough loose stuff for 80% of the time. It ratchets fiercely and locks and unlocks so positively it is annoying to most people and downright scary for an amateur with one wheel on ice and another on rock.

If a clutch-type limited slip doesn't quite give you all you need, a positive-locker may get you through troublesome low-traction situations.

Go Soak Your Rope—I keep about 15 feet of rope behind the seat of my pickup. Rope is plenty handy for a lot of little jobs—on or off-road. Unfortunately the stuff gets stiff because I don't use it much. If you are faced with the same problem, soak it in hot soapy water for about 10 minutes. Uncoil it and let it dry in the shade. This will make it pliable again. After it dries, work a couple of cups of linseed oil—for 15 feet of rope—into the rope with your hand. Now it will stay soft a lot longer.

Little Hole in the Gas Tank—If a sharp rock jumps off the ground and smites the gas tank smartly you can have a leaking gas tank in short order. Normally when this happens, the leak is not a gush, but a fine stream smaller than pencil lead. The leak needs to be fixed, quick. Dick Cepek and some other off-road outlets market a compound to do a pretty fair job of sealing a small puncture in either an oil pan or gas tank. If you don't have some of this goop, remove a small sheet metal or trim screw from the interior. Shove the screw through a metal washer and then through a rubber pad made from a tire patch. Coat the rubber pad with the "sticky" that comes in a tire patch kit and then screw the whole combination of screw, washer and coated rubber pad into the offending hole. Fix the tank or pan when you get home.

A Red Light? If you do a lot of night driving in a van or camper type vehicle and get bugged often when the kids turn on the interior lights, add a light fixture or two and screw in a red-colored bulb. This allows junior to find his snuggy and bubble gum, but allows you to see out and continue driving. If you can't find red bulbs—and they are rare in 12 volts—check with a marine supply house or electronics store for a little bottle of red paint designed for this. Fingernail polish goes on too thick to be of much use.

RUNNING GEAR, OPTIONS & ACCESSORIES

We've lumped running gear, and most of the accessories and options together in this one chapter except for things related to the drive train. Those appear elsewhere in the book. With today's long list of options and accessories it is possible to spend thousands of dollars on accessories for a brand new 2WD or 4WD vehicle. It is just as possible to have all of that equipment take away from the performance rather than enhance it. As we have tried to point out in the rest of the book, equipment will not "save" an idiot or just plain bad driving off the road. Our suggestions and comments should always be tempered by your judgment of how the vehicle will be used and what will really be required to meet those performance demands.

Over the years we've met a substantial number of enthusiasts lumbering around in the puckerbrush scratching up pin striping and custom paint jobs and enjoying it. To those who care for this side of the sport we can only offer encouragement. To those who feel this is foolish, we would point out that no one is forcing them to scratch up custom paint jobs and mag wheels . . . and they are getting enjoyment out of using their equipment. In other words, "What ever turns you on, man."

To a certain degree, we feel the same about the rest of the vehicle. Whether you buy for use or show—or both—is strictly up to you.

SKID PLATES

Adequate skid plates are among those items you assume you are getting when you step into a new $8,000 rig and drive from the dealer's lot into the nearest rock and log-infested dry wash. Don't wait until you've broken down, been stuck, run out of gas or Gawd-knows-what before you stop assuming anything about anything to do with off-road driving and equipment. Skid plates are neat pieces of 3/16-inch or 1/4-inch steel or aluminum plate placed between vulnerable items of running gear

Underside of a Blazer outfitted with an extra capacity gas tank protected by a skid plate. When figuring the cost of such a tank—include the price of a skid plate. You'll need it.

Here's a homemade aluminum skid plate fitted under the engine of a two-wheel-drive pickup. A wide-area plate like this really cuts down the amount of water or small rocks that "float" in the engine compartment during hard running in the rough.

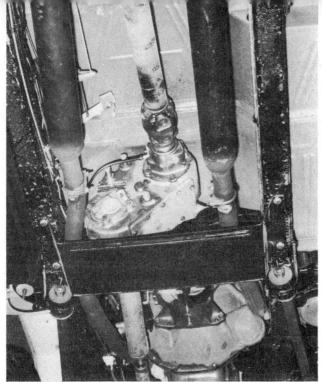

Notice how Bronco transfer skid plate bolts to frame. It lips upward in front to keep rocks from jamming between plate and case. Just watch it when you back up in the rough. A pair of stock mufflers would be much quieter and would not lose any horsepower. Loud vehicles bring the wrath of the public on off-roaders and limit our access to suitable playgrounds for our toys.

Before you start laying out a lot of long green for a 4WD vehicle, make sure it's equipped with a skid plate for the transfer case—if not find out how much one costs and the trouble it is to install. You won't even believe how expensive transfer-case repairs can be.

Typical after-market skid plate: ¼-inch thick steel, sheared and bent to fit a specific application. Large holes allow easy access to trans and transfer case drain holes.

That transfer case may look durable, but it is pure folly to take a 4WD vehicle into rock or stump country without fabricating or bolting on a steel skid plate. This well designed skid plate from Hickey has holes for filling and checking fluid levels. Beveled end on back protects case when the vehicle is backing.

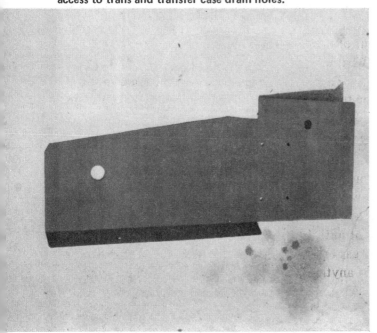

and the unforgiving terrain. Placement and design varies from one vehicle to the next. Some manufacturers offer skid plates as accessories—such as the transfer skid plate for a Blazer. On other vehicles—say the Ford four-wheel-drive pickups—you'll need to fabricate one or buy from an off-road accessory manufacturer. The best guide to what skid plates you need is good common sense. Slide up under the vehicle you intend to buy or have bought and figure out what is going to get in the way the first time you high-center on a log or pile of rocks.

The transfer case is almost a sure bet to need a skid plate, with the next item in line being the gas tank or engine oil pan. Some vehicles tuck the oil pan and engine out of harm's way so they don't need additional protection. Even so, you may want to add protection against a non-standard obstacle or thrown rock which could cause you a heap of trouble.

Another area of concern is the transmission-support crossmember—such as on the Wagoneer. This is a problem when it's being run hard in rocks. For tidbits of information like this, corner every owner of a similar vehicle you can find and ask questions about what they've broken and damaged and how they cured the problem. Mechanics in the back room of the dealership can also be helpful sometimes.

Common sense must also prevail once the vehicle is properly outfitted with skid plates. Just because you have them, don't think you can back off and ram past any stump or rock in the way.

Rocks can shear off exposed ends of spring U-bolts. This can be prevented with a guard which "hides" the bolts in recesses. Socket wrench is needed for nut removal.

Logic along those lines will find you bellied up to a dealer's parts counter asking for a new transfer case *and* skid plate. The trip to the banker to borrow the loot for the parts should sober you up.

A couple of small things should be kept in mind when you are designing and building or buying a skid plate. Any skid plate for a transmission, transfer case or engine should allow lubricant to be drained without having to remove said skid plate. Any skid plate for anything should be shaped to allow dirt and debris to be cleaned off it with a stream of water from a garden hose or the local do-it-yourself carwash. Also build or buy skid plates which will not trap such items as sagebrush when the skid plate is in the immediate area of the exhaust pipe—a healthy fire under the vehicle in the middle of nowhere is excitement you can do without . . . and it happens!

A skid plate should be bolted on—not welded on. Don't wind up with some ill-designed, worse-executed piece of fish plate which forces you to pull the engine to check the fluid level in the transfer case.

Don't lose sight of the purpose of the skid plate: To deflect or absorb energy—not to pass it on to the component you're trying to protect. There should be a minimum of one-inch clearance between any point on the component being guarded and the skid plate. Let the plate get gouged, buckled or bent—but don't let it contact the part it's supposed to protect.

HEAVY DUTY SUSPENSION—SO-CALLED

If you are buying a new four-wheel-drive vehicle and plan to keep it off-road for even 25% of its life, we highly recommend getting a heavy-duty-suspension option if one is listed by the factory. This is especially true of 4WD trucks. Some vehicles—such as a Jeep—don't have a suspension option.

On the other hand, a Blazer can be ordered with standard or heavy-duty-suspension. If your pride and joy is equipped with standard suspension you may find it constantly bottoms out. Although heavier and/or dual shocks on each wheel may help, they will not cure all of the problem. Shock life will be short simply because they are being overworked due to a lack of spring. Don't think you can overcome too little spring with a lot of shock. Doesn't happen! And adding all of the parts

Not only has an additional shock been added to the front of this four-wheel-drive Chevy, stock shock has been replaced with a coil-wrapped unit to improve load carrying capability of the front end.

Some firms offer a spring hardware kit to preload the lower ball joint of a four-wheel-drive vehicle. This reduces front-suspension wander or "hunt" at highway speeds. Effectiveness varies from one vehicle to another and from one kit to another. At top is a steering "stabilizer" shock absorber.

Many firms sell auxiliary shock kits for pickups and off-road rigs. If you're carrying a lot of weight off-road you might consider this method of stiffening-up suspension.

Accessory rear shock assembly—coil-wrapped—features an angle mounting to reduce body roll. Upper mounting bracket is designed like a crossmember and bolts into the '73 to '76 Chevy trucks.

for the seemingly cheap option can cost a bundle—so much more you won't believe it when the parts jockey hands you the bill.

Spring and shock requirements vary greatly from one vehicle to another and from one kind of driving to another. An old flathead military Jeep has more than enough spring for a vehicle of that weight and performance. More spring—or shock—will simply make the vehicle ride like a buckboard and destroy predictable handling at any speed above a walk. A Blazer with standard suspension will bottom out frequently in even moderate-speed desert running. Although dual shocks help, their installation will not cure the problem of too little spring.

We'd get any heavy-duty-suspension options listed by the factory on any new 4WD or 2WD we ordered and let vehicle usage determine what aftermarket pieces were required. Heavy-duty steering stabilizers, as manufactured by Heco, are definite assets to any 4WD vehicle and can help on 2WD's as well. One of these units will go a long way towards eliminating front-end wobble, shake, and tire wear. Vehicle control at freeway speeds is also improved.

Have a clear understanding of what any handling device is supposed to do and why it is supposed to do it before you buy. Cut through all of the wish-book propaganda and make a judgment as to what you really need before bolting on every GeeWhiz item in the store. The Oversteer/Understeer section in the Tire Chapter will help you to understand the problems involved *before* laying out the long green.

Vic Hickey offers dual shock kits for both trucks and 4WD's. Front and rear setup for a Bronco requires no welding to install.

This is not a book about off-road racing, but we couldn't resist showing off some of these tricks on a racing off-road rig. Chain to limit downward travel of the axle is not recommended—use cable! Air bag—arrow—contained in a coil spring will soften the upward travel. Axle tubes are braced and stressed to center section and an accessory shock has been added.

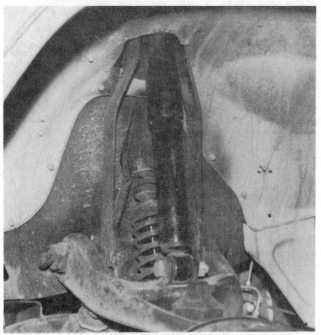

Inner fender well shot of the LUV shows how Doug Roe
Engineering added a shock to each front wheel. Stock
shock was moved to new location and a coil-wrapped
unit placed in original location.

Loop of chain under the rear axle keeps the axle from
yanking downward hard enough to damage the shock when
the truck leaves the ground. A good idea in hard, rough
running—but a far better idea is to use 3/8-inch cable. It
has a lot more strength, doesn't make nearly the noise, is
not apt to break.

Inner fender panel has been sliced open to accommodate
upper mounting hardware for new shock on the LUV.

Lots of off-road vehicles are being equipped with disc
brakes on the front axle. They don't always stop much
quicker than drum brakes, but they are far more resistant
to fading due to heat or water. This is a Blazer unit Vic
Hickey adapted to a Scout.

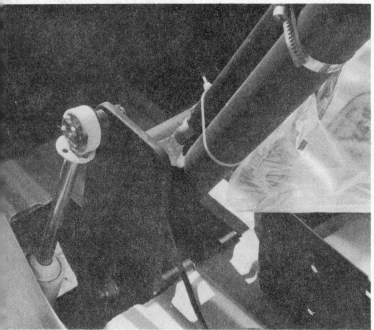

An opening sliced in the bed of this racing pickup allowed mounting an additional shock and tying the roll cage into the frame at this load point. Just an example of what can be done when you get serious about running very fast in the rough. This Blazer also had spare tie rods lashed to the roll bar with worm-drive clamps.

Shopping for replacement shocks? Take a close look at the size of the shaft—if it's exposed. Generally speaking, the bigger the shaft, the more rugged the shock. Free length should be approximately the same as stock shock. If not, keep shopping.

Fast-running, high-jumping off-road race trucks have to be plenty rugged to take this treatment. Check the size of those shocks and the amount of travel available. Also note how the plug wires have been lashed down to keep them from burning on the exhaust headers.

An off-road racer's trick—front shackles have been replaced with fabricated item cut from heavy plate and joined in the center by a short section of box tubing. This makes for a very durable unit which will stand up to tremendous side loads.

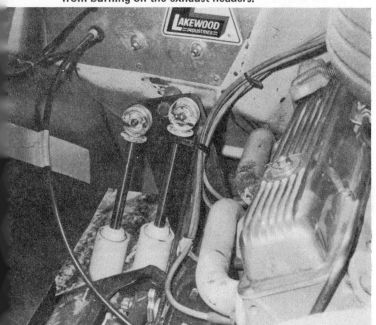

Placing the leaf spring assembly on top of the axles instead of below them gains another six inches of fender—not ground—clearance. This lets you use larger tires, raises the center of gravity and increases the possibility of rolling—pays your money—takes your choice. Jeep vehicle at right has springs atop axles.

AIR SHOCKS/AIR BAGS

A number of firms now manufacture air shocks to raise or lower the rear of a vehicle with air pressure. Air lines run from the shocks to a fitting on or near the bumper and by adding air pressure the rear of a tail dragging car or truck can be brought up to level again. Some of the fancy shocks are even supplied with lines and fittings and a small compressor operating off of engine vacuum. A small control panel on the dash allows the vehicle to be leveled out while being driven. Street strokes have taken to this like a duck to water—it allows them to jack up the vehicle at will. In other words the ride height goes up and down with the current fad. These shocks are very functional for leveling out a vehicle which gets overloaded from time to time. All of this is fine for the freeway—but you don't want them for off-road. Component loading

Truck outfitted for Baja has extra shocks and air bags inside the coil-springs. Air bags keep the coils from collapsing fully on a hard bump, extending the life of the spring without making the ride a lot stiffer. A good deal.

goes out of sight when a 5000-pound vehicle starts hopping a wheel around in the rock. The rubber air chamber on the shock simply was not designed for this and will blow out. This eliminates the function of the shock.

Air bags should not be confused with air shocks. The air bag is a small, tough inflatable rubber bladder which can be pressurized 6 - 10 psi—after being placed inside a coil spring. As the spring is compressed by vertical suspension travel, the air bag is also compressed and gets harder—higher internal pressure—as the load increases. Thus, the bag offers progressive resistance because it only works during the last two inches or so of travel. This saves the life of springs and shocks by softening the blow. Air bags are also available with all the brackets needed to locate them between a leaf spring pack and a frame.

DIFFERENTIAL BRACES

Off-road vehicles subjected to heavy loading can often benefit from differential braces or trusses. The heavy loading we speak of can often be in the form of weight caused by jumping the vehicle as opposed to simply loading the back of a truck down and driving it. For this reason a lot of 2WD and 4WD trucks used for rough and tumble off-roading and racing are outfitted with a truss. The truss is a healthy sized piece of steel—either bar or flat strap

This is one form of differential brace—a piece of bar stock welded to the underside of the axle housing—preferably heli-arced. Under most driving conditions you'll never need this.

There are several designs of axle truss assemblies. These devices go a long way to prevent axle bending when it is subjected to treatment depicted on our cover. You'll note that vehicle is equipped with a Hickey truss.

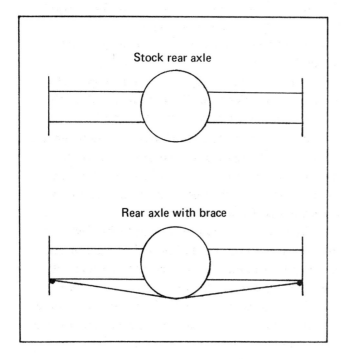

Stock rear axle

Rear axle with brace

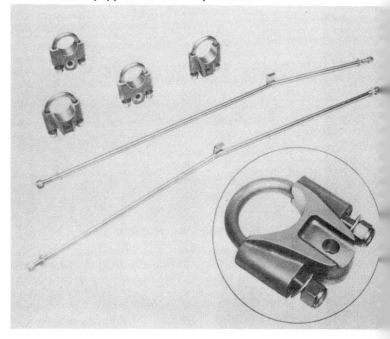

attached to both ends of an axle and coming in contact with the bottom of the differential housing. Several firms such as Hickey sell these trusses for the front axle—because that's the axle most likely to leave the ground. They bolt in place.

On racing vehicles, a truss is often fabricated and welded onto the rear axle. To do this correctly the axle must be removed from the vehicle. The outer axle bearings must be removed and heli-arc must be used to secure the truss to the axle housing. More than just a few axle housings have been ruined over the years by using regular arc welding and getting enough heat into the axle housing to either seize the bearing by warpage or ruining the heat treat on the critical components.

A rear axle housing almost never breaks no matter how it is abused, but front-axle housings coming off the ground a lot are prone to bend and finally break.

HD ALTERNATOR

Leece-Neville Company builds an alternator designed for heavy-duty-truck service. It should be of great interest to off-roaders who really need electrical power for operating a winch or other heavy-duty equipment. The 105-ampere alternator features a built-in regulator. You can hook up to the existing electrical system with only one power lead. Designed for either positive or negative ground, the regulator used silicon solid-state devices to withstand high engine-compartment temperatures. The alternator bolts to the standard mounting arrangement and is completely interchangeable with other makes without redesigning the mounting brackets.

110-VOLT CONVERTERS

A number of firms offer conversion units that connect into your 12-volt electrical system to provide 110-volt output. You can run appliances—nothing like an electric toothbrush whirring away on a chilly morning—or power tools. Make sure you understand what RPM the engine has to be turning before you start peeling off the long green for one of these units. I had one once that would make a 75-watt bulb glow pretty nice—when the engine was turning about 3500 RPM! No thanks. If that's the choice I'd rather work in the dark. It's best to buy the type which has output wattage clearly stated. Above all, ask before you buy, as the unit may not be returnable for a refund.

AUXILIARY GAS TANKS

Before going very far off-road you should find out just how far you and your rusty trusty steed can go and get back without refueling. In this day and age, that's not a completely useless piece of information if you are just running a Cadillac back and forth to the market. At any rate, figure out how far you can go and get back without refueling. Make a realistic appraisal of your travel plans and then shop around before plunging into the "red-hot, super-double-throw-down-deal-of-a-lifetime on increasing your gas carrying capacity."

Consider the following:

1. In an increasing number of states, it is illegal to strap GI-type gas cans to the outside of a vehicle being driven on a public road.

2. Putting a loose can of gasoline inside the vehicle with you ain't too swift either.

3. Gasoline weighs about 8 pounds per gallon—*plus the container.* Adding 40 gallons of gas to what you already have sounds neat until the springs start creaking and shock life goes away from the 350 pounds or so of extra weight.

4. Some tanks reduce the ground clearance of your vehicle. Are you willing to put up with that? The extra weight will also cause the springs to sag; thereby reducing ground clearance.

5. Exactly what has to be done to mount the tank to the vehicle? Are the necessary hardware and instructions provided?

6. What provisions are made to install a sender in the tank and use your present gas gage to indicate the stock tank and the auxiliary tank?

7. What provisions are made to get the gas from the tank to the carb?

8. Will the auxiliary tank cause you problems at an emission check? Does the tank retain all of the vapor-collection devices required by law?

A lot of questions, huh? Yes, and there are a lot more. First figure out what you need in the way of extra gas capacity—not just what happens to be available—deal or no deal. Weigh the advantages and disadvantages carefully.

Any gas tank you buy should be baffled—something else you should know. Eight gallons of gas banging around in a 20-gallon tank is a lot of weight hammering at the tank—and your nerves.

Any auxiliary tank should be hooked to some sort of on/off switching system to give you positive control over which tank is being used.

GI can carriers come in a variety of styles. This one holds spare tire and one five-gallon can. Other carriers hold only the can—allow more room inside the vehicle and swing away for access to the bed.

To get more room inside the vehicle, move the spare outside. There are several designs for most vehicles. Shop around . . . there are differences.

Any gas tank should have a fairly straight filler neck. A neck crooked as a dog's hind leg will "belch back" and be a pain in the gas to fill.

Any gas tank should be mounted firmly to the vehicle so there is no movement and subsequent chafing.

Before installing the tank, slosh a couple of quarts of lacquer thinner around in the tank and examine the thinner when you pour it out into a large bowl. If the thinner is super-dirty, you may want to run a couple of more quarts through it. Some yo-yo on the shipping dock could have been shelling peanuts into the filler neck for all you know. That sort of thing, plus welding slag, spiders and cigarette butts can do all sorts of unspeakable things to fuel pumps and carburetors. I run an in-line filter between the auxiliary tank and the fuel pump.

There is an increasing number of "plastic" gas tanks on the market. They are lighter, don't rust and can be shaped in ways most impractical for welded-steel construction. Seriously consider a skid plate for a plastic tank you choose—assuming it mounts under the vehicle.

The safest, best way to transport large amounts of gas in an off-road vehicle is a fuel cell

There is a better way to carry gas than some lashed-on GI cans. Many manufacturers build high-capacity tanks to replace the stock unit. This 32-gallon tank for the Scout II is baffled, built of 1/8-inch steel and does not hang below differential. If at all possible look at an accessory gas tank mounted on a vehicle similar to yours before laying out the cash. How much does the tank reduce ground clearance and are all of the emission-control fittings incorporated in the tank?

When buying a replacement or auxiliary gas tank make sure you get all the hardware needed to mount it and find out exactly what is needed to use the gas gauge.

Tanks which mount inside the bed of a pickup aft of the rear wheel wells are fairly new. They give good weight distribution and occupy a space in the truck not normally used. These quality units from Hickey are designed for the various mini-pickups.

of the type used in race cars. They come in a variety of standard sizes and can also be custom-made to most any shape. They consist of a metal box holding a bladder which holds the fuel. The bladder, in turn, is filled with a porous foam which acts as a baffle and also slows the flow of fuel down to a trickle should the metal box and the bladder be ripped open in an accident. Needless to say this type of protection does not come cheap. Fuel cells can be obtained from a couple of firms in the suppliers list: ATL and Donn Allen.

A lot of guys don't seem to give much thought when plumbing an auxiliary gas tank—another one of those haste-makes-waste activities. The quick way to do it is neoprene hose. The right way to route the line is to use steel fuel line, flare the ends and clamp the steel line to the frame just like the original line was anchored. Just running steel line along the frame rail doesn't get it. Spend a couple of bucks at the local auto parts store and get a tube bender—now you can bend and route the steel fuel line so it will be away from exhaust and away from a direct stream of rocks thrown up by the tires.

A steel line should be secured to the frame with clips or clamps to prevent it from chafing, getting caught on underbrush or cracking from

Most race cars are now required to carry their fuel in fuel cells. They are the ultimate in safety and sold in a variety of sizes and can be fabricated in most any size and shape. Expensive—but a safe way to carry fuel off-road.

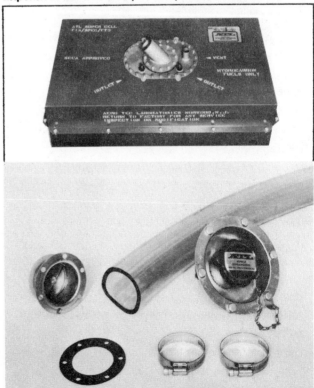

being worked back and forth.

Plumbing shops have lengths of asbestos sleeves which can be fitted over short sections of fuel line which must pass close to exhaust manifolds and rubber hose can be slipped over parts of the fuel line prone to damage by rocks. Get the hose of the correct inside diameter at the local auto parts house and slip it over the fuel line before you flare the end and install the fitting. If the hose is difficult to shove onto the line, coat the line liberally with mechanics' hand soap—works like a charm.

SPARE PARTS, TOOLS AND PERSONAL SURVIVAL

Deciding what parts, tools and fixit gadgets to take with you off-road is a matter of common sense. Unless you drive a real piece of junk off-road, you'll never use 90% of the items you take even once. What you take depends a lot of where you go, how long you stay and how far you are from help. Items I would always take—even for a one-day outing include:

2 jacks—one bumper, one hydraulic
1 inflated spare tire to fit the vehicle
1 valve core and a cap that will serve as a valve-core wrench
1 lug wrench—a good one
1 tow strap
1 pair of work gloves
1 set of open/box end wrenches
1 screwdriver
1 10-inch adjustable wrench
1 pair vise grips
1 pair jumper cables
1 sparkplug-type tire pump
1 roll of plastic electrical tape
1 short handle straight neck shovel
1 tube of RTV Silastic rubber
1 two-pound sledge hammer
2 pieces of ¾-inch plywood about a foot square for the jacks
1 length of 14-gauge electrical wire—about six feet
1 box of fuses
1 small roll of mechanics' wire
3 shop rags
1 aerosol tire inflator
1 quart of oil
1 tune-up kit—points, condenser and rotor
1 tube of gas tank/oil pan leak sealant
1 tire-pressure gauge

If I plan to go a little further away from civilization or stay out for an extended period of time, I get a little more serious about carrying all of that neat stuff allowing you to work on a vehicle instead of having fun. To the above list I then add:

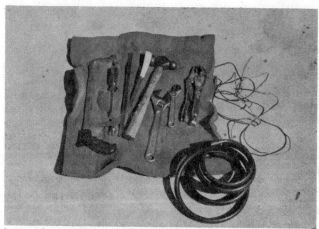

I consider this the absolute minimum tool collection to take off-road. This was all rolled up in the piece of foam rubber and tied up with some electrical wire. Extra fuel line is handy for siphoning gas. A better quality electrician's knife would be nice. Oh yes, and don't forget bailing wire and super tape!

1 set of tire irons
1 extra tube
1 big tire boot
1 tire repair kit for tubeless tires
1 tube repair kit for tubes
1 fuel pump—and a tubing wrench of the right size
1 ignition coil
1 box of assorted nuts, bolts and washers
1 hacksaw
1 short roll of duct—racer's—tape
1 can of radiator stop leak
1 fan belt
1 spark-plug wrench
2 spark plugs
1 length of chain—about 4 feet

I go off road to have fun—enjoy myself and the less work I have to do to a vehicle out in the middle of nowhere the better I like it. Obviously you can take a lot more than what I've listed—an alternator, axles, driveshafts, springs—and so on, but I'd rather travel light and a little slower. If you plan a little off-road adventure with another couple of vehicles, pool your resources and space on all of this stuff. Why should you have three hacksaws, three coils, etc. out there in the middle of the woods when the chances are slim you'll need even one of them? Store the stuff in an old canvas knapsack or duffle bag unless you want to mount a steel toolbox to the vehicle. A box not anchored rattles, moves around and is a pain in the youknowwhat.

In addition to what I take to get the vehicle back, I take what I think it takes to get me back. I have never completely abandoned a vehicle to the sands of time, but I have had to do a little walking before I drove out. I either wear or have with me in the vehicle: Hat, gloves, heavy coat, blue jeans and boots. I stuff the zip-up pockets of the jacket full of a lot of stuff. You can do that or get a surplus survival bag of canvas that clips to a belt. The stuff I carry includes:

1 canteen of water—about a teaspoon of mint flavored mouth wash in the water is refreshing
1 waterproof match box kit with tinder
1 hunting knife in a sheath
1 small metal mirror
1 metal police whistle—I broke a plastic one
1 snake bite kit—read the instructions *before* you get bit, dummy!
1 roll of 3-inch gauze—take it out of the box, but not the wrapper
1 reflective space blanket
1 compass
1 small map of the area if I have any doubts at all or have never been to the area before
1 smoke bomb
1 small tin of aspirin
1 small can of fruit cocktail, peaches, etc. with a pull tab top

If you really get in trouble—the vehicle dies or you get injured what you need is help—not more trouble. The fast moving American is not blessed with an overabundance of patience and that is a killer. Panic, leave the vehicle in a huff and set out to find help so you can get back to work by Tuesday—at least!—and you could easily wind up holding a lilly you can't smell. If you plan to walk out for help, follow your tracks back to the main road. Short cuts turn into big sweeping circles that will soon kill you because you run out of food, water and energy before you run into help. If you are weak, hurt, lost or scared—admit it, dammit, we're all human!—stick with the vehicle. Even an open Jeep can be your shelter, your shade. You can take a seat out or a spare tire and set fire to it with the aid of gasoline to use as a signal if you spot a low flying airplane. This will attract more attention than the mirror and smoke bomb. I highly recommend that before going off on your own to the wilds of nowhere

that you read: *American Red Cross First Aid Textbook* and a book sold by Dick Cepek called *To Hell on Wheels—The Desert Mobility Manual.* This last book contains a vast amount of survival information about the desert—but much of it is basic and can be applied to most types of environment.

Basic knowledge and a cool head is the best thing you can have when the chips are down. If you are new to this game of off-roading, maybe you should make an assessment of this before backing out of the driveway.

Ground Clearance—or things that go bump underneath—this subject crops up in every campfire session. Phrases such as "mutha ain't got no ground clearance" are common. Simply stated a lot of ground clearance means you go farther before getting high-centered. Ground clearance is measured from the lowest part of the chassis or running gear to the ground. Normally this is the bottom of the differential—front or rear. If the exhaust system or a gas tank hangs lower than this, then you measure ground clearance from *that* point.

Looks are often deceiving. The prime example is the current crop of Ford four-wheel drive trucks which appear to have gobs more ground clearance than other makes. Actually, they don't! They do have a lot more fender-to-tire clearance. In turn this means they can be outfitted with some very large diameter tires—and this will increase ground clearance. Never lose sight of this—if you want to increase ground clearance, install larger diameter tires. Disregard campfire talk about ground clearance—99% of the off-roaders I've ever met couldn't tell you how much ground clearance they had—although every one of them had more than the guy standing next to him in the flickering light of ignorance.

Tiny Tips For When The Going Gets Rough—Maintain momentum when driving or towing through sand, streams or mud. There are many situations in which momentum will save the day—when stopping would stick you for sure.

If you have to pass a stalled vehicle on a narrow, semi-road situation in the middle of nowhere, take the route which circles the high side of the road.

A simple bumper hitch on the front bumper of any off-road rig will let the driver manuever any kind of trailer with ease. Mount the hitch six inches to a foot from center toward the passenger's side so the driver has forward vision along one side of the trailer.

If you meet someone head-on on a narrow dirt road, who has the right of way? Every situation is different so common sense dictates that you talk it over and take everything in consideration if the situation is really tight. Keep in mind that backing downhill is dangerous.

If you get stuck while towing a trailer, unhook and get the towing vehicle free and then go to work freeing the trailer via tow strap or building a better path back to the trailer for the towing vehicle to negotiate.

If you are running a camper rig of any kind on washboard or off-road terrain, stop every couple of hours and check for damage in the interior. Spilled food or drinks really make a mess if they're not caught in time. Duct tape, masking tape or rubber bands across cabinet knobs help keep doors closed when the going gets rough. In this same vein, never leave small children alone in a camper or trailer in an off-road driving situation. They can be seriously injured in an instant in a pitching, bucking rig.

Highway accidents I've seen where campers were involved convinced me that a camper is not to ride in. Stay in the truck cab. If you need more room for your family or friends, get a crew-cab truck. If someone has to go to bed, stop and everybody rest for awhile. A camper shell is not adequate protection for your family in an accident.

In a camper or trailer, it is all too easy to bury emergency equipment, even to the point you forget what you have or where it is. Store jacks, axe, shovel, tire chains, tow cable and tools where they can be reached without major unloading. Use a check list and remember to check it before *every* trip.

If you run a camper rig off-road with some frequency, periodically check the floor bolts to make sure they haven't loosened up. Carry a spare bolt, large washers and nut in case one should pull apart or pull through!

If you run a cab-over camper or large trailer off-road, measure the height of your rig before leaving home. Carry a carpenters' 10-foot folding rule on the dash, under the seat or in the glove compartment. When you get to an overhanging limb or rock formation, get out and measure. Don't just blindly drive under a tree—even leaves just low enough to dust the roof can hide a limb large enough to rip an aluminum roof wide open. And that can be expensive!

Resist that temptation to park in a dry wash or gully—no matter how dry it is or what the weather looks like. A flash flood in the mountains many miles away can turn an outing into a nightmare. Stay on high ground. On the other hand, don't camp under tall, dead trees or tall trees with a lot of dead limbs. A wind during the night can break off enough wood to damage a camper or trailer or demolish a tent.

JACKS

There's more than one way to skin a cat—or get unstuck. A high-centered vehicle can be returned to solid traction with a sheepherder's jack by getting one axle at a time off the ground and then tipping the jack over. There's no need to get the vehicle way up off the ground for this action. It's safer and often easier to take several jackings and move the vehicle sideways 8 or 9 inches at a time.

Even if you never drive off-road, you should always carry a working jack in your vehicle. Although this may sound like the "snow is cold" statement of the year, I personally know of five separate incidents of motorists having flats and no jacks to install the spares. If I can bring that many incidents to mind, think how many there must be in the course of a year. The only trick dumber than not carrying a jack at all is to carry one that doesn't work or won't fit the vehicle.

If you've had your vehicle for a while, had it off-road and stuck it—you probably have a certain feel for it—including the jack. If you just bought a new truck or four-wheeler, chances are you promptly peered behind the seat or popped the hood to locate the jack. Maybe you even glanced at the little decal or owner's manual to see how to use it. Note that the drawing does not show you how to use the jack when one tire is flat and half way into a muddy ditch. Neither does the decal provide any help on how to use the jack in the rain. We do, right here! Read the instructions carefully. Remove the jack from the vehicle. Try to use it in your own driveway. Does it fit the vehicle? Will it work in more than two locations on the bumper if it is a bumper jack? Honestly now, just how high can you raise a tire off the ground to shove under brush, rocks and logs—assuming you are stuck? Does the handle fit the jack? Is the base of the jack so small that it will sink in anything other than solid concrete?

These are all very ho-hum questions until you need real answers smack in the middle of nowhere.

If you've never been through the off-road jack scene before, we suggest you use the stock vehicle jack for a doorstop or rowboat anchor and acquire a sheepherder's jack. These items are sold under a variety of brand names such as Hi-Lift or Handy Man. These devils are heavy—a minimum of 30 pounds compared with eight for a stock bumper jack. They are long! The shortest we've seen is 48 inches. Boy, do they work! The 48-inch jack has a continuous lift of 38 inches and can raise 7,000 pounds.

Bury one end of a vehicle in soft stuff and the jack can start four inches from the base plate to pick up one end of the vehicle, lift it 38 inches and then you can shove jack and vehicle sideways to surer footing. If that technique won't work, raise the vehicle to maximum height and start

Transfer case and differential are hung up on the edge of bank—hidden by weeds. Four-wheel-drive is NO help . . . .

. . . but a sheepherder's jack will go up far enough to relieve the load and hopefully the driver can pull away. If not, the jack can be tipped away from the bank to drag the vehicle off.

Check out the size and design of the baseplate on this sheepherder's jack. All the countersunk holes make it easy to attach to a very solid base. Also note how low the jack can go to slide under a bumper that is really buried.

Ever seen a bumper jack that would raise something 40 inches? Here's one. With a vehicle that far up you could stuff a couple of logs and three Boy Scouts under the wheels for a little added traction.

building up the terrain with brush, logs or rocks.

The jack will pull as well as push. A chain can be connected to either end between vehicle and deadman and the mechanism can be jacked to pull on the chain—36 inches at a time before running the jack back down and resetting the chain. When used as a winch the sheepherder's jack is a far cry from a real winch but for the difference in price and the versatility, the jack is hard to beat. The base plate is as large as any bumper jack and it is easily attached or lashed to a larger plate because the base plate looks like swiss cheese. The jack can be used as a vise because the top can be rotated. If you travel the ranching country of the northwestern United States you'll find a sheepherder's jack in most of the muddy, fender-torn pickups roaming the range. That should tell you something.

In the middle of Baja one afternoon I came upon a Ford pickup which turned on its side when the driver shorted out the connection between his foot and brain. He did have a sheepherder's jack though and was well on his way towards getting the truck back on its wheels. The sheet metal on one side was pretty well roached by the time we finished, but he was able to drive off—thanks to that big ugly jack. With a little imagination, a sheepherder's jack is just plenty hard to beat.

If you are dead set against carrying the sheepherder's jack, check your local auto parts store for a good hydraulic jack. The one I carry is a Hein-Werner rated at 8-tons capacity. Fully collapsed it is 9 inches high and it extends to 20 inches height, an 11-inch lift. This is a lot more capacity than we need but the price of these jacks doesn't seem to go up in proportion to the capacity—thus for only a few dollars more we got the 8-ton instead of the 4-ton model. Keep an open mind on the subject when you start shopping. Some hydraulic jacks can be operated in a horizontal position. If they can, it will say so on the jack. It will also tell you which side to point upward. Obviously, get the most versatile jack you can for the money.

Regardless of the jack you carry, *always* have a jack pad in the truck. A jack pad is a do-it-yourself item: One piece of 3/4 or 1-inch thick piece of plywood about a foot square. We say plywood because it is less prone to splitting than a straight board of the same dimensions. The jack pad goes between the ground and the jack to keep the jack

Upper pawl on the sheepherder's jack can be unbolted and mounted up or down so jack can be used to squeeze or spread. Look at all the holes to come in handy when you need to hook on a piece of chain.

We carry this 8-ton capacity hydraulic jack along with the sheepherder's jack when going to Baja. When you need a jack, you'll find substitutes are hard to come by.

from going down at the same time the vehicle is going up—or worse—the jack just going down and the vehicle NOT going up. Watching a jack bury itself in sand or mud is something you should avoid at all costs.

Shove the piece of plywood under the seat and wedge it into place with a hatchet or tow strap or some other piece of off-road gear so it won't come sliding out and stick under the accelerator pedal when you slam on the brakes. Yes, it did scare the applesauce out of me when it happened.

Without a Jak-Rak, hauling a sheepherder's jack can be a nightmare. Even if you don't want this device figure out some way to lash down that 38 pounds before going off-road. These can be built with or without a lock. Author Waar built his own.

Neat jack that comes with an $8,000 pickup is fully extended at 16-inches if you have the patience and the jack doesn't sink in the ground.

Here's that big, ugly, super-useful sheepherder's jack again--this time being used as a winch. The base of the jack gets lashed to the vehicle with a chain, the rachet head is reversed on the jack bar and the tow strap is attached to the arm on the ratchet head and to an anchor. That 30-inch jack handle provides a lot of pulling power.

Sheepherder's jack bolted to mounts on front bumper uses cable-lock through jack and one bracket to discourage rip-off artists.

To lift a wheel—not just the body—you have to place the jack under the axle or raise the wheel with a wheel jack bracket. Just remove one lug nut to use.

COLD-WEATHER OPERATION

If you do your off-roading in the deserts and mountains of the southwestern United States, you can easily be lulled into thinking you have all of the problems in off-roading and that running in sleet and snow is no problem at all as long as the heater works. Maybe, but the grass always looks greener, right? When operating in sub-zero and near-zero temperatures, small problems get big in a hurry. And, like the "115 in the shade and no shade" conditions of the desert, the environment demands a great deal of respect.

Operation of any mechanical equipment in freezing temperatures presents problems which make precautions and careful servicing mandatory. In some respects you are not offered the leeway in recovery and repair in cold weather that is afforded in extremely hot weather. For instance, if you break something in the middle of the day

Running the snow is a ball if you have the right equipment. I can't get excited about doing much of this alone. One more vehicle on an outing in this country is playing it safe. Photo courtesy of Jim Hanna, Back Pack Shop, Spokane, WA.

in the desert, you can always wait until night when the temperature drops to make repairs without the danger of keeling over with a heat stroke. That luxury is not available in the middle of North Dakota in January. Nights are even colder!

One of the most basic—and easily overlooked —problems of cold temperatures is that of moisture from the "wet air" condensing out and collecting in the gas tank. Water in the gas causes erratic running, loss of power and hard—if not impossible —starting. At very low temperatures, the water turns to ice crystals and clogs fuel lines and/or the carburetor. Today's fuel-return lines in the emission-control systems further compound the problems.

A little thought and you may never encounter the problem. Use a paper-element fuel filter and carry a spare one. This is the best type to use to collect water from the gas. Keep the gas tank just as full as possible at all times. The more gas in the tank, the smaller the volume of air from which moisture can be condensed. Don't be stingy about adding ½ pint of alcohol—shellac thinner, not lacquer thinner—to a full tank of gas now and again during cold weather. This simple step goes a long way towards reducing the hazard of ice formation in the lines, tank and carb. The alcohol combines with any water in the tank and the combination passes through your paper-element filter to be burned in your engine. Isn't that nice? Be sure to wipe all snow, ice and mud from dispensing equipment and from around the fuel tank filler cap *before* removing the cap to refuel. If you drop a tablespoon or two of water in the form of ice or snow in the gas tank each time you refuel, you'll have a cupful of water in the gas tank in a hurry and that will cause trouble.

Adequate warm-up time in sub-freezing is quite critical if you care about component life. Once the engine comes to life let it idle. First on the carburetor's fast-idle step, then faster until the engine temperature comes up. This calls for a thermostat which is operating—something else for your check list. After the engine is warm then you can get into gear and move slowly around the area to warm up lubricants in the transmission, transfer case and differentials. Cold-weather operation is a lot harder on bearing surfaces—of any kind—than you might think. A little thought and prudence at the beginning of each day might save

a long walk at the end of one week or months from now when something gives way.

A thorough inspection of the cooling system and the adding of an antifreeze solution is another one of those little easily overlooked basics. A 50/50 mix of modern-day ethylene-glycol antifreeze will take a cooling system down to about -30°F without freezing. This same strength mix will run on up to nearly 230°F at sea level before boiling. Keep in mind that you can increase the boiling point three degrees for each pound of pressure provided by the pressure cap. The point of all this is that today's antifreeze is plenty good stuff to have in the cooling system all year round. There is one catch to all of this. Most everyone falls into the habit of replacing the coolant with water and this dilutes the mixture. We were guilty of this but solved the problem quite simply. We now buy far more antifreeze than it takes to prep a vehicle for off-roading—or anything else for that matter. Feeling badly about it sitting around in the garage not being put to good use, we used every excuse to check the coolant level and top it off each time with more antifreeze. Use whatever psychology you wish, but make it a habit to top off the cooling system with antifreeze—not water. If the vehicle is used by more than one person or if you have to replenish the coolant with water during the winter months, periodically check mixture strength with a hydrometer. We can't get enthusiastic about investing in one of these gadgets because most reputable service stations have one and will gladly check the coolant for you in hopes of selling you a couple of gallons of antifreeze.

The electrical system, and the battery in particular, takes a substantial beating in severe cold. The first sign of trouble will be hard starting; after that things go downhill in a hurry. The large surges of current necessary to start a cold engine require good contact between brushes and commutators. Wiring and connections should be kept clean and dry. Even slightly pitted points can prevent an engine from firing on an extremely cold morning. The same goes for tired sparkplugs or a weak-sister coil. Corrosion where the cables join the battery posts is another common trouble spot. All of this adds up—a small short here, a bad connection there, one weak cell in the battery and a temperature around zero—and all of the cussin' in the world won't help. There just isn't any substitute for a fresh battery.

Battery warranties aren't worth much during the last couple of months so buy early and you won't be caught with your volts down.

We feel it to be imperative to carry a set of good battery jumper cables for winter running because that's when the battery is probably going to quit. By jumping a good battery to a bad one, a vehicle can be started in a hurry. In fact this is the only easy way to start a vehicle with an automatic transmission and depending on the terrain may be the *only* way of starting a dead vehicle. If an automatic-transmission car fails to start off-road and you do not have jumper cables you are left with the choice of either pushing it or pulling it fast enough to do the job—assuming the engine can be fired by pushing. We mention that because most late transmissions—such as GM's TurboHydro simply will not twist the crank—even if you pushed the vehicle 100 mph. The warning is simple. Carry a good set of jumper cables when you go off-road.

In addition to all of the other stuff you would normally stuff in your tool box for off-road use, consider several other cold weather items. For icy roads, nothing else is quite as effective for traction as chains. Pack a set for the front wheels as well as the rear if you have 4WD. When the going gets rough, chains on the front can make the difference between *go* and *no-go*. Before packing the chains away in the tool or emergency box, jack up the vehicle—in a nice warm garage at your leisure—and install the chains on a tire. Do they fit? What's the fastest way to do it? Read the instructions. What tools are needed? If the chains are used, are they in good condition? This is all yawnsville until you have to bail out of the vehicle when it's stuck, jack it up (lots of luck!) in the dark (flashlight battery good?) in a howling blizzard (hope you're warm) and install a set of chains for the first time—just what makes you so sure they'll fit over those oversized tires you bought last summer? Get the point? Once again now, install those chains several times till you can do it in the dark by feel with your fingers ready to snap off from the cold.

Pack along a roll of heavy bailing wire to use to tie off loose flailing chain ends. A handful of rubber chain tensioners also come in handy.

The other item we carry in our tool box for

		WIND CHILL FACTORS								
					Wind Speed					
		0	5	10	15	20	25	30	35	40
	35	35	33	21	16	12	7	5	3	1
	30	30	27	16	11	3	0	-2	-4	-4
	25	25	21	9	1	-4	-7	-11	-13	-15
	20	20	16	2	-6	-9	-15	-18	-20	-22
Outside	15	15	12	-2	-11	-17	-22	-26	-27	-29
Temp (°F)	10	10	7	-9	-18	-24	-29	-33	-35	-36
	5	5	1	-15	-25	-32	-37	-41	-43	-45
	0	0	-6	-23	-33	-40	-45	-49	-52	-54
	-5	-5	-11	-27	-40	-46	-52	-56	-60	-62
	-10	-10	-15	-31	-45	-52	-58	-63	-67	-69
	-15	-15	-20	-38	-51	-60	-67	-70	-72	-76

cold-weather operation is a pint can of wood alcohol to be dribbled directly into the carb as an emergency starting measure, poured in the gas tank to keep collected moisture from turning to ice, or smeared on the windshield to unfreeze an iced-over windshield.

WIND CHILL FACTOR

Because most of us do the majority of our living indoors, cold weather out of doors can be a brutal shock. If you're new to the cold outside world—note we didn't say cruel—chances are you've peered at a thermometer and figured something was wrong because it sure felt a lot colder than the indicated reading. It might not actually be colder than the indicated reading, but wind lowers your body temperature very quickly and makes it seem colder. This is known as the *wind chill factor*. Looking at a wind chill chart we find that 30-degree weather with the wind blowing 25 miles an hour means you should be dressed for 0-degree weather.

MANIFOLD HEAT(ER)

You can put that cast-iron exhaust manifold(s) to good use in chilly weather. If you have a wee one with you, the exhaust manifold is just ideal for bringing a baby bottle up to temperature while the adults are sipping on their coffee. Just place the filled bottle on the hot exhaust manifold. We've even wired cans of hash and soup to the manifold so supper would be warm and ready when we stopped. Chances are you won't want to make a habit of eating this way; but if you're running late and don't care to build a fire and fix a meal a warm can of soup tastes pretty good when the wind is howling. Don't expect the food to get hot—just warm.

With the energy crisis maybe we should throw dinner on the engine before we start home from work every night. Exhaust stoves may be just around the corner.

With the emission control systems of today, enough exhaust heat is being piped into the intake manifold to burn the paint off—so don't overlook the top of the intake manifold as an area to which you can lash your cold turkey. No, not your wife—the gobble, gobble kind!

HOT WEATHER

The hot dry weather of the Southwest is pretty hard on a vehicle so give it a helping hand before grinding to a stop in a sandwash with that horrid hissing sound coming out from under the hood and the temp gauge in the red area next to the big H.

The first thing not to do when prepping a vehicle for hot weather operation is to take out the thermostat. The thermostat not only acts as a valve to let water in and out of the engine according to temperature but it also acts as a restrictor to keep the water in the radiator long enough to be cooled. So *leave the thermostat in.* If you start having some heating problems, pull the thermostat out, put it in a pan of water and start boiling the water. Before the water comes to a boil, the spring should compress and the valve should open up wide. This tells you the thermostat is working. You can now put it back in the engine with a new gasket. If the valve doesn't open wide, get a new thermostat.

Before heading for Death Valley in August, take a look at the radiator cap on your rig. Somewhere on the cap it will tell you how much pressure the cap was designed to hold. Chances are it is somewhere between eight and 15 pounds. Waltz down to the local garage, radiator shop or service station and borrow their cap checker. This handy little device tells you how much pressure the cap will actually hold. It should hold what it says it will. If not, replace it. Pressure raises the boiling point of the water three degrees for every pound

of pressure. Thus a "heating problem" can sometimes be cured by replacing the cap with one that holds pressure.

If you have an eight-pound cap on your Jeep now, why not replace it with a 15-pound cap and raise the boil point even further? Fine, until either the radiator or a hose lets go at 12 pounds. A radiator shop can pressure check a radiator for you and tell how much the core will stand. Use new hoses and good clamps. When replacing radiator hoses—replace the heater hoses, too.

A radiator shop has a set procedure for rebuilding radiators and if your heating problems persist—take it to a shop. Don't waste time and money with a lot of little cans of magic stuff claimed to cure overheating. They probably won't, but you'll have spent your money which could have gone toward fixin' the problem.

A 50/50 mix of a brand name antifreeze solution should be in the cooling system at all times. This keeps the boiling point pretty close to 260 degrees in conjunction with a working pressure cap. Follow the directions for putting the antifreeze into the cooling system. If it says flush the radiator—do it.

Cooling down a hot running engine can most always be helped with a shroud to funnel the air from the radiator to the fan and by running a five- or six-blade fan. If your vehicle doesn't have a fan shroud, see if the dealer has one. If not, a good sheet-metal shop can make one. A wrecking yard can take care of the six-blade fan.

When driving in hot weather keep an eye peeled on the temp gauge. If it starts to move over into the hot zone, back off the throttle and turn off the air conditioning. Both tactics do a lot to bring the temperature back down. As a last resort turn on the heater full blast. The heater core is a small radiator core. When you turn the fan on the little radiator really starts radiating heat—taking heat out of the water. If you stop to let the engine cool off, raise the hood but never, ever take the radiator cap off a hot engine with a pressure system. If you have water to spare, pour some on the top of the radiator and let it run down the outside of the core, but don't take the cap off to add water until the engine has cooled down.

A coolant-recovery system sold at any parts store and most discount houses is a good deal—and they are inexpensive. They do not make the engine run cooler. Their function is to capture coolant when the engine gets too hot and coolant overflows. Then when the engine cools off, the lost liquid is drawn back into the main cooling system by vacuum.

If you are out in the middle of the desert for several days, open the hood every morning before firing up. With the engine cold, checking all of the fluid levels takes only a couple of minutes and it is one less thing you have to worry about during the day. Battery water has a way of evaporating in a hurry in hot weather. Don't check just one cell—check them all. The plates should always be covered with the water/acid mix.

CARBURETION

Unfortunately, there's not enough space in this book to cover everything you need to know about your carburetor and how to make it work better off-road. In a separate book, *Rochester Carburetors,* H. P. Books has 11 pages on off-road carburetor problems and fixes. While devoted to the 2G and Quadra-Jet Rochesters, this info by expert off-road racer Doug Roe can be applied to any carburetor. Float shape, fulcrum, leverage and setting are discussed as are inlet-valve size, plastic bowl stuffers, linkage, vibration, dams and partitions. Angularity and its effects on the discharge nozzles and venting are also covered. If you have a Holley carburetor, you'll want to buy the *Holley Carburetor* book, too.

In general you should keep the carburetor size (flow capacity) as small as is consistent with the majority of the use you give your vehicle. Switching from a two-barrel to a four-barrel will probably aggravate your stalling problems unless you choose a carburetor especially designed for off-roading, say one of the Q-Jets described in *Rochester Carburetors* or a Holley 600 CFM RV-type. These carbs will handle fairly high angularity. Many four barrels designed for racing or high-performance street machines tend to flood out or lean out in rough running, especially on hills.

Keep the smallest possible inlet needle/seat allowing acceptable accelerations within the usual use of the vehicle. Run the fuel pressure as low as you can. In these cases, road tests are essential. Keep reducing inlet valve size until performance drops off in accelerations on a smooth road, as measured with stop watch. Do some seat-of-the-pants checks over rough stuff, too. When acceleration drops off, go back up one size and you've got

it. Do the same with a fuel-pressure regulator: Keep reducing pressure until acceleration drops off, then back up to the previous step with no performance drop-off.

In off-roading, bigger or more is not usually better in carburetion. Smart runners use small carbs designed for off-road angularity, coupled with small inlet valves and low fuel pressure. I'll bet they laugh a lot at the campfire bench-racing sessions where the know-it-alls brag about their super sized fuel pumps and carburetors! Most guys I know will admit their rigs run worse and give awful mileage as compared to the original carburetor they swapped for a different unit.

Assembly and tuning info for all 2- and 4-barrel models including replacements. Covers manifolds, fuel pump/filters/lines too. 208 pages, 300 illustrations.

Includes off-road, economy and race tuning info to make your engine run right. Q-jet rebuilding section alone features 70 photos, 300 pages, 832 illustrations.

VEHICLE AILMENTS

By now, we're pretty well convinced that 95%—or more—of all off-road-vehicle problems not related to tires could be avoided if the owner would religiously follow a planned maintenance schedule. As soon as you unpack from a trip, clean the vehicle—really a scene if you've been in mud—then inspect from stem to stern. Get in the habit of checking lug nuts for tightness, tie rods for straightness, all cotter keys and nuts and bolts in place, etc. Did you bend the tailpipe on a rock? Are all brake lines still clamped down securely? Did you crease a skid plate? Take it off and straighten it *now*. Spend even more time under the hood. Is there a wire chafing against the inner fender panel? Remove the air cleaner and give the carb the onceover. Is the throttle linkage tight? Is the radiator secure or has a mounting bolt backed off? Lubricant just barely seeping from the end of an axle or transmission is no problem at all in the driveway, but it can turn into a nightmare 50 miles from the pavement. How about the radiator hoses? All clear of any belts? Remember the battery mounts, too. How about the fuel tank?

If you discover a number of small items that you plan to take care of before the next outing, make a list and tape it to the windshield right now. Being stranded with a broken vehicle is a jarring reminder that you forgot to do something.

Follow the factory recommendations on routine service to the letter. When in doubt, do maintenance sooner—not later. Anyone running a set of sparkplugs, points and condenser for more than 12,000 miles is just kidding themselves on two counts. Any money you think you are saving by using them longer is costing you in reduced gas mileage. Secondly, despite how smoothly the engine may start and run, the components are living on borrowed time. Replace them and carry

Bulging billfold on this guy indicates the money he's saved by checking the vehicle *before* he goes off-road. This is downright unpleasant in the dark when it's raining.

spares. You needn't carry a full set of sparkplugs but pack along two or three and a set of points and condenser. Make double durn sure the spares fit the vehicle! Dumb as this may sound, we've seen spares that didn't fit more than once. Radiator *and* heater hoses should be replaced every 15,000 miles regardless of how they look. Same goes for the fan and accessory-drive belts.

Batteries are programmed to expire just before the warranty is up. Keep ahead of the situation and replace the battery three months before the guarantee is up. You're betting pennies against the ability of starting some morning. The most you'll save is whatever portion of the guarantee is represented by the three remaining months. Guarantees are prorated so you only recover that small part of the replacement cost. Chances are you can watch for sales and more than make up for the "loss" you'll take on replacing the battery early.

Attend to grease, oil and filters on a regular schedule unless a long or hard trip dictates the routine be stepped up. Use quality components intended to see service in a severe environment. Just because the items are expendable, doesn't mean they should be of poor quality or just whatever you can find on sale.

If it sounds like we are a bear on preventive maintenance, you guessed right. Curing an ill or preventing one from occurring is so easy to do at home and a frustrating—sometimes impossible— task when you're up to your hubs in snow, mud, dust, water or rocks.

There is one last, but most important, factor you should consider before taking a vehicle off-road. Know the basics of how your vehicle operates. Just because the rig costs $7500 and is brand new does not make it—or you—all-powerful and all-conquering. Do you know how to get it in— and out—of four-wheel drive? Have you actually done it? Have you locked and unlocked the hubs? A $600 winch does precious little good if you don't know how to release the cable and don't understand how to use it.

We point this out because more and more people are traveling off-road! *Many of them for the first time in new vehicles.* In other words, they are facing an unfamiliar environment with an unfamiliar tool—not an ideal situation at best. If you a   in that catagory, admit it to yourself and othe   Then store away every scrap of informa-

tion you can about the area you'll be traveling in the vehicle you'll be taking. You should have a basic knowledge of how an internal-combustion engine operates and you should be more than just a little familiar with your vehicle. Libraries and bookstores can get you started on the automotive basics and a dealer can supply a service manual— different from an owner's manual—for your vehicle. Knowing the points are inside the distributor really won't help very much if it requires a very long, narrow screwdriver to remove the distributor cap and you didn't pack one because you didn't know one was needed. This kind of information may not be in any service or owner's manual. Spend some time—like a lot—with the hood up and the service manual in hand. What is that? Where does that wire go? Where is the fuse block? Where is the ground strap? In other words, get to the point where you can open the hood with confidence that you know what you are looking at, what each part is for—and why it's there in the first place.

If you are a prudent off-road driver and a real fuss-budget on preventive maintenance, chances are quite good that you'll never have any serious vehicle trouble off-road. Knowledge of basic mechanics and a cool head can save many a situation. Should your beast of burden suddenly die like a well drilled dove, be prepared to do many things, but don't panic. Don't cuss. Don't scream. Don't tell the passengers that this is all their fault. Don't tell yourself that it is all your fault . . . even if it is. Accept the fact the vehicle died and will not restart. Now think about how it died. Was it suddenly or with a cough? If it died "cleanly" without warning, suspect electrical problems. If it sputtered and wheezed, caught, and then died: Suspect the fuel system, but don't discount ignition problems yet.

Let's say it died cleanly and will not restart. Don't even get out. Don't even open the door. Just sit there and think about how it all happened. Did you hit a super big hole or rock? Did the engine seem to miss at all before it died? Did your big fat knee accidentally hit the ignition key and turn it when you jerked the wheel to avoid that big rock? Don't laugh—strange things happen. *Now* get out and open the hood. Start with the battery—check both terminals. Now check the "other end" of the ground cable that most likely runs to some

When it breaks it breaks—and you might as well make the best of it. A cold beer and a good night's sleep will give you a clear head to make the job a lot easier the next morning.

place on the engine block. Next comes the hot lead from the battery to the starter. Now go to the coil. Shove down on the big fat wire that runs from the center of the coil to the center of the distributor. It should be tight at both ends. There are two smaller wires running from the coil. Check both of those terminals. Trace them down and check both ends of these wires. In most all cases you'll find that there is a terminal loose—the nut or screw backed out, fell down in the dirt and the current came to an abrupt halt.

When you are bouncing down a rough road, wires under the hood and under the dash move around a lot more than you might imagine. If it happens to be the right wire that gets rubbed bare of insulation and makes contact with a metal part—the engine stops. Check out the radio, the lights, the wipers. Take a look at the fuse box. If a fuse is blown, look for what may have caused a short to overload the circuit. Obviously these are the simple and routine things that can go wrong with an electrical system. Bear in mind that these are the things that most often go wrong. Be thorough, cool and logical in your approach to locating the trouble. Do not start jiggling wires at random and yelling at someone in the truck to keep cranking it! About 90% of the wiring in a

vehicle has absolutely nothing to do with the engine running. The typical ignition circuit is very basic, very simple. Find the diagram in the vehicle service manual and understand it long before you go off-road.

You should be aware that some unusual things can happen to an ignition system in an off-road vehicle. A coil can fail—especially true with an older item. Sometimes a coil will fail when it heats up, then work OK almost instantly thereafter—after the engine has stopped. Substituting another coil may help you detect whether this is the problem. We have seen the case on a battery break open, the acid ran out and the engine quit.

We once failed a distributor rotor. Seems the cowl section twisted enough to get into the distributor cap which flexed just enough to create an obstruction for the rotor—which refused to flex. Part of the metal tip broke off and sparks refused to flow out of the distributor. Points can close up because of heat or dust—but this will most often result in sporadic misfiring and/or loss of power before the engine dies—if it ever does.

QUICK IGNITION CHECK

Always start with the ignition. It is the easiest to check and most off-road engine troubles happen in this department. Pull any plug wire off a plug. Do this carefully, especially with the stock TVR carbon-string-type wire. Pull the wire off by pulling the plug connector—not by yanking on the wire. Lay the wire on the engine about ½ inch away from something metal. The rubber boot sometimes makes it difficult to see the spark, so you might have to shove a nail or screw or wire up in there to make an extension. Or, you can install a spare plug and lay the base of the plug against the engine. Turn the ignition switch ON and have someone crank the engine several times while you watch the end of the wire, extension or plug for a spark. If you get good healthy sparks, you can go directly to the fuel system. Let's say you didn't get a spark. What now?

Pull the center wire out of the distributor—the coil wire—and place the end about ½ inch away from some metal on the engine. With the engine turning over on the starter you should be getting a bunch of spark from the wire end.

If your battery is low and you want to make this check without using the starter, snap the distributor cap off and take off the rotor. Turn the engine over somehow until the points are closed. Turn the ignition ON. Pry the points apart with a screwdriver. You should get a healthy spark from the coil wire end.

If you get sparks from the coil wire end with either of these tests, the chances are you have isolated the trouble to be in either the rotor or the distributor cap—or both. There's not much you can do here because about all you can do is to clean the pieces with a little gasoline on a clean cloth. Rub out any dirt or carbon you see, then dry everything off before putting it all back together. Try again with all wires installed except for one plug wire. If you still have no spark, start looking for a guy carrying a spare cap and rotor with his tools.

If you decide the problem is with the points, condenser or primary circuit, pull the cap and rotor. Keep the coil wire laying on part of the engine. Either stop the engine with the points open or open them and slide in a piece of paper or cardboard—paper match covers work fine—between where the point arm and the distributor shaft rub. The idea is to get the points open and hold them that way. Now turn the ignition key ON. With pocket knife, screwdriver or a coin create a short

across the ends of the points. What you are now doing is bypassing the points with whatever you are using to create the short. If you now get a healthy spark out of the end of the coil wire—still held close to the engine, you know that the trouble lies in the points. They are probably badly pitted or full of dirt. If you don't get a good spark; the condenser or coil is bad. If you have a condenser with you, replace it, if not, start looking for outside help. Building a condenser out in the middle of nowhere is like "building" a couple of quarts of oil out of rock and sand. Don't go through life though waiting for a condenser to go bad . . . they do of course, but normally they don't go all at once. I'd say a condenser is the least likely failure in an ignition system.

If your little test revealed bad points you'll need to insert something between them while they are in the "open" position and jiggle it back and forth to file the "mountains" off and/or remove the dust and dirt. A couple of bottle caps full of gasoline, white gas from the camp stove, or lighter fluid will help wash away a lot of dust, grit and dirt if that is the trouble. Then to aid in the cleaning and drying, break out your hanky and shove it around the points with a thin knife blade. Be careful, don't bend or break the point arm.

If you can get an eyeball down close enough to the points you can determine if they are pitted. If they are, the abrasive coating off a book of matches can be used to file down the high places. Don't get carried away with this. Several passes between the points should be sufficient. With the points still open, blow or wash out the debris left by the filing. Clean everything up as best you can and put it all back together.

While we still have that *"as best you can"* phrase in mind, we would warn you to do every off-road repair job as best you can the first time around. Haste makes waste has to be the dullest, oldest axiom around, but off-road it has to be one of the most meaningful. A half-way repair job the first time around can easily lead to one that simply cannot be solved without outside help. Keep that in mind, no matter what you are repairing.

The last area to suspect in the ignition circuit is the coil. They do fail. If you spot goo dripping out the bottom or end of a coil then you can assume that something shorted out inside and that

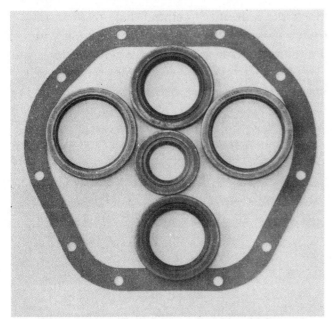

After a long trip or even a short weekend in which running through a lot of water was involved, you'd be wise to check the front differential and the hub assemblies to see if you have taken on water. A sharp off-roader will always have the necessary seals and gaskets around so he won't be dependent on a dealer's parts stock.

you'll need a new coil to get moving again. If you get no spark and know the battery and wiring is good, then the coil is dead and that's that.

If the battery and wiring is OK, and the coil gives off a miserly, weak spark then there is one little trick you might pull to get you a few more miles down the trail—but only a *very few miles.* Short across the ballast resistor to give the coil directly on full battery voltage. If the coil has anything left it will produce a pretty healthy spark for awhile—but only for awhile if you have to leave it this way to make the engine run. This may be difficult or impossible to do if the ballast resistor is part of the primary ignition wire from the ignition switch. Here's where that study you've been doing in the workshop manual pays off. You should know whether the ballast resistor is exposed and easy to get at—or built into the wire. If it is built into the wire, you will have to jumper direct from the battery to the primary terminal on the coil.

Another thing to consider is the possibility of a worn-out or failed ignition switch. This is usually detectable by observing other items which normally work with the switch—such as the fuel gauge, ammeter, oil-pressure gauge, etc. If the switch is the problem, you may have to jury-rig

some wires from the battery to the coil and to the starter solenoid. Study your vehicle. If you know how it works, you can fix it a lot easier.

High resistance at the battery terminals is another likely problem—pull the cables off the battery and scratch or sand both battery posts and the contact surfaces of the battery cables to make sure current can flow from battery to the wire.

Let's say you still haven't located the trouble —big healthy sparks are coming out of the spark-plug wires and the engine won't start. This is the time for you to get a little colder and a little more logical about tracing the source of the trouble. For instance, let's say you pulled off the main highway about 15 miles back and have been traveling down a dry wash and were doing just fine until the engine died. You can't be out of gas because you filled up your 28 gallon tank only five miles before pulling off the highway. You've got plenty of gas. Maybe. You might nonchalantly amble back to the rear of the truck just to make sure the tank didn't get ripped off on that last big rock, or that a line didn't come loose or that a gouge hasn't been sliced from breakfast til next week right in the bottom of the tank. Get the point? You may know in your mind that you have plenty of gas —but does the engine know that if there is no gas in the fuel line?

This brings us to the fuel system check out. The first step is to disconnect the primary coil wire that supplies voltage to the coil. Disconnect it at the coil and tape the end so it cannot ground against any metal. We just may have a goodly amount of gasoline sloshing over the engine in a minute and we don't want the engine to fire, and we don't want an engine compartment full of sparks trying to occupy the same space as the gasoline. Something might go wrong and you would have the misery of learning how much futile effort can go into trying to extinguish an engine fire off-road.

With the coil wire off, remove the air cleaner so you can disconnect the steel or rubber line running from the fuel pump to the carb. You'll need two wrenches to do this. Both may have to be special ones and one must be a tubing wrench or you are not likely to be able to get the tube nut loose from the carburetor. On a lot of carbs this will reveal a filter built into the carb where the fuel line goes in. You may have to loosen a fitting on the side of the carb to get to it. A fuel filter has to be pretty dirty before it won't pass sufficient fuel to keep the engine running. Examine the filter, wash it out with gasoline and re-install it. Now direct the open end of the fuel line toward the open end of a tin can or soft-drink bottle and have someone crank the engine over while you watch the end of the fuel line. Intermittent surges of gasoline should come from the line. Keep cranking the engine until you see about four of these surges. They should be pretty evenly spaced and all should produce about the same amount of gasoline. If this is what you get, then the fuel lines are OK and the pump is OK. If you don't get any fuel, you are out of gas, a line is plugged, the pump is dead, or the filter in the pump is plugged. On some early design fuel pumps the filter was enclosed in a thick glass jar arrangement. If you have this kind, make sure the glass is still intact.

If you don't get the fuel out of the fuel pump, then disconnect the line between the pump and the tank. Usually it is pretty easy to do this on the fuel pump, especially if you have a tubing wrench like I mentioned a little ways back there. If you have not parked on the side of a mountain to make this impromptu pit stop, gasoline will normally flow out of this fuel line—assuming the line between the pump and the tank is not plugged and that you have fuel. If you can hear fuel sloshing in the tank when you rock the vehicle, then you can rightly suspect that the fuel line is pinched or plugged. A careful examination of the line from pump to tank will tell you if it's pinched—but not if it's plugged. If you don't have a tire pump to feed air pressure into the fuel line, you'll just have to figure out how to get down there and blow very hard in the fuel line. If the line is plugged and you free it with air pressure blown toward the tank, the crud just goes back in the tank and you may have more of the same trouble later on. Lotsa luck though on blowing hard enough into the filler neck of the tank—pressurizing it enough to clear a line.

If you are getting fuel out of the fuel pump in healthy spurts, then you can go back to the filter in the carburetor or start looking elsewhere for trouble. Other than peering down the carburetor to see if gas is squirting in when you move the throttle linkage, don't get into the carburetor unless you know enough to put it all back together without help. If there is enough trouble inside the carb to keep the engine from firing you will have been nursing along a very sick engine for a very long time—and nothing short of a carb clean up and perhaps a few replacement pieces will get you moving again.

Depending on what kind of driving you were doing just before the engine died, the engine could be flooded. A lot of severe bouncing around can slosh enough fuel over into the manifold to make the engine sputter and then die—especially if you were running at low speed. If this is the case, hold the accelerator pedal flat to the floor and crank the engine over. This allows the engine to "drink" a lot of air in proportion to gasoline. This eliminates the "flooded" condition so the engine can start.

If you have been driving in very hot terrain, gasoline can vaporize in the fuel lines and pump—so the carburetor just never "sees" the fuel. Called *vapor lock,* this causes the engine to stumble for several minutes before it dies completely. Sometimes it will never die—it will just continue to stumble along erratically at greatly reduced power. If this is a chronic condition, you can install an electric fuel pump near the fuel tank and run it in conjunction with the stock fuel pump. Tinfoil or other insulation around the fuel lines will also help. I've used wet rags wrapped around the fuel pump and line leading to the carb to keep the fuel in a liquid state. A continuing vapor-lock problem is most annoying and you may elect to find something else to do until it gets dark and temperature drops. This will also eliminate the problem . . . until it gets hot again tomorrow.

Off-road trouble shooting can be a real test of your mechanical knowledge and skills. Approach it with confidence and not with fear. Above all else, don't panic—and don't stop thinking. Every time you solve a problem off-road you are the richer for it . . . in more ways than one.

Things can happen way down deep inside the engine that will keep it from firing . . . but those things cannot be fixed in 30 minutes with hand tools down in a dry wash—so why worry about it? You do wear your hiking boots when you go off-road, don't you?

AIR CLEANERS

Oil-wetted foam can be very effective as an air cleaner when placed over a stock paper element. Note effective use of bungee cord to tension the air cleaner element, and note small coil spring which holds foam block over breather hole in valve cover.

Too many vehicle owners pay only nodding homage to the service-manual recommendations about changing the air cleaner. This is a costly error for anyone operating in an off-road environment. The other side of the coin is to buy and install (without thinking) every new, trick, heavy-duty off-road air cleaner that can be sold by advertising. This can also be costly and may not even reduce the flow of wear-causing dust into your engine.

Here is some solid background information on air filters from one of my previous H. P. Books, *Baja-Prepping VW Sedans & Dune Buggies*. It should help you weed out the non-Shinola from all the advertising claims and allow you to select and maintain an efficient air-filtering system for your engine.

The effectiveness of the various filter types: paper or foam—or centrifugal with either element type is not soon to be resolved by off-roaders. Al-

liances have been formed and loyalties cemented in this area and opinions are hard to change. Factual information is almost impossible to gather—because of differences in servicing a cleaning system.

Try these tips and you'll be close. Apply a layer of thick wheel-bearing grease to the upper and lower sealing-edge surfaces of either paper or the polyurethane foam elements: Check often to see that the sealing surfaces on the element and on the element holder are not warped or distorted. If the filter element can be cleaned, follow the manufacturer's directions to the letter. Check all hoses, clamps and mounting brackets often for cracks, leaks or possible mount failure. Get a filter element large enough to do the job. The drugstore-cowboy, chrome-topped wonder that was a press fit on a '49 Ford two barrel will not get the job done. Such items are of little help on the street, much less off the road.

The AC Spark Plug Division of General Motors has supplied the following information which helps to separate fact from the fictions to which we have all been exposed. In summary, it would appear that the current trend towards the combining of a polyurethane "sock" around a paper-element filter may be as "near-perfect" a combination as can be had.

AC points out that proper filtration of air prior to its entrance into the engine reduces fouling of carburetor parts and spark plugs, and reduces wear on engine parts: pistons, piston rings, cylinder walls, and bearings.

Even a small-displacement engine can consume an entire "box car" full of air in less than half an hour. If driving conditions were considered hazardous because of dust clouds reducing visibility, then our box car full of air would contain at least a handful of dust.

Air cleaners are classified into general groups based on the principle of filtration and the "condition" of the filtering material. AC makes oil bath, dry paper, wetted paper, polyurethane foam and "dual-state" or paper-polyfoam combinations.

Oil-Wetted Metal—Filtering material is a relatively coarse entanglement of crinkled aluminum ribbon, coated with a film of oil—usually by dipping in clean engine oil and allowing to drain. As a particle of dust tries to penetrate the element, it strikes an oiled surface of the ribbon and sticks. This process continues until all of the oil has been soaked up and the dirt particles no longer stick when they strike the dry, dust-covered ribbons.
NOTE: This filter has a low first cost and is not very efficient. It should not be even considered for an off-road vehicle.

Oil Bath—Here again, dust particles are collected on an oily surface. In this case, the filter element is a pad of densely entwined cactus fibers positioned directly over a pool of oil. The incoming dirty air is forced to reverse its direction over this oil before entering the element. In making a 180° turn over the pool of oil, many dust particles strike the oil and stay there. Oil mist which is carried into the element by the air stream washes off and re-oils the filtering fibers.

Oil-bath cleaners are expensive. They are big and bulky. Some form of splash protection is required to keep the oil from leaving the reservoir when the vehicle stops suddenly, starts suddenly or bounces on uneven terrain. A sustained vehicle attitude such as on a long hill or in a pit will alter the oil level within the air cleaner, impairing its function.

The filter element must be oil-wetted to perform its function, consequently the oil bath air cleaner must be designed to draw oil mist into the element at reasonably low air flows at or near engine idle conditions. On the other hand, at high engine speeds the air flow must not be permitted to draw the oil completely through the element and carry the dirt into the engine.

Unless the oil level is maintained accurately, the oil mist will not be drawn into the filter element at the designed air flow rate, leaving the engine unprotected. If long periods elapse between servicings, dirt displaces oil in the reservoir, raises the level and lowers the pull-over point (the air flow rate at which oil is drawn through the element into the engine). The result is a sudden and infinitely more harmful dose of dirt thrown into the engine, and the filter becomes almost completely useless immediately thereafter. Average efficiency of an oil-bath cleaner at 150 CFM is 95%, increasing with flow.

Dry-Filters—Until the early '60's, dry paper was considered the best air filter on the market for passenger car and light-truck usage. Protection given to the engine in terms of keeping dirt out of the intake system was superior to any other readily available filter on the market.

An impregnated paper composed mainly of cotton and rayon fibers is not in any way oiled and relies on its dense structure to act as a strainer. Its "pore size" is very small and only a few of the "holes" are even as large as a human hair. Although this type of element "plugs up" faster than the other two, this "clogging" action is retarded because many of the dust particles adhere to the filtering fibers.

Overall laboratory efficiency of dry-type cleaners is about 98% and does not vary appreciably with variations in air flow. Initial restriction is about the same as wetted aluminum mesh and somewhat less than an oil-bath unit. Although dust capacities vary considerably with size, an oil-bath unit has many times the capacity of a dry-type unit. However, the dry type will protect the engine religiously even until the engine will no longer run due to lack of air.

If cleaned with expert care, dry-type elements may be re-used several times. AC recommends that these filter elements be replaced by new ones as indicated by an AC paper-element air-cleaner tester.

Wetted Polyurethane—These filters came next, starting around 1960. The wettant gave polyurethane the increase in efficiency over dry polyurethane necessary for automotive usage. This element offered even more engine protection than dry paper. To assure consistent high performance of this element, a special wettant was developed for application at the factory. This wettant had greater adhesion to polyurethane than the oils which had previously been used. This assured that the wettant would be retained on the element and provide high dust-collecting performance.

Even though these polyurethane elements gave superior engine protection, the dust capacity was less than that of dry-paper elements on some road tests. . . there was still room for improvement.

Wetted Paper—For 1964 cars, AC engineered and released improved paper elements with increased efficiency and dirt capacity. The improvement resulted from wetting the paper with oil as part of the manufacturing process.

Numerous tests showed that the dust capacity was doubled and that the oil treatment also increased the efficiency of the paper over a wide range of dust-particle sizes.

The final tests were based on field results in which oiled-paper elements were run in direct comparisons against dry elements at the G. M. Desert Proving Ground in Arizona under extremely severe conditions. The oiled-paper elements consistently out-performed the dry-paper and wetted-polyurethane elements. The dirt capacity of oiled paper is double that of dry paper and more than double that of wetted polyurethane. Examination of interior air-cleaner and carburetor surfaces shows them to be much cleaner when an oiled-paper element has been used.

Dual-Stage—This type was developed as an improvement over oil-bath units used on trucks in heavy-duty operations with severe dust conditions.

The Dual-Stage air cleaner provides improved

Here's an engine that's headed for trouble. The owner of this four wheeler replaced the big heavy-duty stock filter with an accessory filter far too small for the job. On a long dusty trip this could cause a problem. The original equipment may be the best you can buy and since you've already bought it—why not keep it?

protection against engine wear due to dust. This is due to the high filtration efficiency of the wetted-paper secondary stage. Dual-Stage elements have a filter efficiency of 99.5% compared to AC and other oil-bath cleaners which range from 86.6% to 98.6% efficient.

These air cleaners require less frequent servicing because they hold more dust. The following chart compares Dual-Stage air cleaners (used by Chevrolet) with other conventional elements and oil-bath air cleaners for the same engines.

FILTER COMPARISON

Air Cleaner	Dust Capacity @ 5" Restriction Increase @ 200 cfm	Filtering Efficiency
Dual-Stage	772 grams	99.5%
Dry Paper	120 grams	98.2%
Oil-Wetted Paper	263 grams	99.4%
Oil Bath	300 grams	98.6%

Chart courtesy AC/Delco Div. of GM

This data indicates that Dual-Stage elements have over six times the capacity of dry paper, three times that of oil-wetted paper, and two times the capacity of an oil-bath type.

The paper and outer wrap filter design is a two-stage filter containing Glycol-wetted polyurethane (at least 1/2" thick) backed with oiled pleated filter paper. This integral construction of filter paper, polyurethane, backfire and support screens all embedded in plastisol and seals is similar in size and shape to dry-type paper filters containing pleated paper only.

This filter's performance characteristics, particularly its dirt-holding capability, make it suited for severe dust conditions.

RELATIVE MERITS OF AIR-CLEANER TYPES

Type	Efficiency	Service Life	Cost
Centrifugal*	Poor	Long	High
Aluminum Mesh	Poor	Long	Low
Oil Bath	Good	Long	High
Polyurethane (wetted)	Good	Medium	Medium
Paper (wetted)	Excellent	Medium	Medium
Paper-Poly	Excellent	Medium to Long	Medium

*AC's comparison is unfair to present-day centrifugal filters which combine centrifugal action with a paper element to get very high efficiency.

Chart courtesy AC/Delco Div. of GM

AC Dual-Stage air filter has pleated-paper construction surrounded by oil-soaked polyurethane-foam wrapping, one of the most efficient filters you can buy for the dust encountered in off-roading.

CYCLOPAC Air Cleaners are made in horizontal and vertical models by Donaldson Co. of Minneapolis. Truck and heavy-equipment dealers have these available in several sizes to fit dune-buggy engines. These combine centrifugal action with a paper element to achieve 99% cleaning efficiency. Price is about $35 for the 5¼" diameter model which weighs five pounds. Arrows show air flow.

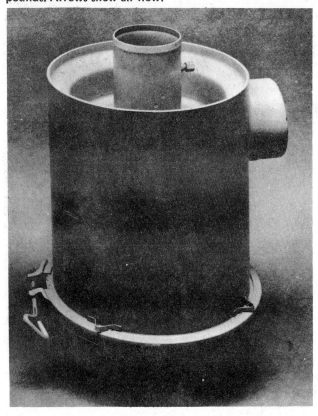

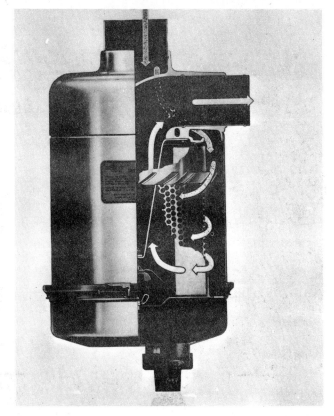

WINCHES

To illustrate the strength of his Sidewinder winch, Vic Hickey pulled off this demonstration for the press—a trick for the professionals to pull. It was no problem getting the Sidewinder to pull the Blazer up the tree—the time was spent bracing the tree! Photo by Tom Madigan.

Regardless of the rig you drive off-road, chances are you do not have a winch. Compared to the number of off-road type vehicles around, the winch is one relatively scarce item. Why so? There's no one single reason. A winch is expensive —about 600 bucks by the time it's mounted and ready to do you any good. That's a lot of bread, but just *part* of the reason. For a lot of off-roaders, a winch is a mystery item. There is a great lack of knowledge about how the winch works and how you go about using one. Couple that with a gnawing that comes before the check writing—do I really need one?

Let's look at the pros and cons. First, the plus side. Simply stated, a good winch can get you or someone else out of one hell of a lot of trouble. You can go places with a winch that you wouldn't dare try without one. Because of all of this you will have the capability of going places alone where you wouldn't go before. With a block and tackle, a winch mounted on the front of a vehicle can be used to lift heavy loads, move timbers, pull engines out of vehicles—even the vehicle in which the winch is mounted on! By far the greatest advantage of having a winch is that snug secure feeling of knowing that when you get stuck in sand, high-centered on a log, mired in mud, or bound up in snow that you can get unstuck in minutes with almost no effort. Without the winch you rely on a helpful yank from another vehicle or hours of digging and jacking. Finally it must be remembered there are times and places where a vehicle can be stuck so firmly that no amount of digging and jacking can free the vehicle. In this case, the possibilities are narrowed to a winch and another vehicle. That's the positive side of installing a winch on your off-road vehicle. It could save you a *long* walk someday.

The negative side of the picture shapes up like this. A winch is expensive—we've already mentioned that. Although a well mounted and maintained winch enhances the resale value of the vehicle, you won't be able to recoup all of its cost. For the most part a winch is seldom used. Months and months of off-roading can pass before the winch is needed. When it is needed will you be getting yourself unstuck or helping some other vehicle out of a bind? That brings us back to the money—is it worth that kind of money to help

someone else get unstuck? Off-roaders running the wide open spaces of the Southwest point out that when they get stuck in the sand, there ain't nuthin' handy to hook a winch to, so why bother? A winch weighs a lot and on some vehicles the additional weight causes the front suspension to sag and bottom with some frequency. This can be cured with heavier springs and shocks, but that costs more money . . . and doesn't do anything to help an already rough riding vehicle.

DO YOU NEED A WINCH?

I don't know. That's one question only you can answer. Do you travel alone off the road? What's the weather like where you travel? Can you freeze to death or suffer from heat exhaustion? In other words, could a winch mean the difference between life and death for you? Do you really yearn to go places you won't travel now because you don't have a winch? Do you genuinely like to help people in trouble? Can you use the winch for work as well as pleasure? Do you want to increase your knowledge of off-roading and become more confident and self-sufficient than you are now?

These are the questions that surround the decision to have or not have a winch. In your conversations with other off-roaders listen carefully to both sides of the question, but be wary of the guy that says he wouldn't put a winch on his truck if someone gave it to him. Be equally wary of the man who says he wouldn't be without one—ever, even if he stayed on the road.

TWO KINDS OF WINCHES

If you start shopping for winches, you should be aware there are two basic types to chose from and several brands represented by the two types. Historically, the power take-off winch is the old Granddad in the game. In advertising and in enthusiasts' books, this type of winch is known as the PTO. A driveshaft from the forward end of the vehicle's transfer case connects to a gearbox mounted in the area of the front bumper. Engagement of this gearbox is effected by moving the lever which controls the transfer case function. You'll have to admit this is a pretty effective way of getting power to a winch. You can winch all day long with no ill effects with a PTO. You are not apt to run across many PTO winches on two-wheel-drive trucks because few of them have a transfer case. Older utility company trucks,

WINCHES AT A GLANCE

MANUFACTURER	MODEL	TYPE	CAPACITY (LBS)	LINE	WEIGHT (LBS)	WINCH ONLY
Hickey	Sidewinder	12V Electrical	9,000	130' 5/16'' Aircraft Cable	122	$550
McCain	Hub	Mechanical	10,000	100' 1/4'' Aircraft Cable	25	$105
Ramsey	200	Mechanical	8,000	150' 5/16'' Hempcore Cable	118	$548
Ramsey	DC200	12V Electrical	8,000	150' 5/16'' Hempcore Cable	152	$480
Koenig	C100	Mechanical	8,000	150' 5/16'' Hempcore Cable	73	$460-$595
Koenig	EC100	12V Electrical	8,000	150' 5/16'' Hempcore Cable	116	$495
Warn	Wrangler	12V Electrical	8,000	150' 5/16'' Aircraft Cable	40	$550- mt. kit incl.
Warn	8000	12V Electrical	8,000	150' 5/16'' Aircraft Cable	130	$450
Warn	8200	12V Electrical	8,000	150' 5/16'' Aircraft Cable	141	$465-$521
Superwinch	PM 4000	12V Electrical	4,600 20% Grade	35' 3/16'' Aircraft Cable	25	$165
Desert Dynamics	T-200	12V Electrical	9,000	100' 5/16'' Aircraft Cable	125	$439
Braden	EC4-1	12V Electrical	8,000	150' 5/16'' Cable	130	$400

1977 Prices

wreckers and gasoline trucks had such setups but they are rare. The possibility of damaging the driveline and the cost involved in installing all of the hardware makes the PTO winch less than the hot setup in today's market. At one time the PTO was the only kind of vehicle winch available; now the overwhelming favorite is the electrically powered winch.

An electrical winch consists of an electric motor—like an automotive starter motor—a drive gear and a drum on which the cable is reeled. The electric winch is powered from the vehicle's electrical system—the battery. Advantages are that the system is relatively simple. Installation is straightforward. Maintenance is low. In many cases the winch can be pulled out of one vehicle and

Bog city! When you get into this situation without a winch or another vehicle standing by, you'd best start walking for help. Nothing short of draining the swamp solves this problem.

On an electric winch with a remote-control switch, the operator has full control while out of the vehicle. This is Vic Hickey showing off. Careful how you throw "percentage" and "degree" around when referring to a steep hill. This vehicle is at about a 45-degree angle on a 100-percent grade. Don't do this just to be doing it. If anything happened the Bronco would go back and straight down about 60 feet.

Think twice before you get yourself in this position. The winch would pull the vehicle over the top, but drew immense amounts of current from the battery; hence the engine had to be running—but oil pressure failed at this severe angle.

We don't advise winching over this terrain if you can help it, but when you can't help it, it's nice to know you can.

mounted in another when vehicle number one gets sold.

A disadvantage is that the electric winch consumes enormous amounts of current. Its appetite can be compared to placing a vehicle in gear and trying to start it. In other words, trying to use the starter motor to start the engine and pull the vehicle at the same time. How long would your battery last under that punishment? Fortunately, this rarely gets to be a problem. You start your engine and bring it up to a fast idle so the alternator/generator can feed current into the battery while the winch motor is using it. On an extremely long, heavy pull the electric motor will sometimes overheat. This is also rare. Prudence when operating and an occasional pause for cooling during a long pull will solve the problem. Obviously, if you burn out the motor you ain't gonna be able to finish your winching, which may or may not be important to you at the time.

You'll need all of the winch and cable capacity you can find in this situation. Bronco is high-centered and none of the wheels can get enough of a bite to be any help until the winch pulls the vehicle another five feet or so.

You gotta be kidding!! Nope. This is the sort of thing a winch can do for you. Pretty scarey, huh? Notice the straight pull. There is no hint of the vehicle moving to one side in this situation.

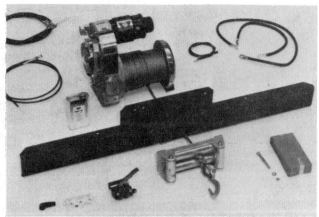

A winch mounting kit is a lot more involved than you might think. Unless you are an excellent metal fabricator, buy the mounting kit from the winch manufacturer—you'll be dollars and time ahead. They come with electrical controls and hardware to locate and secure the winch assembly. This is a Warn unit.

A heavy-duty push bar designed to protect the Sidewinder winch is a good idea.

Hickey Sidewinder winch installation on a Jeep Wagoneer. All hardware is behind and below the level of the bumper— yet the winch skidplate is above the lower edge of the front differential. Skidplate is part of mounting kit.

Underside of Sidewinder shows a clean profile. Entire unit is protected by the wraparound skid plate.

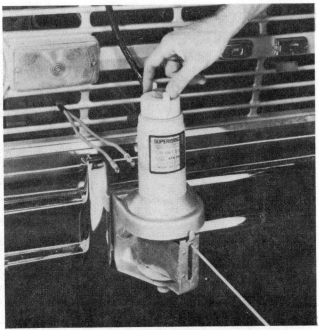

Superwinch is a small but powerful electric winch. It can be controlled at the winch or from inside the vehicle. It pulls more than two tons—rolling—up a 20% grade without a pulley block.

A pair of Superwinches mounted on a Bronco. These items are so light they can be quickly removed from the mounting brackets and stored inside the vehicle. To do this correctly, a backing plate must be placed behind the bumper to distribute the load.

If you need a winch with which to get unstuck or perform other chores, the electric type is the one to buy. If you plan to use a winch for constant effort with hours of grinding away, get a PTO winch—if you can find one for your vehicle.

WHO BUILDS WHAT?

Hickey builds the Sidewinder—so named because the cable spool pivots about a vertical axis. No other winch sold does that. A light, powerful winch, it can be installed between the frame rails of most 2WD and 4WD trucks. About 20 kits are available to mount the winch in various vehicles. This winch can be equipped with either 100 feet of 3/8 cable or 130 feet of 5/16 cable.

The McCain winch consists of a spool bolted to the outside of one of the vehicle's driving wheels—either before or after the vehicle is stuck. By applying a cable and the power to the driving wheels in the normal manner, the vehicle pulls itself out. A number of accessories are available from McCain such as a roller plate that can go under a wheel to allow the hub winch to lift an object or pull another vehicle.

Ramsey is a large company—active in making all sorts of winches and winch-like devices for industry and the military.

Koenig is another large company involved in hardware other than winches. They offer several accessories for and versions of their mechanical power-take-off type winch.

Warn builds a full line of electrical winches and mounting kits for most all domestic and some foreign trucks. They also list accessories such as remote-control operation and snatch blocks.

There are several sizes of the Superwinch— one of the most popular is found at the front of boat trailers to pull the boat snuggly into place on the trailer. All of the winches are small and light and can easily be taken off the vehicle and stored inside when not being used. Remote controls and snatch blocks are listed as accessories.

Over the years, the license to manufacture the Thor Winch has bounced from company to company. They are available through Desert Dynamics. The basic design of the winch has not changed. Mounting kits are available for most all domestic trucks—2WD and 4WD.

USING YOUR WINCH

We don't profess to have all of the answers to operating a winch . . . but we do know using a winch can be as simple or as complex as you want it to be. Vic Hickey—who lent a great deal of

With a winch installation like this—notice all that overhang —drive low in the rough stuff. Far hanging weight really punishes front suspension. This Warn winch required a non-stock bumper. Fog lights are mounted alongside the winch.

Shop for a winch unless you want one that weighs a bunch and hangs way out front of the vehicle—imposing a heavy load on the front suspension.

A remote control cable for this Warn M-8200 winch allows you to get out of the vehicle and operate for better visibility or to move away from a dangerous situation.

A deep hole hidden in a stream can lead to a mean situation—especially if the engine stalls. Here's another place where a winch pays off. The driver sits behind the wheel and lets the electric winch do its thing. Someone had to get his feet wet attaching the cable to an anchor. Warn unit.

Sometimes the only way to get past a log is to go over it. With a little help from 4WD, most winches can handle this with ease. Use a little common sense and don't leave the entire exhaust system and transfer case stuck on the log.

advice and help in this book—suggested a winch be used at every opportunity—that the owner go out of his way to find ways to use the winch until he develops confidence to hook up and pull with no hesitation.

Vic hammered away at one point: The operator should know his equipment from stem to stern. If you buy a winch, read the literature that comes with it, reread it and then save it. Know what the device does and how it does it. Have respect for the equipment. You should. A full-size electric winch mounted on the front of a vehicle is usually capable of pulling a minimum of 8,000 pounds and perhaps as much as 13,000 pounds. This pulling power can be doubled with a snatch block when the snatch-block with its pulley is attached to an anchor and the pulling cable is routed through the pulley and back to the vehicle. The pulling goes from slow to super-slow when using a snatch block this way.

If the vehicle is really stuck and jammed up against something, you can stack up the snatch blocks and pull over a pretty good size tree if the ground is damp. In other words, a winch is powerful enough to do things you don't want it to do. Needless to say you don't need to generate 13,000 pounds of pull at a 45-degree angle for very long before you'll twist the frame of your vehicle. Use common sense.

Cable breaks slowly and will give you warning if it is under a steadily increasing tension. You'll see the cable starting to part and small wires will start sprouting in the area that will soon give way. That means the cable is getting weak. Stop pulling! Replace the cable or get someone else to do the winching. The fraying cable will never get any stronger!

Despite the fact that cable gives plenty of visual warning before it parts when in a steady pull, keep yourself and others as far back as possible. If you have doubts about the pull or the cable, tie jackets, blankets or hang an old tarp on the cable near the end away from the vehicle. If it does snap, all of this cloth will keep it from moving very far or very fast.

Cable can be a real mess to work with—and if you don't keep a pair of heavy work gloves in the glove box, console or shoved under a seat you'll regret it when messing with that gritty cable in the mud. Seems like I always wind up with no

Control on most electric winches is a simple plug-in arrangement under the hood.

If you install your own winch, mount the switching junction and relay box high enough to keep that wiring dry and close to the battery for minimum current loss.

Winch controls vary—be sure you have complete understanding of the controls before getting your vehicle in a sticky situation and then figuring it out. These particular controls are for a Warn M-8000 allowing operation from inside the vehicle or from winch side when needed.

When used as a deadman—shown here—a snatch block will effectively double the capacity of any winch. If you carry one, be sure to take along a tow strap or extra chain so the block can be lashed to a solid object.

When using an extension cable on a winch use one with a loop several feet from the end. After the normal winch cable is fully retracted, connect the extension cable hook to the vehicle to hold it—then release the winch and re-extend.

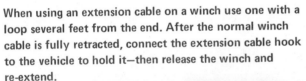

gloves and as a consequence come away with some healthy nicks and scratches on my hands.

If the vehicle really appears to be in a dangerous situation—like in danger of rolling or sliding in the river—get on the high side of it. Sit down and think for a minute—even if it is pouring rain. A cool head can turn a bad situation into a workable one.

Before winching up mountains, fording creeks and tearing down barns with your winch, read the instructions. We've said it before, but we'll say it again. Hopefully, the people who built it know more about it than the average user—so read what they have to say when you dunk the winch in the water or have to use it in water. Maybe it wasn't meant to work there.

Don't oil the cable—that's a mistake a novice often makes. Every piece of grit and grime in the world wants to stick to the cable then—something you sure don't want.

Don't try to second-guess a manufacturer as to how the winch should be installed. What I have in mind is the electrical circuit. Never install a circuit breaker in an electric winch wiring hookup. On some winches when the breaker clicks "off" with a load on the line, line immediately starts flowing out of the winch. This situation could get tight in a hurry!

Ever so often I hear about someone who accidentally hit the power button from inside a vehicle and the winch started operating while being hooked up to itself. The other version of the story is that the wiring shorts out at 2 a.m. while the camp is quiet and before anyone can disconnect the battery, the winch has pulled the front bumper halfway through the radiator. I laugh a lot at the stories—because either of the stories would make a neat cartoon, but the remote possibility of either one happening does exist. For this reason the clutch or gear should be completely disengaged when the winch is not being used. This is normally as complicated as moving one lever.

If the vehicle is being used on the street most of the time and the winch will not be used for awhile, disconnect the power line to the winch motor. That way inquisitive folks are not apt to get something messed up for you. People who do such things are never around to 'fess up when the damage has been done.

No one said a winch has to be used strictly for getting a vehicle unstuck. An 8000 pound pull can come in mighty handy around a ranch or farm.

Here's a situation where the Jeep can't go down the loose rocky grade and tow the pickup out—so the winch is put to use with the Jeep clamped to terra firma. That guy with his hands in his pocket is in the wrong place if the cable snaps—for sure!

Can you see hanging a winch off the nose of your passenger car just for an occasional back country drive? No? Then consider a hub winch to store in the trunk for just this sort of mishap.

McCain hub winch is so simple in concept and design everyone wonders why they didn't think of it first. Hub unbolts when not being used.

Land anchors come in a variety of shapes and sizes. This pointed one is cast-aluminum.

We used a sledge hammer and piece of pipe to drive the anchor ten inches into the ground. Then the cable was connected to the winch on a pickup.

There's not another vehicle in sight, so the winch cable is played out and lashed to a tree to the side of the vehicle. With the winch doing the work, the operator saws the front wheels back and forth to get a bite with the tires. Note the cable is stretched about 90 degrees away from the vehicle.

With truck in neutral on level ground and brakes not set, power to winch was applied. Result: Truck did not move, land anchor started moving through hard ground. Moral: Plan on sinking a "land anchor" pretty far down if you plan to use it as a deadman to get unstuck.

After less than three feet of pulling to the side, the wheels are able to get a bite and unstuck.

There's a ditch adjacent to that bluff and the Bronco dropped both right wheels in and is now immobile . . . .

This is a nasty one. Winch cable is run at a 45-degree angle to the tree, pulling the vehicle into the brush instead of straight up the bank. Another vehicle with a winch·or acting as a deadman would help here.

When you're stuck, with or without winch, make sure the wheels are pointed straight unless there's a good reason to do otherwise. If they're cocked, unnecessary and detrimental drag results. With power steering this is hard to feel, so hang out the window and take a look before putting a lot of effort into getting unstuck.

This 4WD pickup still needs help getting up that loose hill. An alternate solution is to use the winch on the truck, take the cable under the vehicle and hook it to an anchor up the hill. The winch on the Jeep does make it handy.

In looking for the ideal campsite this guy got carried away. This is the sort of situation you don't dig or jack out of— not with the weight of that camper on board—and two-wheel drive to boot. Call the Auto Club—or hook up the winch.

Winch operation drawings courtesy Vic Hickey

Many times it is impossible to pull straight ahead with a winch. There's nothing wrong with pulling nearly 90 degrees to the centerline of the vehicle. To get where you want to go, it may be necessary to unhook and re-anchor several times. When pulling from an angle, turn the wheels in the direction of the pull and apply power slowly—this is where an automatic trans comes in handy—and smoothly to help the winch.

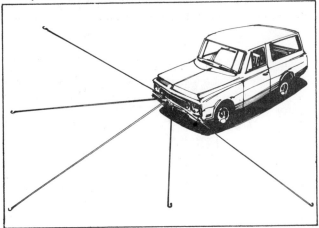

A lot of work and time is involved—but a large log or even a spare tire can be buried several feet in the ground to serve as an anchor. If you do have to bury a tire, plant it vertically on a plane of 90 degrees to the vehicle. A couple of axles lashed together may work as an anchor in loose dirt or mud.

You want your anchor to be plenty solid like a big tree or rock. Get the most solid thing within reach of the cable. You want to get unstuck—not unstick the anchor! Two trees can be lashed together with a length of chain. Any boulder should be firmly embedded as you don't want to winch the rock out of its foundations!

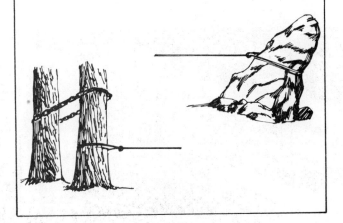

I ain't too keen on this—but it did work once for me in soft dirt when I wasn't badly stuck. Slam a big shovel down in the ground as far as you can—angle the top of the handle away from the vehicle and attach the cable to the metal shank where it grips the wood. Wrap a heavy coat or a blanket around the cable near the shovel so if the cable does snap it won't flail around. Just make sure the guy on the shovel keeps shoving down and keeps the upper end of the handle pulled back.

As you become more and more familiar with the winch and develop more confidence in your ability to operate it safely, you'll discover all sorts of ways to use it. Several snatch blocks may be needed to route the cable exactly where you need it. As always the key is to plan your pulls.

The pulling power of any winch can be doubled by using a snatch block (1P) with a single pulley. As the pulling power goes up the cable speed is cut in half. This takes twice as much cable. If you have enough cable, a single-pulley snatch block and a double-pulley snatch block, you can quadruple the pulling power of your winch. Cable speed is cut to 1/4 normal and it takes an awful lot of cable. If you want to pull something other than the vehicle equipped with the winch and the load is really heavy, consider anchoring the vehicle before starting the pull.

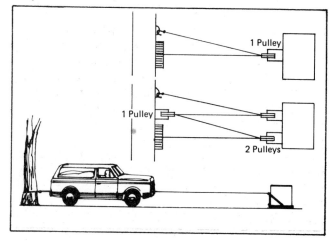

A winch comes in just as handy for lifting as it does for getting you out of the puckerbrush.

CABLE TYPES

Two types of cable are offered by winch builders. Aircraft cable is galvanized so it won't rust and is the strongest type available. Hemp-core is less expensive, not quite as strong and is a little more pliable. Two sizes of cable are commonly used—3/8 and 5/16-inch. If you have a big truck—stick with the 3/8-inch cable.

SNATCH BLOCKS

Snatch blocks are also known as pulleys. A snatch block will double the pulling power of any winch *when the pulley is attached to an anchor and the pulling cable is routed through the pulley and back to the vehicle.* There are a couple of things to remember about a snatch block. You want to make sure the device is strong enough to stand the pull of the winch—in other words the pulley assembly must be rated at double the winch capacity. The pulley should be easy to take apart and put back together. Hickey has one that can be disassembled by pulling on one big lock pin—no tools required. If you can't get the snatch block apart, how are you going to get the cable on it? To use the snatch block as a "dead man" and double the capacity of the winch, the snatch block must be securely attached to something—

The guys that depend on a truck for maintaining a ranch or farm discover in short order that a winch can be used to apply tension to fences, dilapidated buildings and hard-to-budge parts on farm machinery.

The hunter or fisherman can launch and retrieve a boat in an area that simply won't support a vehicle. This is often where the fish or ducks are thick.

One man and a vehicle mounted winch can clear a lot of brush timber and rocks in a day.

One of the most common uses of a winch is in getting a fellow off-roader back on the trail. Boy, is that guy ever glad to see you with that cable hook hanging out of the bumper.

With a good winch and a sheepherder's jack a guy can move a vehicle out of a pretty nasty situation. Consider all that weight on the front end though before strapping it into place. Thor winch.

If you run a winch always carry these accessories: 6-foot choker chain with a hook on each end, 15-foot double-hooked cable and a snatch block. These will double the flexibility and power of a winch.

Hickey probably makes the best pulley block. It handles 3/8 or 5/16-inch cable and comes apart for inserting the cable just by pulling the lock pin. Hickey used one to hang that Blazer from the tree. There are also double-pulley snatch blocks.

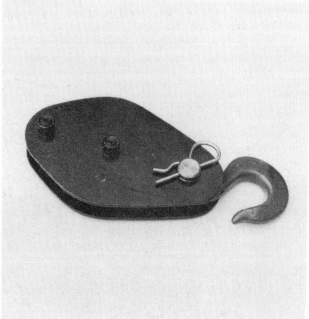

like a tree. Which brings up the next point. Don't bother carrying a snatch block along unless you have a big piece of chain or cable to attach the snatch block to an anchor.

POUNDS OF PULL—WHAT'S THAT?

Winches are rated by the force they can generate on a single line pull. The rating always refers to line pull with the first inner layer of cable fully wound on the drum. As more cable is wound on the drum the effective gear ratio decreases. Thus, if you've got the cable all the way out and starting a pull, you can pull say—8,000 lbs. But before very long with more cable stacking up on the drum, the pull is down to 4 or 5,000 lbs.

THE MIGHTY COME-ALONG

There is an alternative to a full-size winch. We've explained elsewhere about how to use a sheepherder's jack as a winch. But there is actually a poor man's winch—called a come-along or ratchet-handle hoist. They are sold by large hardware stores, ranch-supply outlets and some off-road stores. These units come in several capacities —get the largest one you can find—and are easy to use for getting a vehicle unstuck. They are slow, but they are also low-cost. The one I use weighs less than 20 pounds and has a one-ton capacity.

By using a shovel and a come-along you can move a lot of weight. Just don't expect to do it in a hurry.

Big hardware stores and some off-road equipment places sell a rachet action winch called a "come-a-long" for less than $50. It can do a lot of pulling and should be considered if you want some pulling power but don't want to invest in a full-size vehicle-mounted winch.

BUYER'S GUIDE TO OPTIONS & ACCESSORIES

If you contemplate buying a vehicle for off-road use chances are pretty good you have some questions about how the vehicle should be equipped. Although most of the items we'll mention here are touched on in other areas of the book; spend some time here before popping for a high-dollar rig.

First and foremost be honest with yourself about what the vehicle will be used for; know what you want before buying the vehicle. Car/truck salesmen just love to see a guy come wandering in the door who doesn't know what he wants. You will get such a "deal"—and the salesman will get such a commission!

WHEELBASE

If you have three kids and like to camp for a week, you'd best get something with a long wheelbase—like a Blazer/Jimmy or long-wheelbase pick-up. The reason should be fairly obvious—room to carry stuff. A long-wheelbase vehicle will go most any place a short-wheelbase vehicle will, but sometimes you have to back up and take another cut at a sharp turn. Three or four sleeping bags and one cardboard box full of camping gear take up a lot of room in a small vehicle. On the other hand if you don't camp and don't haul a lot of people around look closely at what's available with a short wheelbase.

PAINT AND TRIM

The darker the color the warmer the interior is gonna get from heat absorption. The darker the color the more small scratches and dings will show. Chrome trim on the side of a vehicle is just asking to be ripped off by brush. If the brush doesn't take the trim off, twigs and leaves get jammed between the trim and body. On the other hand, if you never get off the pavement with your off-road rig, chrome trim helps sell the vehicle when you get tired of playing with it. Consider both sides of the picture and know what you want before signing the big note.

ROLL BARS

These are neat items. The times I've been in a vehicle rolling over I just knew it wasn't going to roll—but it did anyway and there was not a thing I could do about it. If the vehicle comes equipped with a roll bar make sure the thing is out of the way as much as it possibly can be and still be effective. Is it back far enough so the driver doesn't whack his head on the top of the bar? Be honest—you are going to get very tired of the bar and the vehicle if something like this annoys you. Does the placement of the bar interfere with getting into the vehicle or into the rear area? Think about these things before crowing about your neat roll bar.

Even if you can afford an off-road vehicle you might want to consider renting for the one or two weekends a year that you do get back to nature. I've seen more than one rent-a-racer in the puckerbrush. This guy was trying out one with a long wheel base.

The fewer bends in a roll bar the better. Keep that in mind when shopping and also find one that gets right up there within an inch of the vehicle top. This one's in a Bronco.

An advantage to a soft top is protection when you need it and the wide open spaces when you want it.

If you are buying a roll bar to install in a vehicle we'd suggest you find out exactly what has to be done to get the bar in. Do you have to remove the top? That's not so much fun on a vehicle with a removable hard top! Do you have to remove the doors to get the bar in the cab? Know what you are getting into before laying out the cash.

TOPS

On some vehicles you have a choice of no top, soft top or hard top. Hard tops offer more comfort, less noise, and items can be locked up in the vehicle. You have far better control over interior temperature. Hard tops are heavy—compared to the other options. They are a time-consuming pain to take off and they are difficult to store.

A soft top offers maximum protection with minimum weight and expense. Interior noise level is up and there can be some difficulty in getting the temperature just right for all occupants. If you plan to be running in a lot of dust, you should know that the soft top will not keep all of the little stuff out. A good top will keep out water—but not dust.

No top is for the guy who really enjoys the great outdoors and is willing to put up with inclement weather and sun bearing down on your headbone—or park the vehicle. Running with no top is a lot of fun if you are willing to put up with a few discomforts. Having a top of some kind is essential so far as I'm concerned. Just being

The advantage of a hardtop is freedom from dust and the rest of the elements. Make an honest appraisal of how the vehicle will be used for most of the time you own it.

Some brightly-colored burlap, several lengths of cord and the rear section of this Blazer is transformed into a bedroom with privacy.

Hard to beat off-road ingenuity. Slide a piece of plywood half way out of the tailgate and prop it in place for a longer bed. May be crude and simple but it must work. This guy was still snoring and the sun was up.

able to get out of the blazing sun can sometimes make the difference between a fun trip and one that's truly grim. Sometimes a top could save your passengers from heat stroke while you work to fix the vehicle.

AUTOMATIC VERSUS STICK SHIFT TRANSMISSION

An automatic is easier to drive and easier on the engine, axles and tires than a stick. An automatic and the right driver will get through soft stuff that the same driver can't get through with a stick-shift machine. The automatic is not as good as a stick when the engine/transmission must be used as a brake and because today's automatics don't have a rear pump, a vehicle equipped with one cannot be started by pushing.

POWER STEERING

Power steering won't give you the feel for the ground that a standard box will but that is a small price to pay for effortless steering. You have to fight a standard steering box for half a day in the rocks to really get an appreciation of power steering. If I bought a Jeep for running back and forth to work with an occasional trip off-road, I wouldn't get power steering—cause the Jeep is light and easy to steer. If I bought a full-size pick-up for any use, I'd get the power option. If power steering costs $100 from the dealer on a new car or truck, you can figure it will cost $300 to get it put on later.

Another word or two about power steering– Power steering as a factory option is a relatively new item to off-roading. As a consequence, there are the usual number of kits to put late power steering into early vehicles. A great number of older vehicles have been modified with "home-brew" power steering. Ask a lot of questions before getting involved in any of this. Overlook the apparent sales price and "easy installation" ad copy long enough to find out how a kit works, what it does and whether everyone is happy who has installed one. If the guy selling it won't give you the phone numbers and names of several satisfied owners, you might wonder to yourself what he's hiding. An older vehicle can be safely equipped with power steering–just make sure yours is done that way.

Keep in mind that it is one thing to brace a frame and add a power steering box–which might dangerously alter suspension geometry–and another thing to add a hydraulic slave unit to force a manual steering box to become a power steering box. In short–about the only power steering I want is the one installed by the factory–or one put on by a guy I trust.

POWER BRAKES

Because of the damping effect of the vacuum booster, the shock loads imposed by your big foot are not as great as with a standard master cylinder –yet the brakes get down to work with less effort on the part of the driver. I like power brakes and always order them but will be the first to say they are a lot handier on the pavement than in the dirt.

WINCHES

This is an expensive, heavy, seldom-used device. It shortens the life of front-suspension components and increases tire wear. But brother when you need a winch–I mean really need a winch– nothing else will quite do the job.

HEADERS

On a properly tuned engine being used for racing, headers can give a little bit better gas mileage and improvement in horsepower. But don't expect a great amount in either department if your vehicle gets driven most of the time at engine speeds below 4500 rpm. And don't be surprised if you get *worse* mileage. Headers are lighter in weight than the stock exhaust manifolds. Headers do make a lot of noise which can

Most late Ford power steering pumps have this small cooler attached. You can get one from a wrecking yard and use it on any power steering assembly to reduce its oil temperature when you're sawing through a sand wash.

be annoying when you have to live with it for hours on end. Headers should be considered for any off-road vehicle having a chronic problem of exhaust-manifold cracking–and some do have this problem. Just make sure the exhaust system doesn't hang down low enough to snag a rock.

Actually, most off-roaders will be better off in the horsepower and mileage departments if they'll install large mufflers and 2-¼-inch-diameter exhaust and tailpipes. The Corvair Spyder mufflers are fairly small and have big entry and exit holes.

ENGINES

On some off-highway-oriented vehicles you don't have a choice of engines–such as the Toyota 6-cylinder, for instance. On those where you do have a choice, consider the following. It is very costly to add horsepower to an engine by hopping it up. If you have the horsepower to begin with, no one says you have to use all of it. A tiny engine that is straining all of the time will get about the same gas mileage as a small V6 or V8 that isn't working so hard.

If you are thinking about a hop-up project on your present vehicle, be sure to consider turbocharging as one possibility. This offers the most power for the least dollar investment and you can find out all about it in HP Books' *Turbochargers,* available for $4.95 where you bought this book.

LIMITED SLIP

A great item for on or off-pavement driving. Never stick one in the front axle of a four-wheel drive vehicle unless all your driving is off-road in super-slippery terrain. Like power steering, limited-slip differentials are modestly priced on a new vehicle—but a pain in the pocketbook to install later.

AUXILIARY GAS TANKS

Most factories offer optional tanks for their vehicles—factory installed in a sanitary manner. This is far less expensive than buying an after-market item. However, you can get more carrying capacity with after-market tanks.

WHEELS

Aluminum wheels weigh about the same or sometimes more than the steel items they replace. Aluminum wheels get scuffed up in a hurry in rocky terrain. They look great! If you want "mags," shop around before laying out a lot of bread for mag wheels already mounted on the vehicle by the dealer. You'll probably pay through the nose for what he has on there—and you may wind up with some after-market tire you didn't want to boot.

Spoke wheels are built for appearance. That's it, period.

TIRES

If you buy a new vehicle, you'll get at least four tires. Read our section on tires slowly and continue to drive the same way—*slowly*—on the tires you have. They may be far from being the tire you'd like to have, but by playing with the tire pressure in the soft stuff, you might be surprised how good the stock tires are. You may also be surprised at how bad they are.

AIR CONDITIONING

Generally speaking, under-the-dash, after-market AC units are lighter and less expensive than factory-installed items. They might not look as neat but they work about as well as most factory stuff. The exception here is GM air conditioning—which is absolutely and undeniably the world's best. In the desert Southwest, AC can literally be a lifesaver. When running through dust and silt the AC can be used to pressurize the inside of the vehicle just enough to keep most of the dust out of the cab. Noise and wind can both be very fatiguing—AC can be of great help in this department. Using AC definitely worsens gas mileage, as detailed by another HP Book, *The Whole Truth About Economy Driving* by Doug Roe, available for $4.95 where you bought this book.

SKID PLATES

If you plan to go off-road at all, I'd say get every skid plate the factory offers. Compared to after-market units, the price is right.

There are a number of well-designed, well-built tow bars on the market. If you plan to tow a vehicle on the highway, invest in a good bar, safety chain, light hookup and some time in the service manual or dealer manual about what driveshafts need to be removed.

RADIO

Yeah, I'd get an AM—but not an FM. I had an AM/FM in a truck and I couldn't even get good static on the FM out in the sticks. Had a Blazer once that came with a tape deck. Worked plenty good—just turned up the volume and let Buck Owens be my buddy on the way to El Arco.

CB radios are neat and help keep everybody together if you like to caravan with a small group. The range is limited so don't expect much from them in mountainous terrain. Power boosters are available but they're illegal.

We're back to the nitty-gritty of buying the vehicle. Figure out what you need and then stack the practicality of each item against your need. A black truck with no air and a six banger with a three-speed may be just fine for a rancher in Montana. But if you live in Arizona and use the truck for commuting and weekend outings—lotsa luck. Buy what you need and want—not what someone has for sale!

AFTER-MARKET ADD-ONS

When you order a vehicle from a dealer, you sit down and go over the long list of options offered for that particular model. Keep in mind even if you get everything on the list, there may still be a lot of items you still want to get. For the most part, after-market parts don't compete with factory offerings. Such items as super-capacity fuel tanks and high-intensity driving lights may not be offered as a factory or dealer option on any vehicle you plan to buy—but if you really think you need the item, you should know that most anything you can think of does exist.

Suppliers such as Cepek, Hickey, Desert Dynamics, Stroppe, etc. can provide you with just about any item known to off-road man. Other suppliers are so specialized they may only carry one or two items. The best way to keep up on what there is for the off-road market is to subscribe or buy on a regular basis those magazines dealing with off-roading. We've listed these publications and the major off-road suppliers and manufacturers in the Suppliers section of this book.

Heavy metal brush guards are available which will protect a lot of that front sheet metal when you start plowing through the underbrush. These things are heavy though—do you really plow that much? They can seriously affect handling, as discussed earlier.

If you care about the appearance of your vehicle and add larger than stock tires, you'll probably want to make—light aluminum sheet—or buy gravel guards to keep flying rocks off the rocker panels.

119

There is a limit to how much tire can be shoved under a vehicle before the wheel wells must be enlarged. Many accessory firms sell fender-flare kits to simplify this operation.

Many off-road vehicles are short on interior space for carrying bulky camping items such as cots and sleeping bags. A roof rack is a great idea. Once you start looking for such items, you'll discover there are a lot of roof racks around and one of them might just fit right on your rig for increased carrying capacity. This is a Pinto rack on a Bronco.

If you run out of storage space inside the vehicle, the roof is the logical place to go for more room. Shop around to get the best quality. With three hundred pounds shifting around on the roof, it can be a real scene.

Owner of this Blazer found a tape-cartridge holder on a Chevy in a wrecking yard. Low-cost, slick idea for those with a tape deck.

Should you mount off-road driving lights on the roof? They add depth to holes and dimension to rocks at night— just as they produce glare off the hood. The plan is either a pencil beam up here or a flat metal shield mounted under the lights. Flat-black paint on the hood also helps. You must remember the lights are there when running under low-hanging limbs.

There are several versions of a switch to allow using two batteries in a vehicle. Either battery can be used for starting and either can be charged at the flip of the switch.

If you've never tried to back a trailer in the rough, you can't appreciate what you've missed. A rather simple, inexpensive solution is to install a hitch on the front of your off-road vehicle to make the job a little easier. This is also helpful for handling a boat trailer on a launching ramp.

Hickey sells this hardware to raise a bucket seat 1½-inches from the floor—a simple solution to increase forward visibility.

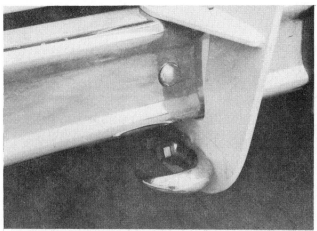

You might not think you need a tow hook attached to your off-road vehicle because there are plenty of places to hook a chain or cable. Even when you are up to the headlights in water or snow? These hooks sure save a lot of groping around.

Here's a slick little item you can make. A small piece of spring steel closes the "eye" of a tow hook so the rope, chain or cable won't fall out when the line goes slack. Saves a lot of time in a back-up, try-over-again situation.

After bending bumpers and sliding under trucks in the mud to find a place to put a tow strap, I heartily recommend forged steel tow hooks. Bolt them on with Grade 8 bolts.

OFF-ROAD INSURANCE

What happens if you roll your Jeep over in some dry wash skinning up the sheet metal and breaking a passenger's arm? Who pays the bill? Who pays the bill if you kill a prize bull with the push bar on the front of your Blazer? Chances are your insurance will cover all of this but check with your insurance agent. Normally, liability coverage goes wherever the vehicle goes—no matter who is driving. But there are always exceptions, so go over this with your agent. When you wrinkle all of that expensive sheet metal off-road, insurance will normally cover it. Sure it's expensive—but it could be the best bargain of your life. I say that—and like everybody else I groan and mumble everytime I pay a premium.

My advice is to sit down and have a long chat with your insurance agent. Depending on the value of the vehicle, he may advise you to forget collision insurance and simply carry liability. Rates vary from one state to another and as always your age and driving record have a lot to do with how much you pay for protection. If you have another vehicle insured by the same company, you can get a discount—but how much varies among companies.

If you have your off-road vehicle insured in the United States and plan a trip out of the country—by all means take time to call or visit your agent to tell him of the trip. Chances are if you are going to Canada he will not advise additional coverage, but Mexico is a different case. The liability insurance will probably be in effect in Mexico, but not the collision. Normally, U.S. insurance companies don't have lawyers in Mexico which makes any U.S. written policy of doubtful value if you have to file a claim concerning something that happens south of the border. If you travel to Mexico, I strongly advise buying a short-term policy from one of the Mexican insurance companies that have offices near all of the border crossings. Contrary to popular belief, a Mexican insurance policy will not keep you out of jail if you do have a mishap, but if might. Buy the Mexican insurance in addition to what you already have and . . . DRIVE CAREFULLY.

If you plan to do any driving with any of your vehicles in another state of the U.S., new no-fault insurance laws have complexified out-of-state insurance requirements. Your present cover-age may not meet requirements of other states or countries you'll be traveling through. While many insurance companies extend benefits on their policyholders to cover unusual out-of-state requirements on trips, some do not. If you are in an accident in a state where you are not fully covered, you may have to prove you can pay for all damages involved and perhaps even risk having your driving privileges suspended in that state. This could make it difficult to continue a trip—or even get home. As of the end of 1974, a policy for at least $40,000 bodily injury and $10,000 for property damage would probably let you meet all U.S. and Canadian requirements. Double-check this with a competent reliable insurance agent and get his opinion in writing on his company stationery if you possibly can.

The Ten Commandments of Jeeping

1. Thou shalt not dismantle jeep engines in thy living room.
2. Thou shalt not pirate parts from thy family auto for use on thy jeep.
3. Thou shalt not park thy jeep in the garage and let thy family car sit out in the rain.
4. Thou shalt not use thy grocery money to repair thy jeep.
5. Thou shalt stay home at least once a year to mow thy lawn.
6. Thou shalt not covet thy jeep and forsake thy wife and children.
7. Thou shalt not take strange and beautiful girls for moonlight jeeping trips—unless they are married to you.
8. Thou shalt not steal thy wife's black lace undies to use for oil rags when thou breakest down.
9. Thou shalt not look at new vehicles until thou has paid at least one payment on thine own.
10. Thou shalt wash thy family car once for each fifteen times thou washest thy jeep.

Author unknown

122

CAMPER BODIES & SHELLS

Let's say you are the proud new owner of a long wheel base 4WD pickup. Your pride and joy is less than two weeks old, you haven't made a payment yet and already you think a 4WD pickup is the neatest thing since sliced bread. Of course you do want some kind of camper to bolt onto the bed—but that's no big thing because a friend of yours knows a guy that can get you a deal on one right from a factory. Uh huh. Camper bodies can weigh so much that you'll have to go to bigger big tires—and usually wheels—to get the thing safely down the highway. Then, when you start to go off the road the truck is hopelessly under-powered. You are also liable to get stuck with all that extra weight too. So pass up the deal for a day or two and figure out what you really want the truck for and what you really want the camper for.

If the camper is too heavy to be lifted off the truck by yourself and one other adult, do you have the necessary jacks and supports to take the camper off once you get to the campsite? If you ride a motorcycle, can you get the motorcycle in the bed of the truck in an upright position without rotating the handlebars downward? Do you plan to leave the camper on the truck all of the time or do you plan to store it and use the truck for work or play without the camper? If you plan to take it off, do you have a place to store it? Are you aware of the beating things take in a camper when running off road? Food spills, cabinet doors come open and nails, staples and glue start working loose within the structure. If you don't plan to go far off road and are willing to take it slow and easy, none of this is a big problem. But if you plan to do a lot of off-roading then you should select a camper with care. How much does the camper weigh? Sales literature will tell you—but it may not tell you what is included in the "weight." If a refrigerator and portable toilet are options on that particular model, bet big money the weight listed does not include them. The wife may have her heart set on a four-burner stove, refrigerator, shower, toilet, sink and 35 gallons of water to take along on a camping trip. That's fine, but if that's what you get you might as well throw in a TV set and some easy chairs 'cause you ain't going very far off the beaten trail. Look at it

These guys unloaded a cab over camper and a shell from a couple of pickups—plus about a thousand pounds of gear. With camp set up for the family, they then went off-roading. Unreal.

There are a lot of advantages and comforts to a big 4WD rig like this. I wouldn't get excited about a lot of fast or rough running though—getting it unstuck is an experience to avoid.

another way—maybe you really don't want to get out into the wilderness; you just think you do. Your wife may have other ideas.

Before buying that camper, consider the costs. Maybe the recreation areas you use have enough motels so you can stay there nights and buy nice meals instead of merely giving your wife a "change of sinks." You can buy a lot of nights' lodgings for a pretty big family for a lot of years before equaling the price of some of these campers. Think about it! Or, you could travel light like a back-packer does. Either way, you keep your off-road mobility.

A shell no higher than the top of the truck cab will hold a lot of gear, is light, creates a minimum of drag—which kills gas mileage—and can be taken off by two men instead of jacks and supports. If a shell will fit your needs, consider one having a conventional door in the back instead of one which swings upward from the tailgate. Now that you've located one with a door in the rear, find one built so the entire rear panel—containing the door—can be lifted off. This comes in handy for loading all sorts of bulky items—like a motorcycle or a fat girl friend.

I had an ideal shell—except it didn't have the

Most hardtops are a lot heavier than they look. Five guys have this top in hand.

Figuring out where to store a lot of gear—or beer—in a small vehicle gets to be a pain after while. If you don't have a vehicle yet, take this into consideration before making a final decision.

lift-off door—on my Chevy pickup. It was an *Aztec* with windows and insulation throughout. Weighed about 250 pounds.

There are some pretty effective devices around to lock a camper or a shell to the bed of a truck. Make sure you have what it takes to clamp that "Oakie Palace" securely to the vehicle. Once the camper or shell starts moving chances are pretty good that the clamping devices will be sheared apart by the movement. Check the tie-downs, clamps or bolts at least once a day if you are in the rough stuff.

One last thought on campers and I'll quit preaching. When figuring out what to get to take off-road, figure out how little you can take with you and still have a good, safe time—not how much will the truck haul.

Rugged one-ton chassis with frame-mounted camper offers a lot of comfort for a family on the go. However, you won't do any serious off-roading with a rig this size. All that weight will get you stuck in a hurry.

Vans are becoming popular off-road. Little overhang and reasonable ground clearance allows some off-roading. You'll need all the tire you can get though to provide adequate flotation for the soft stuff.

Motor homes have become increasingly popular during the past several years. They really are self-contained homes—but lack of ground clearance, long overhang and weight make them unsuited for anything other than pavement or hardpacked dirt road.

125

BUYING A USED OFF-ROAD VEHICLE

There is a great variety of used off-road vehicles on the used car market. Whether you buy from a dealer or individual, spend plenty of time and energy checking out a prospective purchase.

The advantage of buying a used vehicle is a much lower cost than driving a new one off the dealer's lot. The disadvantages are you don't get to select equipment—the truck has a stick-shift, you wanted an automatic—and you don't know how the previous owner treated the vehicle.

First rule of thumb for buying any used vehicle is to wear dirty clothes when you go look at it. If you are bashful or lazy about crawling around under the vehicle, then you have no one but yourself to blame if you find after you buy the vehicle that one motor mount is broken, a tie rod is bent and the gas tank is held in place with bailing wire. Don't be so hasty to take the vehicle for a spin around the block. Crawl under, in and out of the vehicle several times. Is there evidence of a crash? Have some of the body panels been straightened? Have some of the panels been replaced and now don't align properly? Have some of the body panels been attacked by rust? Does it look like the underside of the vehicle has been treated to a spray of salt water? Does it appear the oil filter is fairly new, or is it the one supplied by the factory? Is the oil clean? Is the radiator water rusty or is it clean? Are the battery terminals corroded? This is the sort of thing that helps to tell you whether the owner took care of the vehicle. If the vehicle was not serviced on a regular basis, then figure you are going to pick up some problems sooner or later due to the previous owner's neglect.

You can't expect the underside of an off-road vehicle to look like the underside of a street-driven Caddy, but then it shouldn't be a patchwork of welds, bailing wire, dirt-impregnated grease and worn tires showing evidence of a bent front-axle assembly. When you get around to driving the vehicle, turn off the air conditioning and radio and listen to the vehicle. If the owner goes for a ride with you and he chatters away, tell him you want to listen for a minute—please be quiet. A rear end howl is different than a tire howl. Off-road tires make one noise on asphalt, another on concrete; rear end howl stays the same. If the vehicle is equipped with four wheel drive, take it off-road— even a grassy field—engage 4WD and the hubs, if there are any. Is there great difficulty in getting the transfer case engaged? Any strange noises when the vehicle is being driven in 4WD? If you plan to drive the vehicle at freeway speeds, you'd better find a freeway and do a little driving. A noise can show up at 55 that simply was not there at 30 mph. Handling problems can show up too.

Take your time. If you look at the vehicle in the evening, plan on taking another look at it in the daylight. If you don't trust your judgment in evaluating the vehicle, take along a car nut friend. Failing that, pay a mechanic—your choice, not the seller's—to check the vehicle over. Twenty-five or thirty bucks spent here could save you several hundred.

People sell vehicles for many different reasons. Just never lose sight of the fact one of the reasons is the vehicle is giving trouble and they want to unload it before they have to pay for having it fixed. Buying used often works out great, but it has been referred to as, "Buying another man's troubles."

SURPLUS 4WD?

With the cost of new four-wheel drive vehicles rising with each model year, many enthusiasts at one time or another give thought to buying an old surplus military 4WD vehicle, doing a little work on it and heading for the sticks. Sometimes this is a good deal; at other times the entire experience turns into a nightmare. In most cases the price of the vehicle is dependent on its condition, so the cheaper it is, the more work it probably needs. There are a number of things to consider before getting involved.

How much work are you capable of doing yourself? If the engine needs to be rebuilt or replaced, can you do it yourself? If the answer is yes, how long will it take—six weeks or six months? Do you have a place to work on the vehicle? Do you have a place to store it when it is not in running condition? Do you have the majority of tools needed to work on the vehicle? Will your wife grow cold to the whole idea of off-roading while you give it a year or two of your total spare time?

If you're looking at a vehicle with a thought towards buying it, make a check list as to what needs to be replaced and what needs to be repaired. Do this *before* you haul it home. Keep revising your estimate—always upward. Is it all there? Transfer case, levers, clutch linkage and radiator all there? Do you know of a source for parts for the beast you might buy? Much has been said and written about buying an old military Jeep, replacing the engine with a late V8 and blowing the doors off much more expensive, late-model equipment. There is some merit to this line of thinking—but it only holds water if the transfer case and front differential are in good working order to start with. If these items need to be repaired or replaced and it takes outside labor to do so, costs will soar. A ballpark figure on having a transfer case rebuilt is $150 to $200. Depending on the parts needed, the same figures can be applied to the front-axle assembly. Thus you could be looking at a $400 repair bill and you haven't touched the brakes, transmission, clutch or engine. The possibilities of engine and transmission swaps seem to be endless. Many of the

suppliers listed in this book can provide all the hardware you need to install V8s, Pintos, Vegas, automatics, four speeds—you name it and it has probably been done under the hood of a Jeep.

If you are not inclined towards engine swaps and plan to stick with the stock military engine, you should be aware that military hardware is normally set up with a 24-volt electrical system. If the generator fails, the price can be between $65 and $125—either used or rebuilt. The distributor is $45. Regulators are tough to find and even tougher to pay for—figure close to $40.

There are two versions of the 24-volt system: waterproof shielded and the regular system. Most are of the waterproof version. To convert to a 12-volt system means changing distributor, generator, regulator, starter, wires, plugs and all lights. A bracket will have to be fabricated to hang the generator from the engine and because that is the case, serious consideration should be given to installing an alternator. From time to time you may run across a surplus military jeep with an 8-

We won't take sides on this—but with little overhang, gearing like a goat and no chrome to rip off in the brush we'd find it hard to argue.

Refurbishing an old military vehicle from a boneyard can be full of fun and frustration. Look before you leap. Most electrical systems are 24 volts, registration may be difficult and the cost of restoration could soar past the price of a new similar vehicle.

volt electrical system. There are waterproof and standard versions of this system and everything we've said about the 24-volt system holds true for the 8—change it to 12 volts in the beginning to save later hassles.

What happens if you don't change to a 12-volt system? Nothing, so long as everything operates correctly. But what happens if the regulator or generator dies on you 38 miles south southeast of West Outerback, Idaho? Even if you can get a tow back to town your chances of finding parts in the next week or so are not very good. When you do find the parts and have them shipped to you, the cost will be so high you'll start kicking yourself for not converting to a 12-volt system when you had a chance.

Fortunately, most running gear and body panels on late-model military Jeeps interchange with components used on civilian versions of the same model. Thus if you break the mainshaft in a transmission case 80 miles from Noplace, Montana, parts obtained at a local Jeep dealer may work. Naturally, there are exceptions and these might cause you to start wondering all over again whether you really want a surplus vehicle. Most military Jeeps have a T-84 transmission. The civilian equivalent of the same Jeep came with a T-90 trans. The *transmissions* will interchange with no problem—but the internal parts won't. Thus you could be forced to change an entire transmission in a situation only calling for a couple of parts . . . if you had to get it running to get it back home. The same

Look before you leap into restoring a 4WD military vehicle. Price might look right going in, but unless you don't value your time, total cost could be high. This body has been hot tanked—yes, the whole body!—and still needed many hours of scraping and sanding to be ready for primer painting.

Thirty years after this was government issue over half the world; a flathead military, shovel and ax are still pretty good companions for getting you in and getting you out.

goes for the transfer case. There are cases with a 26-tooth output shaft and then there is the 29-tooth version.

The interchange existing between civilian and military Jeeps is very fortunate for the surplus buyer because we haven't said anything about the shape the suspension is liable to be in. And you might as well plan on rebuilding the brakes while you're at it.

If you're still interested in the prospect of owning an old military Jeep, obtain a bidder's card from:

> Department of Defense Surplus Sales
> P. O. Box 1870
> Battle Creek, Michigan 49016

It's probably the only *free* thing you'll ever get related to a surplus vehicle.

After getting the bidder's card and a list of instructions on how to bid, you'll be put on a mailing list and start receiving information on surplus equipment up for bidding in your part of the country. In typical military fashion you'll be given a cursory description of each piece of equipment, where it is located and when you may inspect it before bidding.

If your bid is accepted, you then have to come up with the purchase price in a given number of days and have the vehicle removed within a given number of days. The sanitary, no-nonsense way of getting the vehicle moved is to rent a car-hauling trailer from a nearby rental firm. Trailers large enough to haul a Jeep normally rent for $12 to $15 a day. Be sure to take along enough chain and load binders to lash the Jeep securely to the trailer. Good luck—you've got your work cut out for you.

There is another way of buying a surplus Jeep —and you won't even know it until you already have it. Buying off a used car lot or from an individual can have all of the intrigue of a Turkish train ride if you are not sure of your vehicles. An engine swap, a paint job and a few aftermarket accessories can turn an old military into an attractive looking package. This is certainly OK, if the package is OK. This is a case where you should take a buddy with you who knows Jeeps. If you don't have such a friend, recruit a mechanic from a nearby garage. Paying $20 for an inspection now could save you many times that later on. Consider the fact the Jeep may be for sale because the current owner is fed up with pouring money into it.

This old reworked, rehashed military truck is outfitted with 36-inch-tall tires and gearing we couldn't even believe. A very impressive, low-cost vehicle for low-speed fun.

TIRES

Any off-road enthusiast who has ever managed to crest a dune or slog through a muddy field is a tire expert without peer around the campfire. This is not surprising because most off-roaders— 2WD or 4WD—realize tires can make or break the performance of any vehicle off-road. But what makes a tire good or bad for off-roading? Why is one tire so much better than another? Is there a best all-around tire? We could fill this chapter with questions about off-road tires and in the end that's all we'd have—just the questions. What you and every other off-roader need is a list of answers. For the first time we think we have most of them nailed down on a scientific basis for you.

To get expert opinion and cold, hard, factual information on tires you must go to professional tire testers—not tire kickers. Our choice of tire-testing firms was DataMotive, Inc. of Reno, Nevada. They are in business and professionally equipped to do specialized vehicle testing. About half of their work is tire testing for major tire manufacturing firms. Unlike some other firms, DataMotive does off-road tire testing as well as highway-type testing.

DataMotive's Chief Engineer and President Bill Janowski mapped out our test procedure. He spent many years with Lockheed developing and testing the famed Twister and other military-oriented off-road vehicles. As an avid jeeper Bill is more than a little familiar with the joys and problems of going off-road.

DataMotive gathered the hard engineering facts and helped me to interpret the results. Opinions on the various types of tires are mine, but I've checked them with the Cepeks and Janowski to make sure I wasn't getting too far off base.

The tire testing procedure presented here was

For each action there is a reaction and in this case the action is firing sand rearward and the reaction is moving up the hill. This is a relatively unexplored area of tire knowledge.

designed just for you, with your interest in off-roading. To do that we had to make some assumptions or we'd still be testing. We assumed you would be using your off-road vehicle on the highway or graded roads as well as off-road. We also guessed you'd care about how the various tire sets would affect your vehicle's ride and handling. We made the assumption you are concerned about the performance of the various tires on wet asphalt as we know much of your time is spent operating on hard-surfaced roads and wet ones are potentially the most dangerous. Because of the great popularity of running in sand at beach or desert areas we figured you and most other readers would be interested in how the tires performed in soft dry sand. These are our assumptions about what you wanted to know—and DataMotive did the testing accordingly. Test data is presented in the chronological order as it was done—with the exception of

With those super wide rims, dual rears and thin-skinned, grooved tires on all corners (ex-dragster types), this old military is setup just for sand running. Nice sensible height for a roll bar too.

This stack of test tires may be capable of providing orgasmic response to an off-roader, but to the professional tire testers at DataMotive, this is all in a day's work and the latest thing in tires very quickly assumes the anonymity of a letter or number code.

the tire measuring. In the test procedure, all tire-measurement data was obtained at the end of all the testing because data obtained after break-in is far more meaningful than that from fresh new tires.

If you search in vain through our tire-test section for your favorite tires, we can only tell you these pages present the most off-road-tire test information ever assembled in one place. We know there are many more off-road tires. Some we tested are now obsolete but they are still being used on lots of off-road machinery. You'll note we've tested at least one tire from each type of construction: bias, bias-belted and radial. Our selections of tread design range from milk-toast to mean. The point of all of this is that with a little off-road savvy, common sense and the data presented here you can pretty well size up how a tire will work off-road before laying out cold cash for a set of four. Although tire advertising and marketing types would argue this—naturally!—the brand name on the sidewall ain't nearly as important to the off-roader as tread design, construction and *inflation pressure*.

We did not deliberately exclude any tire from our test group. There simply was not enough time or resources available to carry the testing any further. We'll gladly accept support—dollars and tires, that is—from any tire manufacturer who wants us to run similar tests at DataMotive. Better yet, tire makers can have DataMotive do the work and authorize them to release the test data to us for the next edition of this book.

THE BASICS OF TIRE TALK

We cannot think of another off-roading factor as important as the tires—which is at the same time so little understood. Feel confident and understand tires and you'll be going places others fear to tread or you'll be unstuck while others are stuck. Tire knowledge is fundamental to fun and troublefree off-roading—it's that simple.

Campfire conversation or not—you should know the three types of tire construction available to the general public today: Bias, Belted-Bias, and Radial. Bias construction refers to the manner in which the plies of fabric are placed about the circumference of the tire. The fabric cord is "on the bias" or placed on an angle of 30 to 40 degrees to the radii. The bias-ply tire is the oldest of the three types listed. Strength can be gained simply and

effectively by the expedient of adding plies. It should be realized that adding strength in this manner stiffens the bias-ply tire.

The majority of tires sold in the U.S. replacement market today are of bias construction. Their popularity has been severely eroded in the past several years by the increasing use of bias-belted and radial tires as original equipment. Even so, you can count on bias-ply tires being around for a long time because they feature strength, versatility of design, and comparatively low manufacturing costs. In other words: They are cheap! Radial tires will be original equipment on most U.S. cars and many U.S. trucks starting in 1975.

Drawings below show cross-sections of typical tire construction. Note the extra sidewall plies in the conventional tire and the added tread plies in the radial.

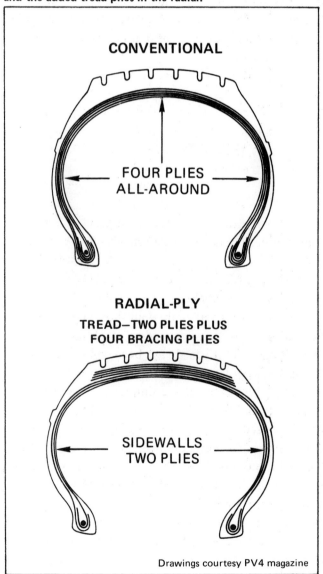

CONVENTIONAL

FOUR PLIES ALL-AROUND

RADIAL-PLY
TREAD—TWO PLIES PLUS FOUR BRACING PLIES

SIDEWALLS TWO PLIES

Drawings courtesy PV4 magazine

Historically, the radial ply comes next in our line-up. On radial tires the fabric plies go across the tire from bead to bead, with a continuous fabric or steel-wire belt around the circumference of the tire under the tread. This tends to make the tread "lay down" and gives vastly superior traction under all conditions due to less squirm and a greater amount of tread on the ground. The lessened squirm also contributes to better economy because less horsepower is used to overcome the drag induced by tread squirming. A radial is long-wearing and smooth riding. It is considerably more expensive than a bias or bias-belted and is usually more vulnerable to sidewall damage than the other two types. Radial tires with tough sidewalls can and are being built today. The Armstrong Norseman Radial steel tire is a good example. It's discussed later in the next chapter. Another point in the radial's favor is it usually wears less and lasts longer—usually enough so to offset its greater cost, especially when the improved gas mileage is taken into consideration.

Bias-belted tires are an attempt on the tire builder's part to try to bridge the gap between radial and regular bias construction without making the vast investment required to manufacture a radial tire. The basic bias-belted construction is a bias-ply tire with a preformed "belt" of cording placed around the circumference. The sidewall remains totally biased, but the tread area gets tougher, smoother running and longer wearing than ordinary bias construction. This is the current "in" tire, due mainly to the wide, "low-profile" look which street enthusiasts really appreciate. It is also cheaper to make than a radial tire.

If you don't understand all those words on the side of a tire these days, don't feel like the Lone Ranger. This has always been somewhat confusing and may be getting more so by the day. Actually, things are getting simpler but there are a few lines to learn before you go on stage. Layers of fabric used in tire construction are called plies. Plies are used in even numbers. You buy two, four, six, eight, etc. ply tires. The more plies the stronger—and stiffer—the tire becomes. This was simple enough until the mid-1960's when tire makers boasted they could make a two-ply tire as strong as their old four-ply tire. They advertised two-ply construction at four-ply rating—the rating being a measurement of strength. This was about the time

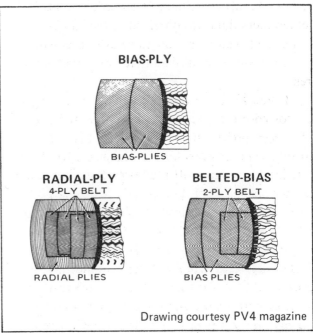

Three tire types show construction differences which give each its particular characteristics.

When buying any tire—take the time to read some of the valuable information molded into the sidewall. Federal laws require all this information to be there—so you don't have to listen to all of the salesman's double talk.

Direction of rotation arrows are on many special-duty tires. Rotation should follow the direction of the arrow to gain maximum tire effectiveness.

There's a lot of information found on tire sidewalls these days. That maximum speed limit means just what it says—this special-duty tire's tread will separate from the carcass at higher speeds. Tire could be ideal in a swampy situation.

the Federal government was taking a little closer look at the automobile industry anyway and tires got shoved under the Fed's microscope. As a result we now have something called *Load Ranges.* Today's new tire imprinted **Load Range A** means the tire will hold as much load as a two-ply tire; Range B, four-ply and so on. Because a lot of tire buyers are still scratching their heads over this one, companies are trying to help out by printing the Load Range AND the number of plies along with the old ply rating. Thus you get **Load Range B 2ply/4ply Rating.** Hang on, it gets better.

If you see a series of numbers on the tire sidewall like **6.70-15,** you can tell two things about the tire. First, that's the size of the tire. The **15**—or **14** or **16**—is the rim diameter. The **6.70** part tells you whether the tire is a big fat one or a skinny one relative to other tires. A **6.70** is smaller than an **8.25** and larger than a **6.00.** That number **6.70** refers to section width of the carcass in inches. If the entire number **6.70-15** is wholly numerical, the tire is of bias construction. If the number contains a letter such as **G70-15** or **J60-15** then the tire might be bias or bias-belted construction. On tires with this type of designation letter A thru L is tire width, A is the smallest, L is usually the widest. Some **50** series are available in M and N widths which makes them wider than **L's.** The next two numbers—**70** or the **60** in the examples given above—refer to the aspect ratio of the tire. Isn't this fun! Aspect ratio is a fancy term which means you divide the height of the tire by the overall width. Thus the **70** series tires are 70 per-

cent as tall as they are wide. Low wide tires in the **50** and **60** series are fine for that racing appearance, but are not so "racy" in off-road use. Let the air out of a tire with a low aspect ratio (**50** or **60**) and you don't put as much rubber on the ground as an equivalent **70** or **78** series tire. The low-aspect-ratio tires just cannot deflect as much. Stay with the **70–78** series and you will go where the fat cat with the Indy-type low tires fears to tread.

A radial-ply tire always has the letter R somewhere in the size information. It might be something like **LR60-15,** which means an **L60-15** of radial construction. Naturally this is too simple so you find sizing designations like **R225-15.** This also means radial construction but the **225** refers to the section width of the tire in millimeters. As far as we know this only shows up on tires made outside the United States, but that will change as we all learn to speak in metric. While you're standing on your head trying to figure out what kind of tires are on that Jeep you just bought you'll probably run across something that looks like **DOT JAL5 AKMD123.** The **DOT** refers to the Department of Transportation; everything that follows is their method of identifying who built the tire, how it's rated, and when it was built. When it was built can be deciphered from the last three digits. In the example **123** is the key to the date of manufacture. The **12** means the 12th week of the year of '7(3). If a new tire doesn't have a **DOT** designation, the tire may not be run on the highway legally. Highway patrolmen keep up with neat little things like

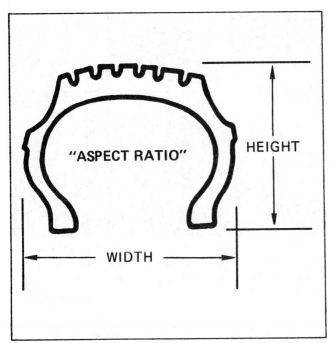

"Aspect ratio" is height of tire divided by width. Hence, a "70 series" tire is 70 percent as tall as it is wide.

this and are aware that certain off-road-type tires do not have the DOT rating. If you are stopped and the patrolman inspects the tires and fails to find a DOT designation you can be cited. There is an exception to this, however. Federal law requires the letters DOT followed by the 10 letter-digit number *or* in the case of the prime manufacturer —its name (Armstrong, Goodyear, etc.) *and* the 10 letter-digit number. Private-brand highway rated tires such as Concorde, Desert Dog, National must have the DOT letters. Also, as of 1974-75 many tires built before the advent of the new law were being sold without DOT numbers and these are not illegal, even though they don't have the numbers. This was done to allow dealers to clear out their old stocks.

It is illegal for a tire dealer to *mount* these non-DOT tires on a vehicle. It can cost a dealer a fine of up to $1,000 *per tire*—plus some time in the slammer if he violates this federal law. He may mount them on rims and you can haul them away in the back seat, drive one block and bolt them on to the vehicle yourself. That lets the tire dealer off the hook, but you are still liable to get that citation. Nevertheless, the DOT designation is for your own safety: You won't have to worry about your tire coming apart at high cruising speeds. When you purchase a highway-rated tire the dealer is legally required by federal law to fill

out or have you fill out a tire-registration card. This is to make sure you can be notified if a tire is recalled. The tire manufacturer can notify you by certified mail that he made a defective or *possibly* defective tire and that he wants to replace it with a safe one! This law works just like the recall program required of automobile manufacturers. You've got a real problem if both your vehicle and its tires are recalled.

One last item concerning the DOT designation. If you see DOT R this does not mean the tire is of radial construction. If the R is adjacent to DOT the tire is a recap.

There is a new system of measuring tires which the general public won't be aware of until early 1978. Naturally it concerns the metric system.

If all of this sounds like a lot of writing on the side of a tire, the bright side of the picture is that you have plenty to read while changing a flat.

Tires come in tube and tubeless construction. If they are tubeless, this will be printed on the sidewall. If they are of tube type, then chances are no mention will be made of the fact. There are three good reasons to run tubeless tires off-road. Many times a flat can be fixed with a plug gun— without even removing the tire from the rim. Just be sure to patch it on the inside first chance you get. Plugs should be considered only as a temporary fix. At extremely low pressures, there is no danger of chafing a hole in the inner tube. At low pressure and high-torque application, such as drag racing in sand, there is no danger of spinning the tire and tube on the rim and snapping off or rupturing the valve stem. I run 'em tubeless and carry a couple of tubes with some tire-changing equipment—just in case.

THE TIRES TESTED: MEASUREMENTS AND DATA

We are presenting the tire-measurement data first to introduce you to the tires being tested.

The *Armstrong Norseman* was selected because of its widespread popularity as an "all-around" off-road tire.

The *Armstrong Tru-Trac* was introduced to the market in '71 and enjoyed instant success with off-roaders using heavy four-wheel-drive vehicles with big wheel wells such as Blazer/Jimmy and the various four-wheel-drive pickups.

The *National Sure-Trac Preminum* is just another name for the *Gates Commando XT*. The tire has been popular for years and is probably found on a greater variety of vehicles than any other tire in the test group. We wanted as wide a variety of tread designs as possible in the test and the Sure-Trac is very aggressive-appearing. If for no other reason that would justify our inclusion of the Gates. This tire is now made under the name: National Commando XT.

The *Armstrong High-Flotation Tire*—for highway service—has a very non-aggressive tread. It is a wide tire highly favored by those who do most of their running in sand. The tire is very smooth except for the several slight grooves which follow the circumference.

The *Formula Desert Dog* tire was selected because it had the most aggressive-appearing tread design of any tire we could find. Neither the author nor any of the tire-testing crew had had any experience with the tire. The Formula Desert Dog tires used in the test had approximately 1,500 miles of on- and off-highway running under a Blazer. Despite the normal number of small nicks and abrasions, the tires appeared to be in good condition at test time.

By far the most controversial tire in the test group was the *Sears Radial*. The tire was expensive, designed primarily for highway use, but had been introduced with a flurry of publicity tying the tire to winning race cars in Baja and Africa off-road events.

The vehicle used as a basis for all of the tire testing was a 1972 Blazer which came equipped with the *General Belted Gripper 780*. This tire was listed as an option from Chevrolet for the Blazer in 1972. It was a good tire to include in the test group because it rounded out the types being tested with a bias-belted tire. The Sears Radial is a true radial and all others of the common bias-construction technique. At the time of the testing the Generals had approximately 5,200 miles on them—all on the highway. Wear appeared to be negligible on the rear; the front two showed slight outer-edge cupping . . . normal for 4WD vehicles. Except for the General and Formula Desert Dog tires, all were brand new.

THEORETICAL CONTACT PRESSURE

When a vehicle moves from a hard surface to a soft one—snow, mud, sand—tire contact pressure is where it's at when it comes to staying up on top of the terrain. There are a lot of fancy ways of defining tire-contact pressure but what it boils down to is dividing the wheel load in pounds by the tire footprint area in square inches.

$$\frac{\text{Wheel load (lbs)}}{\text{Tire foot print area (sq. inches)}} = \text{Tire Contact Pressure (lbs/sq. in.)}$$

Think about that for a minute. What this says—before we even get into it—is that a lightweight vehicle such as an old military Jeep can stay on top of the sand or whatever with far less rubber touching the ground than a heavy vehicle like an air-conditioned Blazer. Nothing startling about this. A guy with size 14 brogans weighing 200 pounds won't be able to make it up the side of a sand dune any easier than his 90-pound wife with size seven tennies. The obvious extension to this line of thought is strapping on a set of snowshoes—the name of the game is *flotation.*

To "put some numbers" to the information gathered about the tires being tested, DataMotive computed the theoretical tire-contact pressure of each tire group at three different inflation pressures. Note that we use the term *theoretical tire contact pressure.* Unless the tire being tested has no tread pattern—such as a drag slick—there are voids in the contact area. Measure all of these voids and grooves and subtract their area from the theoretical tire contact area and you'd have the actual tire-contact area for a hard flat surface. However, as a tire sinks into the sand or mud, these voids and grooves fill and the area contributes its share to bear the load. Thus, when discussing off-road tire flotation it is logical to use the void and groove area as well as the lug area when computing footprint area and contact pressure.

The term *net-to-gross contact ratio* describes the amount of open space in the tread design. Desert Dog has a tread design with a lot of open space and a *low* net-to-gross contact ratio. Armstrong High-Flotation has a *high* net-to-gross contact ratio.

$$\frac{\text{lug area (lots)}}{\text{gross area}} = \text{high net to gross ratio}$$

$$\frac{\text{lug area (little)}}{\text{gross area}} = \text{low net to gross ratio}$$

TIRE MEASUREMENT TABLE (As Tested)

	ARMSTRONG NORSEMAN	ARMSTRONG TRU-TRAC	NATIONAL SURE-TRAC PREMIUM	ARMSTRONG HIWAY FLOTATION	FORMULA DESERT DOG	SEARS RADIAL	GENERAL BELTED GRIPPER 780
SIZE	L-78-15	11-15	10-15	11-15	10-15	225-15	L-78-15
TREAD TYPE	Mud/Snow	Mud/Snow	Off-Road	Sand	Off-Road	Highway	Mud/Snow
LOAD RANGE	B	B	B	B	B	B	B
INFLATION, PSI	24	24	24	24	24	24	24
TREAD WIDTH, INCHES	6.9	8.75	8.6	10.58	9.8	5.6	6.6
SECTION WIDTH, INCHES	9.9	11.52	10.53	10.8	10.31	8.72	9.02
OVERALL DIAMETER, INCHES	29.53	32.92	30.41	30.77	30.22	29.00	29.39
SECTION HEIGHT, INCHES	6.75	8.18	7.09	7.06	7.04	6.17	6.53
CONSTRUCTION	Bias	Bias	Bias	Bias	Bias	Radial	Bias Belted
CORD MATERIAL	4-Ply Nylon	4-Ply Nylon	4-Ply Nylon	4-Ply Nylon	4-Ply Nylon	2-Ply Steel 2-Ply Rayon	2-Ply Fiberglass 2-Ply Polyester
TUBE/TUBELESS	Tubeless	Tube	Tubeless	Tube	Tubeless	Tubeless	Tubeless
DUROMETER*	67	65	67	62	73	64	69
AVERAGE TREAD DEPTH IN INCHES	0.500	0.610	0.488	0.297	0.652	0.315	0.520
STATIC BALANCE WEIGHT, OUNCES	6	3.5	10.5	7	2	4	None
MOUNTED WEIGHT, POUNDS	57	71	57	59	57	58	55

* Durometer - a measure of rubber hardness.

RECOMMENDED SIZE WHEELS FOR TIRE (BEAD-TO-BEAD) For general on and off-road driving.	
Tires	Rim Width (Inches)
7.00-15	5.5
7.50-16	5.5 or 6
L78-15	6-8
10-15	8
11-15	8
12-15	10
13.00-15	15
16.50-15	18
8.00-16.5	6
8.75-16.5	6.75
9.50-16.5	6.75
10.00-16.5	8.25
12.00-16.5	9.75
	Dick Cepek Catalog

Which tires for which wheels or vice versa; after selling and mounting thousands of sets of tires on 4WD, Dick Cepek made this chart. Best recommendations I've seen!

Back to our test. Theoretical contact pressure was based on a hard surface with no penetration of the tire into the surface. Here's how we did it. A load of 1280 pounds was established for the left rear tire of the Blazer test vehicle and each tire was in turn mounted on this wheel, inked, and then slowly lowered onto a large piece of paper on an aluminum plate on the floor. After the print was made, the wheel was jacked up, paper removed, tire pressure altered and the same procedure followed again until three separate footprints per tire had been made.

Where the running surface is soft enough, there will be less contact pressure than the chart shows. The tire will tend to penetrate and, depending upon construction of the tire, will tend to pick up area according to the amount of penetration. Specifically, we have the Sears tire in mind. This tire performed very well in all of the tests—yet did not appear on paper to have a real good, low contact pressure. Radial-ply construction lets the sidewalls bow out so they are parallel to the hard surface as opposed to lying down on the surface. Consequently, the footprint area we measured on a hard surface was considerably less than it would have been had the pressure been measured with the tire penetrating the surface at least 1/4-inch. This is reflected in this tire's performance in sand where it did sink in. The Sears Radial put far more foot-

print on the surface than our contact-pressure graph shows, Graph 1.

Each of the bars includes the inflation pressure used to develop the contact pressure. Note the inflation pressure was lower than the actual contact pressure. This is particularly noticeable at the higher deflection ratios, that is, at lower inflation pressures. At highway pressures sidewall stiffness adds to a lesser degree to the actual ground pressure. A flexible sidewall will allow more rubber to contact the ground, reducing the contact pressure.

The minimum internal tire pressure selected was based upon the beginning of sidewall buckle. We did this for a reason. It is about the only guide to safe minimum pressure when you are off the road. When you begin to get sidewall buckle, the sidewall cords are going into a severe reverse bind. This you do not want. Stop short of that, just as we did to establish minimum pressure.

Of all the tires, the Tru-Trac could be let down to the lowest internal tire pressure which also resulted in the lowest flat-plate-contact pressure of 10 psi. DataMotive engineers felt the Sears Radial at the 8 psi internal tire pressure would have been comparable to the Tru-Trac had we been able to account for the large area of the sidewalls not contacting the paper.

As you pursue the charts, study the photos of the individual tread patterns and the tire footprints at the different pressures. Areas measured were the projected areas, i.e., DataMotive took the ink patterns and went around the periphery of each pattern to determine the area—including grooves and voids. When we say it's the theoretical contact pressure on hard surfaces, that is exactly what it is . . . *theoretical.*

Tires with high net-to-gross contact ratios such as the Sears Radial or the Armstrong Norseman bring the theoretical contact pressures much closer to the actual contact pressures on hard surfaces.

Also as you study the information presented here, you may be interested in knowing that high-performance off-road military vehicles use under 10 psi theoretical contact pressure. For instance, the M-113 armored-personnel carrier uses about 7 psi as do the Lockheed Twister high-performance articulated vehicles. These are not really the hot dogs when it comes to getting through the super-soft soil—often called marginal terrain. Specialized military vehicles run the range of less than 2 psi and the snow vehicles get down in a range of 0.75 psi or less.

When studying Graph 2, Tire-Deflection Ratio, keep in mind this generally indicates overall stiffness. Generally speaking, it is desirable to have a flexible sidewall so reducing internal tire pressure gives a proportional increase in footprint area. The graph shows this is certainly the case with the Sears Radial's relatively low sidewall stiffness. Consequently it is capable of going to very high deflection ratios. Don't buy a tire with a higher load rating—number of plies—than absolutely necessary. Those extra plies in the sidewall will reduce the benefits of letting air out to get a better footprint because the stiff sidewalls keep holding the tire up.

TIRE FOOTPRINTS

DataMotive engineers had the following random comments about the tires following the obtaining of the footprints.

"The Sears Radial tire footprint fails to show the sidewalls were bulged out—but running parallel to the flat surface about ¼-inch up. Had a footprint area been taken of the tire penetrating soil to this depth, footprint area would have been 20 to 30% larger. This tire had the longest footprint—good for off-road use. Steel-belted radials should usually be mounted on a rim not wider than 80% of the section width. Tom Cepek claims the Armstrong Radials work fine on 8-inch rims. Follow the manufacturer's recommendations for rim width. You can damage the steel belt if you use radials on too-wide rims. This is contrary to the typical recommendation for bias-ply tires. They sometimes use rim widths wider than the section width. Both radial and bias-belted tires have rectangular-shaped footprints which are relatively square at the ends.

The Desert Dog and National Sure-Trac gave us a footprint length-to-width ratio of 1:1 over the pressure ranges checked. Both have a very low net-to-gross contact ratio.

This means that when operating on surfaces where there is relatively little tire penetration, ground-contact pressure of each lug is relatively high due to the small amount of lug area.

These tires tend to be aggressive and damaging to soft soils. On the Desert Dog, even at the lowest pressures, the shoulders are not in contact for any

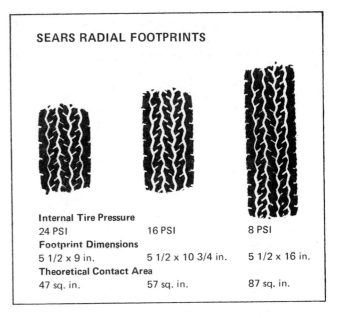

SEARS RADIAL FOOTPRINTS

Internal Tire Pressure		
24 PSI	16 PSI	8 PSI
Footprint Dimensions		
5 1/2 x 9 in.	5 1/2 x 10 3/4 in.	5 1/2 x 16 in.
Theoretical Contact Area		
47 sq. in.	57 sq. in.	87 sq. in.

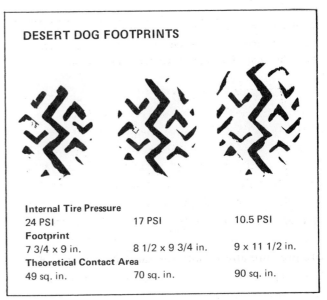

DESERT DOG FOOTPRINTS

Internal Tire Pressure		
24 PSI	17 PSI	10.5 PSI
Footprint		
7 3/4 x 9 in.	8 1/2 x 9 3/4 in.	9 x 11 1/2 in.
Theoretical Contact Area		
49 sq. in.	70 sq. in.	90 sq. in.

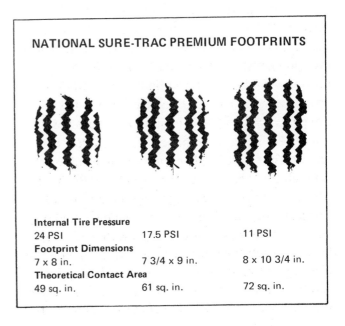

NATIONAL SURE-TRAC PREMIUM FOOTPRINTS

Internal Tire Pressure		
24 PSI	17.5 PSI	11 PSI
Footprint Dimensions		
7 x 8 in.	7 3/4 x 9 in.	8 x 10 3/4 in.
Theoretical Contact Area		
49 sq. in.	61 sq. in.	72 sq. in.

TRU-TRAC FOOTPRINTS

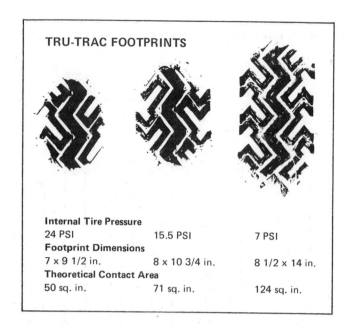

Internal Tire Pressure
24 PSI	15.5 PSI	7 PSI
Footprint Dimensions		
7 x 9 1/2 in.	8 x 10 3/4 in.	8 1/2 x 14 in.
Theoretical Contact Area		
50 sq. in.	71 sq. in.	124 sq. in.

ARMSTRONG HIGH-FLOTATION FOOTPRINTS

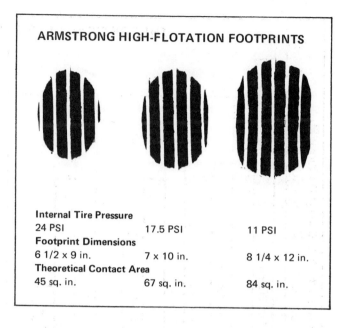

Internal Tire Pressure
24 PSI	17.5 PSI	11 PSI
Footprint Dimensions		
6 1/2 x 9 in.	7 x 10 in.	8 1/4 x 12 in.
Theoretical Contact Area		
45 sq. in.	67 sq. in.	84 sq. in.

ARMSTRONG NORSEMAN FOOTPRINTS

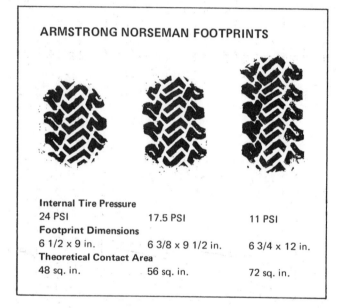

Internal Tire Pressure
24 PSI	17.5 PSI	11 PSI
Footprint Dimensions		
6 1/2 x 9 in.	6 3/8 x 9 1/2 in.	6 3/4 x 12 in.
Theoretical Contact Area		
48 sq. in.	56 sq. in.	72 sq. in.

GENERAL FOOTPRINTS

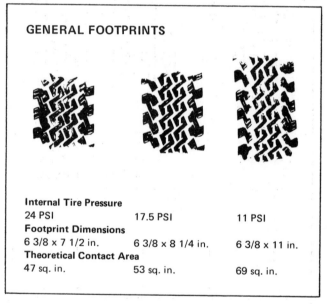

Internal Tire Pressure
24 PSI	17.5 PSI	11 PSI
Footprint Dimensions		
6 3/8 x 7 1/2 in.	6 3/8 x 8 1/4 in.	6 3/8 x 11 in.
Theoretical Contact Area		
47 sq. in.	53 sq. in.	69 sq. in.

length. The patch is still virtually oval although the shoulders touch the surface at the center.

Tru-Trac, Armstrong High-Flotation and Norseman tires have a rounded leading edge to the tire footprint. This gives a gentle entry into the soft soil. In other words, there is little or no distinct edge at the point where the sidewall meets the tread with which to cut or claw the soil. This may or may not be advantageous. It is interesting to note that at the lowest deflection of 7 psi the Tru-Trac actually grabbed the paper due to the tread flexing—thus the contact patch print is very poor.

At 24 psi inflation pressure these tires all have the outer shoulder off the ground: Desert Dog, Tru-Trac, Armstrong High-Flotation, and National Sure-Trac. The balance of the tires— including Armstrong Norseman, Sears Radials and General—held their overall widths throughout the pressure ranges tested. General gives very little contact-patch change until you get below 17 psi because sidewall stiffness does not allow any appreciable bulging of the tire or increase in length.

The reason the General—bias-belted—cannot produce long footprints like a straight steel-belted tire is because sidewall stiffness precludes the laying out of the belt as is the case with the more

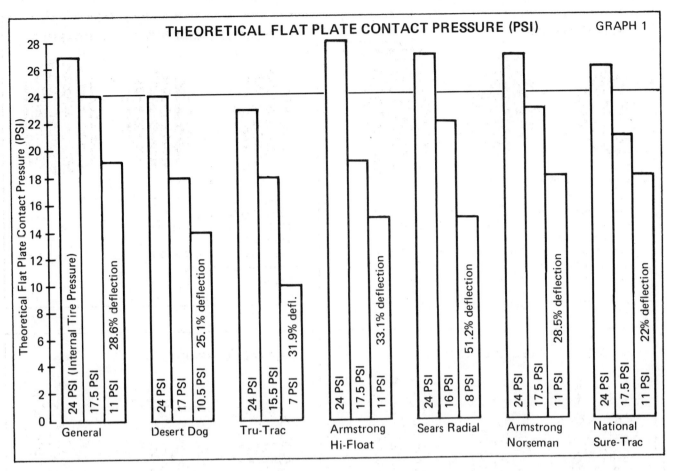

THEORETICAL FLAT PLATE CONTACT PRESSURE (PSI) — GRAPH 1

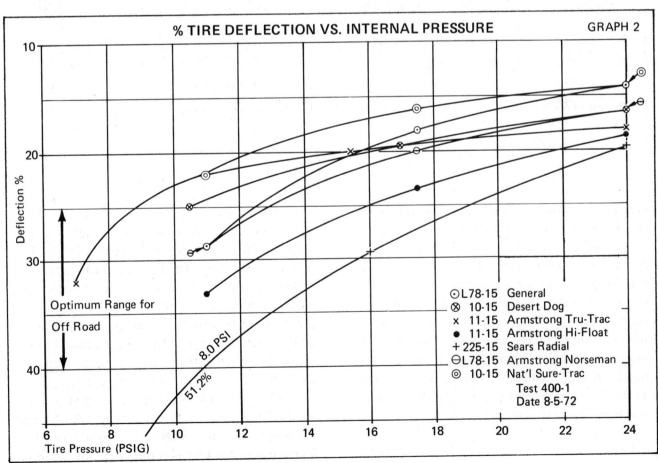

% TIRE DEFLECTION VS. INTERNAL PRESSURE — GRAPH 2

⊙ L78-15 General
⊗ 10-15 Desert Dog
× 11-15 Armstrong Tru-Trac
● 11-15 Armstrong Hi-Float
+ 225-15 Sears Radial
⊖ L78-15 Armstrong Norseman
◎ 10-15 Nat'l Sure-Trac

Test 400-1
Date 8-5-72

radial construction.

Comparing the Armstrong Norseman with the General, both increase overall footprint length slightly as tire pressure goes down. General's belted construction gives a rectangular pattern with severe entry into the soil compared to the Norseman's somewhat oval shape and more gentle entry characteristic.

The Armstrong High-Flotation should have the lowest hard surface contact pressure due to the greatest amount of tread area on the surface. Experience has shown that on the High-Floats you can go to a lower pressure on a narrow rim without getting the buckling encountered with the 8-inch rim. The narrower rim allows a longer footprint generally considered to give more traction in soft soils.

One of the factors to consider in rim-width selection if a lot of rocky terrain is on the menu is to keep the rim inside the sidewall of the tire to protect the rim from rock damage. In other words, let the sidewall hit the rock before the rim. Thus it will tend to glance away without damaging either tire or rim. You hope! If pure sand only is to be traversed then a wider rim can be run without damage.

As previously noted, the shoulders of many of the tires at 24 psi did not contact the hard surface. The narrower the wheel, the less sidewall or shoulder contact at the higher pressures . . . for a bias-ply tire.

Next to the lowest surface-contact pressure is provided by the Sears Radial. As previously mentioned, when the radial penetrates the surface ever so slightly, contact area is substantially increased. When using the tire at 8 psi, extreme care is needed to avoid damaging the sidewalls against hard objects. This is because the edge of the sidewall actually runs parallel to the ground surface. Use of such low pressures should be limited to running in sand which has no rocks.

One interesting facet of the steel-belted radial ply tire: Circumference remains essentially constant throughout a range of tire pressures. Although the apparent rolling radius changes, revolutions per mile remain essentially the same for all operating pressures. On the bias-ply tire, as the tire pressure goes down the revolutions per mile figure changes drastically."

SUBJECTIVE RIDE AND HANDLING

How does one go about putting numbers—concrete information—to tire characteristics such as *nibble, yaw, over/understeer, harshness, noise level, thump and vibration?* It can be measured; information can be drawn and one set of tires can be compared directly to another with established baselines. Why go to all of this trouble? How many times have you heard someone complain a given tire set made an ungodly amount of *noise* on the highway? Ever heard someone say a particular set of tires just didn't want to move out of a tiny rut in the road? That's *nibble.* All these factors are important to a tire buyer—whether he knows it or not. Tires can do as much as and sometimes more to enhance or ruin vehicle handling than major suspension changes.

Keep in mind—after you've bought the tires you are usually stuck with them. Few of us can afford the luxury of five or six sets of tires at a time to bolt onto what is most often a recreational luxury. DataMotive took our seven sets of test tires and gave them a complete shakedown and put some very real but subjective and meaningful numbers on all of the tire characteristics listed above. A cold-start tire pressure of 24 psi was used for all tires tested for ride and handling. This pressure was considered the minimum for the high-speed highway tests.

Using the belted General tires as a baseline tire, a 38-mile-long highway and gravel-surface course was set up. Landmarks were noted, or markers put up to help the driver duplicate the driving conditions for every set of tires. A Data-Motive engineer laid out the course and did all of the driving. Each characteristic was measured for all tires at exactly the same point on the course and same speed. Subjective impressions by a tire test engineer with more than 10 years' experience were captured by a tape recorder carried in the Blazer.

Impressions were number rated on a scale of zero to five for each characteristic and condition for each set of tires. The number rating system was the basis of the two Subjective Ride Study charts prepared by DataMotive. Zero indicates total absence of a characteristic; one through five rates the characteristic from good to bad.

Test tires. New, mounted, inflated, measured, printed, weighed and ready for the ride and handling portion of the test.

Tires identified by letters in subjective handling study below are A) Armstrong Norseman, B) Armstrong Tru-Trac, C) National Sure-Trac, D) Armstrong High-Flotation, E) Formula Desert Dog, F) Sears Radial, G) General Belted Gripper.

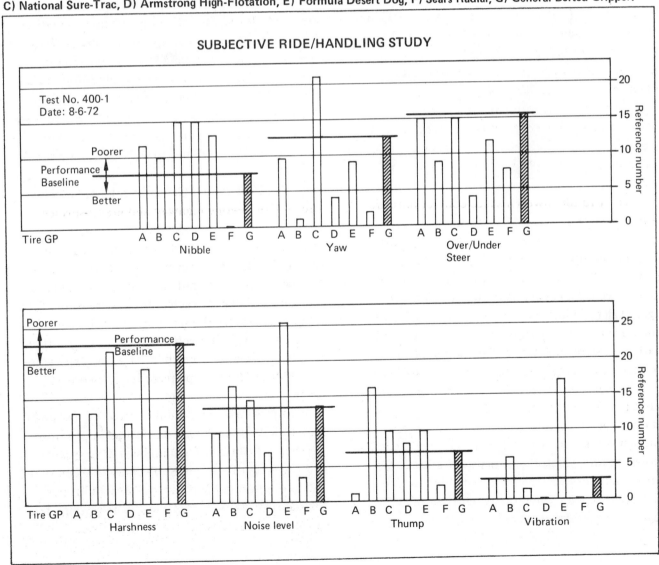

Noise level at various speeds on the different surfaces was measured subjectively and also with a decibel (dB) meter used to make true sound measurements. The meter was mounted on foam rubber on the console between the seats of the Blazer so it could measure the sound level heard by the driver.

To reduce variables in the testing procedure, DataMotive ran the control tires—the Armstrong Norseman—after each two sets of tires tested. Thus the tire testing went like this: Armstrong Norseman, Armstrong Tru Trac, *Armstrong Norseman,* National Sure Trac Premium, Armstrong High-Flotation, *Armstrong Norseman,* Formula Desert Dog, Sears Radial, *Armstrong Norseman,* etc. This gave the test driver a constant close reference back to the control tires.

Before the actual testing began, all of the tires not previously subjected to road use were broken in by running them on the 38-mile course. This was intended to put all of the tires on an equal footing from a testing standpoint. Tires don't stay new and no one runs them new for very long. They are broken in and run that way until being discarded. So why begin the testing with new tires?

Here's a description of the test course by the engineer: "To begin the course, we have 30 and 45 miles per hour highway with the tires cold, measuring harshness, thump, vibration, nibble and the noise level—both on a noise-level meter and a subjective noise level. In other words—what you can hear. From that we go to a 30 mph highway stop to see if the tires cause any vibrations in the vehicle. After the stop, we have a start to determine if there were any problems with the tires in that phase. For the highway-curve portion of the test, we ran 60 mph right and left curves going north and going south through the same curves. These curves were approximately 200- to 300-foot constant radius and about a 45-degree turn angle. The gravel turns were much sharper—about a 100-foot radius. These were traversed at 50 mph, both right and left curves, north and south. A portion of the gravel road was corduroy and we measured corduroy harshness and the skate of the tires on that surface. From that area we went onto a divided expressway and ran a 70 mph passing maneuver to check the yaw cycles at the start and end of the passing maneuver. We then had a 70 mph highway high speed evaluation of harshness, thump, vibration,

nibble and noise level with the tires hot; 45 mph same, 30 mph same. From this subjective data, we then got a reference number for the tires which is a matter of subjectively evaluating each tire by a number from zero to five, zero being none or good or best and five being the poorest or bad condition."

Because I rode on all of the subjective rides and handling runs I feel this description is overly modest about what was done. I would only comment it takes a considerable feel and a great deal of concentration to hold a vehicle exactly at a given speed in a curve while at the same time commenting—number rating system—on the over/understeer characteristics at five given positions in the curve in addition to rating the tire for yaw! Think about it for a minute and mentally put yourself in the driver's seat.

The information we've just discussed appears here in a DataMotive graph as a quick and easy reference to any of the ride or handling characteristics we measured. How can you use these charts? In many ways. Your imagination is the limit. Let's say you are currently running the Norseman tire and they need to be replaced. You desire a tire which has less noise on the freeway and—hopefully—less nibble. Look at the charts. Of those tires listed which have less noise and nibble—what are you losing? This information, of course, must be weighed against what you feel is an acceptable level of performance on wet asphalt and in dry sand. If you never drive on wet asphalt or never go in the sand, then the choice might be simpler depending on whether you let unfounded prejudices take the place of information such as that provided here.

WET ASPHALT TESTS

In addition to the subjective ride and handling testing conducted on asphalt and gravel, Data-Motive felt even more time should be spent on the asphalt to give the potential tire buyer and user more "numbers" with which to carve out a tire choice. The result is a wet-asphalt traction study—which not only shows the tractive effort of each set of tires on wet asphalt—but also how *forgiving* the tires are after they've once broken away. In other words, once you *lose it* on a slick stretch of pavement, how much help will the tire give you in bringing the vehicle back under control? This is an

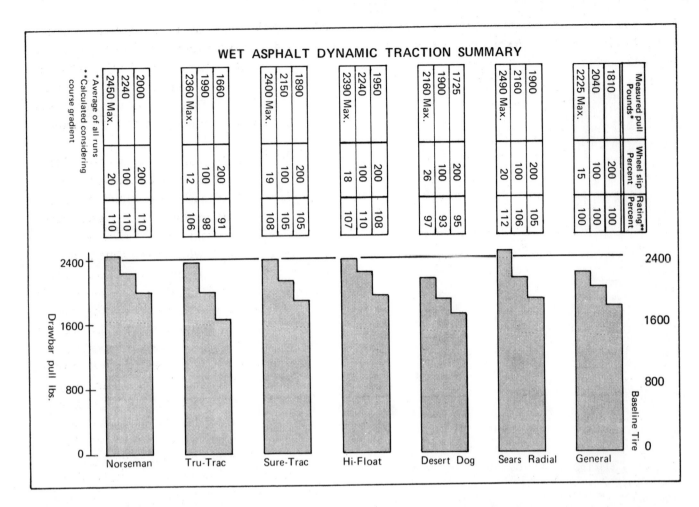

WET ASPHALT DYNAMIC TRACTION SUMMARY

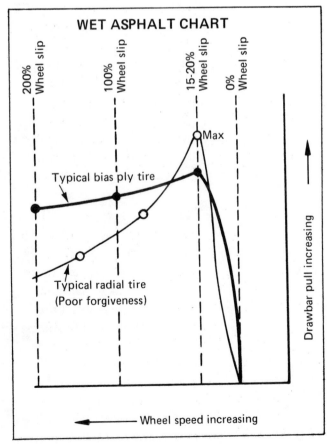

WET ASPHALT CHART

important consideration and often means the difference between going in the ditch and staying on the road.

The tractive effort of the tires on wet asphalt was measured from drawbar pull. Simply changing the rear tires gave the comparisons between the various sets of tires. Specifically, the test tires were mounted on the rear axle only—to simulate normal road driving—of a Blazer which towed the Wagoneer dynamometer car outfitted with a Honeywell XYY recorder model 540T. The dyno car was also outfitted with sophisticated digital readout equipment to ensure each test would be run under the same conditions as the others. All tires were tested at 2.5-mph vehicle speed, controlled by the dyno car. Wheels on the test vehicle were accelerated, starting at the 2.5-mph vehicle speed, until maximum drawbar pull was obtained. At this point, the test tires gave approximately 10 to 30% wheel slip—very slight wheel slip—when maximum drawbar pull was obtained.

Percentage of wheel slip is defined as:

$$\frac{\text{wheel velocity - vehicle velocity}}{\text{vehicle velocity}} \times 100 = \frac{\text{percentage}}{\text{wheel slip}}$$

For instance with the vehicle velocity of 2.5 mph and the tires turning at 10 mph, indicated by the speedometer, the slip =

$$\frac{10 - 2.5}{2.5} \times 100 = 300\% \text{ slip}$$

After maximum drawbar pull was reached, smooth acceleration of the Blazer wheels was continued until the tires went into full slip—approximately 300%. The recorder plotted all of this including that period of the test after maximum drawbar pull was reached.

Plotter mounted in the dyno vehicle records the exact drawbar pulled by a group of test tires in addition to showing how rapidly the tire breaks away once maximum pull is reached. This is perhaps the most sophisticated and accurate instrumentation of its kind in existence.

What's yaw? For our purposes, yaw could be related to "fish-tailing" or the back end of the car moving back and forth relative to the front. The front of the car is assumed to be going straight forward with the rear moving from side to side following a normal passing maneuver.

What's understeer/oversteer? Well, if you want to get picky about it; there ain't no such animal! But again for the purpose of this book we'll use the term understeer/oversteer to refer to the overall analysis of how much effect a set of tires has on the basic steering characteristics of the test vehicle. A vehicle can quite often be both an over and understeering vehicle depending upon operating and surface conditions. In general, an understeering car is considered far safer for the average driver. Most passenger cars understeer for this reason. The *understeer/oversteer* characteristic of each set of tires was gauged subjectively and rated accordingly. *Yaw* in the context used here is primarily an *oversteer* condition.

The term *less under/oversteer* will mean closer to *neutral steer* than a tire with *more under/oversteer*. *Neutral steer* is a condition where the vehicle goes where you want it to without unusual deviation at either end of the car.

There's more about *understeer* and *oversteer* on page 164.

What's drawbar pull? Drawbar pull is the available tractive effort in excess of that (rolling resistance, etc) necessary to propel the vehicle at a given constant speed on a level surface. It is a measure of the force available to accelerate the vehicle, climb grades and pull towed loads.

Plotter readings come from this load cell pivoting from the frame of the dyno (towed) vehicle. Cell is rugged, yet sensitive in terms of providing accurate information—expensive.

Now the overall performance of the tire could be examined. This was essential to learn what the tire did once it had broken traction. Ideally, the optimum tire would reach maximum drawbar pull and continue that effort even as wheel slip increases.

Interpretation of the graphs on page 145 provided the following analysis of the shape of the traction curve.

The Norseman got its maximum drawbar pull at 20% wheel slip, maintaining it through approximately 50% wheel slip and then tapered off slightly. A very good *forgiveness* curve.

Tru-Trac's drawbar pull peaked at 11 to 15% wheel slip and immediately tapered to a lower drawbar figure. When you have these tires, limit spinning the wheels; it looks impressive but isn't very efficient.

National Sure-Trac's maximum drawbar pull occurred at 19% wheel slip, did not hold the drawbar-pull value, and immediately dropped to a lower drawbar value.

Armstrong High-Flotations showed maximum pull at 18% which gradually tapered to a lower value.

Setup for the wet asphalt drawbar testing consists of the towing vehicle on which the test tires are mounted. Wagoneer serves as dyno with load cell in between the two vehicles. Fifty yards of asphalt was kept wet by a lowbuck sprinkler arrangement.

Drawbar test hookup to towing vehicle consists of cable yoke attached to rear axle which connects to a single cable going back to the dyno vehicle. Other line reads driveshaft speed of Blazer so dyno operator can start applying load at same speed for each group of tires.

If you're the guy that has to do the changing, there is a week full of backaches in that stack. Considerably more than a thousand dollars worth of tires is represented here.

The Desert Dogs pulled best at 26% wheel slip and had a gradual curve to a lower figure. Its maximum drawbar pull was less than any other tire tested.

Sears Radials reached their peak drawbar pull at 20% wheel slip, then dropped off to about 80% of its maximum value at 100% wheel slip. This drop off is typical of radial tires. However, due to the high peak traction, they are comparable to a bias-ply tire.

The General pulled best at 15% wheel slip, and only gradually decreased in value. It might be noted that a bias-belted tire has most of the features of a radial tire in dynamic traction, i.e., a higher peak value but with a lesser drop off in traction at high slip rates than a bias-ply tire . . . a good compromise.

The preceding paragraphs tell it like it is, but again give no clue to the amount of work and time. After each two sets of tires were tested, the control set—Armstrong Norseman—was retested to make certain all of the data would repeat and all of the test equipment was working correctly. After all of the tires had been tested using this procedure, all were retested. In other words, not only was a control set used after testing each two sets of tires, but each set of tires was tested *twice* to confirm the data.

Take a look at page 145. You'll note the General tire is used as the baseline tire—different function from a control tire—and the rating on the General is 100%. Thus the performances of all other tires are rated in relation to the performance of the General—some better, some worse.

The Wet Asphalt Dynamic Traction Summary chart applies meaningful numbers to that particular part of the testing. Each graph section represents the performance of one set of tires on wet asphalt. To explain the chart's function—let's look at the baseline tire at the top. That figure of **1,810** represents the amount of drawbar pull at 200% wheel slippage. Because this is the baseline tire that figure then becomes 100% and the performance of all other tires tested is then stacked against it. In the graph immediately below the baseline we find the Sears Radial is rated at 105%. That means in this particular instance the Radial was 5% better than the baseline tire.

2,040 lbs represents the performance of the

tire at 100% wheel slip and **2,225 lbs** drawbar pull is the maximum amount pulled by that set of tires at any time during the test. In this case, maximum pull was obtained at 15% wheel slippage. In other words, the chart figures describe the traction curve of a set of tires at three points. For instance the Norseman would pull you away from the standing start faster than the baseline tire.

Tire traction characteristics at high slip rates come into play when you try to move away from a stoplight too fast when it's raining. See lower chart on page 145. A radial tire with its high drawbar peak can be accelerated faster by feathering the throttle and allowing the tire to remain at its peak performance. When you see that maximum pull is at 20% wheel slip, remember the vehicle is going 2.5 mph and the tire is only rotating 3.0 mph—a very small difference.

DYNAMIC TRACTION ON DRY SAND

The final portion of the DataMotive testing was the dynamic traction test conducted on the sand of Sand Mountain, Nevada. This test differed from the wet asphalt test in that it was a pull-to-stall traction study. The Blazer test vehicle entered the test course in four-wheel drive—low transfer,

Sand drawbar tests were run both ways on a test course. Driver of Wagoneer applied the brakes until the Blazer stalled.

Dick Cepek shows just how flexible a tire can be. If you think you need sidewall flexibility for a maximum bite in the sand, try this test with tire in question.

Accurate data compiled over a long period of time is no easy task. Here a DataMotive engineer gathers a sand sample which will later be lab tested for moisture content. This will be recorded and tire tests six months or six years from now can be compared on equal footing.

low range—at 10 mph. The Wagoneer dynamometer vehicle being pulled by the Blazer pulled the test vehicle down to stall with the test tires spinning but test vehicle stopped by applying the Wagoneer's brakes. The recorder plotted pull at the drawbar as it varied with slip and then stalled. This can be related to real-life driving by assuming a slope gradually increasing until the vehicle stalls or spins out.

The sand test was conducted with the tires brought down to the minimum deflation figure shown. The tire-traction curves looked like this:

The Norseman reached maximum drawbar pull at 50 to 100% wheel slip and held that maximum, dropping only 20% at stall or near-stall. This tire was very erratic in the sand, causing excessive wheel hop as maximum drawbar pull and wheel slip increased.

The Tru-Trac's showed the highest drawbar pull of all the tires tested—at approximately 50% slippage. When slippage increased beyond this figure, the drawbar value immediately decreased. This indicates that once the vehicle starts to sink it really sinks in a hurry. However, due to its high peak drawbar value, the Tru-Trac's high slip draw-

PERFORMANCE CHART

	Tire Footprint*	Max. Sand Drawbar	Max. Sand Drawbar @ 100% Slip	Max. Sand Drawbar @ 200% Slip
Max.	Tru-Trac	Tru-Trac	Tru-Trac	Tru-Trac
	Desert Dog	Desert Dog	Desert Dog	Desert Dog
	Sears Radial	Sears Radial	Sears Radial/ Hi-Float	Sears Radial/ Hi-Float
	Hi-Float	Hi-Float	Norseman	Norseman
	Norseman/ Sure-Trac	Norseman	Sure-Trac	Sure-Trac
	General	General	General	General
Min.		Sure-Trac		

*At lowest pressure

bar value is significantly better than any other group tested.

National Sure-Trac Premiums pulled best at 60 to 75% wheel slip and immediately dropped to a much lower value. These tires will get you stuck in a hurry in loose, dry sand if you're not careful.

Armstrong High-Flotation tires pulled hardest at 25 to 50% wheel slip, had a slight nose on the curve and dropped to a lower value.

Desert Dogs pulled their utmost and immediately dropped to a lower drawbar pull, making them harder to use effectively in sand.

Sears Radials maximum drawbar—quite high!—was maintained through ever higher slip values. Excellent performance in sand.

Generals peaked and kept on pulling for a short period, then dropped to a lower drawbar value. Fair performance in sand.

To summarize the dynamic sand traction using the General tire as a baseline—and thus giving it a value of 100%:

Norseman produced a value of 103%—virtually equal to the General.

Tru-Trac registered 120%. Clearly the best tire tested for the sand.

National Sure Trac fell below the value attained by General. At 92% these were significantly poorer and the worst tires tested in the sand.

Armstrong High-Flotation with the straight grooves produced 106%—slightly better than either the General or the Norseman.

Desert Dogs and the Sears Radials both recorded 108%.

An overall summary of the performance of the various tires in the sand is presented in our Performance Chart on page 149. This ranks tire performance using the footprint as the basic point of comparison. In all cases, the tire at the top gave the maximum in terms of footprint area or drawbar pull and the tire at the bottom gave the least. Data-Motive engineers pointed out that in terms of the overall maximum drawbar pull, the difference between the best tire and the worst one was about 25%. The tire footprints in this chart were obtained with the tires on a hard surface at the lowest pressure just prior to the sidewall buckling (see page 139).

In comparing the footprint with the maximum drawbar column, note that only the Sure-Trac's performance is out of line. A comparison of

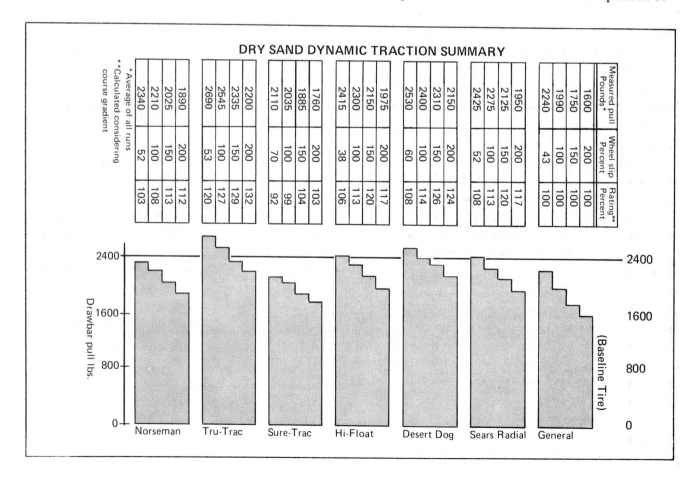

DRY SAND DYNAMIC TRACTION SUMMARY

Ugly, archaic, underpowered and still one of the most useful, lovable off-road vehicles in existence—made even better with the outfitting of today's high flotation tires.

maximum sand drawbar at 100% slip shows the tires lined up exactly as they did in terms of the footprint and the same is true for the maximum sand drawbar measured at 200% wheel slip. Data-Motive's Bill Janowski was quick to point out this is a comparison of tires based primarily upon the friction of the tire against the sand as opposed to a paddle-wheel tire which tends to dig and accelerate sand to the rear. Also, it should be pointed out this comparison of these tires is only for very dry sand. The effect in wet sand was not tested and could very well be different.

DataMotive engineers made a number of observations after the testing. In dry sand, there is no apparent effect of the tread upon the maximum drawbar capability. The top three tires—Desert Dogs, Sears Radials and Tru-Trac designs exhibited an extremely aggressive and deep tread, a street tread, and a mud and snow tread. Simply stated, as long as you can get the rubber down on the sand, the tire will perform effectively regardless of the tread design. Obviously, Desert Dogs' very aggressive lugs were sinking into the sand so the whole tire tread was in contact with the sand. Tire diameter is certainly no basis for judging tire performance in the sand—except for

very small and *very large* diameters. The Tru-Trac's outside diameter is 32.92-inches. Sears Radials were the smallest with a 29-inch diameter. The top three tires also contain those with extremes in overall section width: Tru-Trac 11.52-inches; Sears with 8.72-inches. So the conclusion here is that section width is not a critical consideration—so long as the rubber gets to the sand.

Janowski pointed out that the Norseman tends to float a little on the chart because it developed the most severe tire/vehicle bounce under high drawbar conditions. The tire would create an oscillation due to vertical pitch or bounce, scattering the data points on the graphs so they were difficult to interpret.

The comparison of the maximum drawbar at 100% and 200% slip did not produce anything to surprise DataMotive's test crew. However, it was noted that only one tire developed maximum drawbar at less than 40% slip and that was the Armstrong High-Flotation. At the other end of the scale, the National Sure-Trac, developed maximum drawbar pull at 70% slip. All of the other tires pulled best between 40 to 60% slip. What this is saying, in terms of applying the test information to practical off-road driving habits is: When you start to get stuck and are spinning the tires, you may be able to spin them at just the right slippage to allow you to get unstuck. A good deal of flying sand may be impressive to the troops but if you've crossed over that critical point of maximum drawbar, then throwing sand is about all you are doing. Experiment the next time you are out in the sand. You can actually feel the difference in the tires' pulling power at various slip—spinning—rates. Get to know their capabilities and you won't get stuck so often. Your competent manner in handling your vehicle will also impress your friends.

As the drawbar pull begins to increase the Desert Dogs dig in and . . .

. . . the vehicle begins to sink. All forward movement has ended by now, and it's up to the driver to get off the throttle before . . .

. . . situation gets worse. Notice how much closer to the sand the door sill is then when all of this started.

The driver is off the throttle, but it's too late. The unforgiving tire has dug four holes and carried the vehicle straight down. Now comes the backing and rocking to get out.

After the dust clears this is the depth of the digging. At this point both differentials are nosed into the sand. All of this occurred in about 3½ seconds.

152

Wide, non-aggressive tread pattern of the Hi-Flotation Armstrong disturbs a minimum amount of the terrain.

Weight was added to the log drag arrangement in the form of a "skier" who could shift his body fore or aft in order to dig in with the leading edge and provide a dead smooth surface for the drawbar tests.

Sand drawbar tests were always conducted on a freshly "graded" course provided by a short length of liberated utility pole. This ensured equal running conditions for all tires.

Ah, the glamorous life of a professional tire tester. The temperature is way over a hundred, there is no shade within fifty miles and we only have 28 more complete sets of tires to change before we're through.

Ambient temperature was recorded after each drawbar pull as was the temperature of the sand.

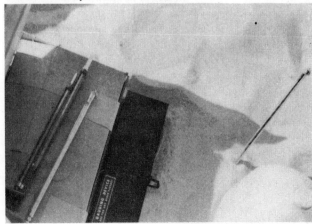

Bill Janowski shows there's a difference of 3.15-inches in tread width here. As mounted, the Tru-Trac weighed in at 71 pounds while the Sears stopped the scale at 58 pounds.

TIRE INFLATION, ROTATION AND WEAR

Despite my philosophy that tires are an expendable item, I feel you should get your money's worth from them. The sad fact of the matter is—very few off-roaders do. Proper inflation is the most important single factor in prolonging tire life. Underinflation causes extra flexing of the cord body, in turn causing breaks and separation of the cord fabric. Overinflation reduces the tire's capability to absorb shocks and increases the possibility of damage from sharp objects.

Follow normal tire wear indications. Too much wear in the center means too much pressure. Too much wear on the edges means too little pressure. If you're buying tires from a savvy tire store such as Cepek's they'll gladly recommend a starting pressure for the tire fitted to your vehicle. Don't take these figures as gospel—only as a starting point. You must always remember that drivers, vehicle weight, loading and variations in use are all different.

Check the pressure with an *accurate* gauge at least once every two weeks. Service station gauges attached to the air hose should be avoided like the plague because they are subjected to all sorts of unspeakable abuse and they are seldom accurate. Don't trust your eyeballs to tell you when the pressure is right or wrong. Use an accurate gauge—often. Don't be lazy about varying the tire pressure as you go from highway to off-road and back again. Run the correct pressure for the environment.

If you're fairly new to the game of four wheeling, you'll soon learn that all 4WD rigs "cup" the edges of the front tires. You cannot entirely eliminate this, but by knowing about it and acting on it you can get several thousand miles more from a set of tires. Whether you have 2WD or 4WD, be sure the front-end alignment is correct. Have it checked on a regular basis. Just hitting a curb will knock the front end out of alignment on a passenger car; think how many rocks and holes you hit on that last outing.

Keep the wheels balanced. This normally can be done at the same shop that checks front-end alignment. Don't waste your money on static balancing. Pay only for dynamic balancing where the tire is spun off the car or truck. Because of the size and tread design of most off-road tires, they're hard to balance and most of them need a lot of weight added. Out-of-balance tires really cut down mileage on a set due to irregular wear—especially if the tires spend a lot of their life on pavement.

The absolute maximum mileage at which tires should be rotated is 5,000 miles. Rotating tires evens out the uneven wear on the front and this is where you can gain extra life for a set. If your rig is outfitted with a limited-slip device in the rearend —such as Positraction—rear tires (not radials, though!) should be swapped side-to-side at least every 2,500 miles. Radials should stay on the same side of the vehicle once they have been run. Unlike the bias and bias-belted tires, the radial takes a set and should rotate only in one direction throughout its useful life. If this sounds like a lot of tire rotation to you—it is. But tire rotation is an essential part of the program of giving your tires several

The Tru-Trac was tested on 8-inch rim and could have been easily mounted on a ten inch. The Sears was mounted on a 6-inch rim and might possibly have been slightly more effective if a *narrower* rim had been used. There's a difference of 2.80 inches in section width here.

Believe it or not, when both tires are inflated to 24 PSI, the Tru-Trac on the left has a footprint area of 50 square inches, while the Radial on the right has only three square inches less. Note the completely different approach to tread design due to the fact the Sears was not designed as an off-road tire.

There's more than one story here. The mounted Tru-Trac had a diameter of 32.92 inches as opposed to 29.00 inches for the Sears Radial. That difference greatly affects fender clearance and gear ratio.

Just once, how'd you like to show up for a desert outing with a load of tires like this? Look close and check the inflation posture of those Tru-Tracs.

thousand miles of good life and in turn this means dollars in your pocket. Use the tire rotation chart in this book, and use it often.

Accept all of this tire maintenance as a real challenge and see just how many extra miles you can squeeze from a set. In the long run you'll be glad you did.

RANDOM THOUGHTS WHILE PUMPING UP THE TIRES

A number of random bits and pieces of information came to light while putting this section together. Hopefully some of them will help set the record straight. Larger than stock tires and wheels will not affect turning radius *if* stock offset is maintained. If not, you can expect turning radius to suffer along with wheel-bearing life.

Dick Cepek, Inc.

9201 CALIFORNIA AVE.
SOUTH GATE. CALIF. 92080

PHONE
(213) 569-1675

TIRE SIZE	RECOMMENDED TIRE INFLATION	TYPE OF VEHICLE

—

		FRONT LBS.	REAR LBS.

ROTATE!
ROTATE!
ROTATE!
ALL F.W.D. RIGS
"CUP" THE FRONT
TIRES UNLESS RO-
TATED AT LEAST
EVERY 5000 MILES.

1. HI-WAY UNLOADED

2. HI-WAY LOADED

3. OFF-ROAD, ROCKS ETC.

4. SAND USE ONLY

**HEAVY FEET KILL
TIRE TREAD LIFE**

Tips on tire maintenance

Proper inflation is the most important single factor in prolonging tire life. Underinflation causes extra flexing of the cord body, which results in breaks and separation of the cord fabric. Overinflation reduces the tire's capacity to absorb shocks and increases the possibility of damage from striking sharp objects.

Check inflation pressure: Pressure should be checked, with an accurate gauge, at least once every two weeks. Appearance alone is not a reliable indicator of tire pressure.

OVER INFLATION	UNDER INFLATION	PROPER INFLATION
Hard ride	Runs hot	Good ride
Poor traction	Loosens cords	Good traction
Fabric breaks	Uneven wear	Even wear
		More mileage

Rotate tires every 5,000 miles

Be sure that your car's front end alignment is properly set and checked regularly.

Keep wheels balanced

Out-of-balance wheel may cause tires to wear irregularly. This can also cause a "bumping" or vibration of the tire.

Check brakes and shock absorbers

Faulty or "grabbing" brakes cause flat and bald spots on tires. Faulty or worn shocks cause irregular tire wear and lead to other mechanical irregularities.

Dick Cepek sends this recommendation form with tires, based on past experience with vehicle size, weight and typical driving. Drivers, vehicle weight, loading, and variations in use are as different as each individual so these are merely recommendations to start with. Keep a close eye on tread wear until you have reached the correct pressures. All pressures are listed as "cold" and not to be set after the vehicle has been driven. Follow normal tire-wear indications. Too much wear in the center, too much pressure. Too much on the edges, too little pressure. You must rotate tires every 4 to 5 thousand miles on a 4WD vehicle. If you have Positraction in the rear you must move the left rear tire to the right rear and the right rear to the left rear every 2,000 to 2,500 miles. *Do not* run off-road pressures on the hiway at high speeds. Run slightly higher pressure in the front two tires of a 4WD vehicle to compensate for tire wear on the edges due to steering. Equip your 4WD rig with a steering stabilizer. Some vehicles need two to stop shimmy problems.

This off-roader threw a bunch of money away in a hurry because he didn't rotate the tires. Cepek recommends 4WD tires be rotated 2500 miles for maximum even wear. Badly worn front tires at left are severely worn on outside edges which points to an inadequate inflation pressure. Rear tires are hardly worn.

Just to speed things up, Cepek runs four balancers—all are the dynamic or spin type. Bubble balancers just won't cut it when you get into the big stuff.

The owner of this tire obviously never checked pressure. He ran it too high. While the center is slick, the very outer edge shows little wear. He loses $$$$$.

Got a bent axle? An alignment problem? You're sure? Here's another case of no rotation and not checking tire wear.

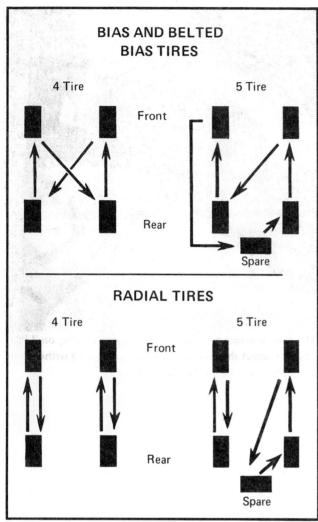

BIAS AND BELTED BIAS TIRES

4 Tire

5 Tire

Front

Rear

Spare

RADIAL TIRES

4 Tire

5 Tire

Front

Rear

Spare

Tire rotation plan recommended for safe, even wear and long mileage.

How's this for graphic proof of what low pressure can do for you. Tru-Tracs were run up the side of the dune at street pressure (24PSI) and the stall point on the side of the dune marked . . . .

. . . . with the pressure brought down to minimum safe running pressure (7PSI) the Blazer attacked the same dune and went more than a hundred yards past the first stall point.

Rarely will any tire you buy be in perfect balance after initial mounting. Special, handmade racing tires come close, but even they need to be balanced once they're mounted.

A tire is far more vulnerable to cut damage when wet than when dry. This is because the water lubricates the sides of the cuts and allows far easier and deeper penetration of the cutting object. Don't believe it? Thoroughly soak a discarded tire in water, then see how easy it is to slice—compared to the same treatment when it's dry. If you're running amidst sharp rocks in the rain—go slow or stop to wait for things to dry off.

LOWER THE PRESSURE—BUT THEN BRING IT BACK UP

Throughout this section you'll see a lot of evidence that taking tire pressure down when running off-road gives a significant increase in performance. However, running an off-road pressure on the road can be a disaster. Here's what happens. You pull off the road and play in the sand and rocks for a long weekend. Comes Sunday afternoon, you load up all the gear and family and get back out on the highway. The plan—in your mind—is to run nice and slow until you get to that service station just down the road. Just down the road turns out to be 23 miles and by the time the station is in sight, everyone concerned is fed up with running the pavement at 30 miles an hour.

The wise off-roader will pull that air pressure down *before* he gets stuck. Low-geared, lightweight Jeep can run even lower pressures than can a heavier vehicle. It all adds up to better flotation.

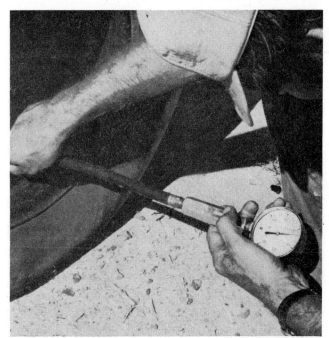

That big, accurate and easy to read gauge is sitting on 7 PSI which is about the limit for any serious running without danger of spinning the tire on the rim.

The Armstrong Tru-Trac is as impressive to view mounted on the vehicle as perusing the test data on paper.

This is the secret of the effectiveness of the radial tire in the sand. Lower pressure causes the sidewall to deflect far more rapidly than on the other test tires. This simply means more footprint.

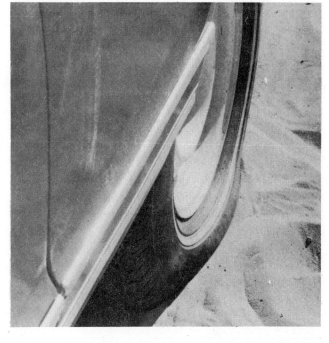

So with a mile and a half to go you speed up to 50. Whamo! A sidewall lets go. The Cepeks said they were seeing an increasing amount of this. Get a spark plug tire pump or mini-compressor and use it. A tire can do a lot of things, but it can't think for you.

Among other items imprinted on the side of your tires is a line about inflation pressure, usually something like: Max load 2200 lbs. at 32 PSI max pressure. This means one tire inflated to the stated pressure will support the listed amount of weight.

In this case, four tires could support 8,800 lbs.— a pretty heavy vehicle. You do not have to run 32 PSI all the time. In fact, you *shouldn't* run the maximum listed pressure unless your vehicle's weight equals or is close to the tires' carrying capacity. Bleed some pressure to improve traction *and* the ride of the vehicle.

Many an off-roader takes pressure down to 10— 12 PSI when running off road—then brings it back up to 24—26 PSI for around-town driving. Get an accurate tire gage. Keep it in the vehicle and use it. Experiment with various pressures.

Tire engineers and testers generally agree that very few people get their money's worth out of their tires because they do not rotate them and don't check pressure often enough. The attitude that, "If it ain't flat, it'll do," or "That looks pretty good, let's run it," simply cuts performance and life from your tires. In an attempt to educate tire buyers, the Tire Industry Safety Council offers a neat little kit containing an air-pressure gage, a tread-depth gage, four tire-valve caps and a 16-page Tire Guide booklet. At $2.25 for the kit, it is obvious they are not trying to make money on the deal. If you want one, here's the address:

Tire Industry Safety Council
Box 1801
Washington, D.C. 20013

WHICH SIZE TIRE AND WHEEL FOR WHAT VEHICLES?

Without the vehicle and tire and wheel assembly it is impossible to determine the largest size tire and wheel that will fit on a vehicle without running into clearance problems. Dick and Tom Cepek did draw some broad parameters though. We've scaled the vehicles in three groups—going from light to heavy.

TIRE WEIGHTS

When someone mentions tire weights you probably think about those lead balance weights which get clamped to the rim. Many times you should be concerned about the weight of the entire wheel and tire assembly. If you anticipate running at pretty high speed in rough terrain, a heavy tire and wheel assembly can fatigue springs and shocks just as quickly as a heavy vehicle. Getting a 100 pound tire and wheel assembly on and off a vehicle

TIRE/WHEEL/VEHICLE CHART

Light

CJ5 Jeep-size vehicles and old military Jeeps	Minimum wheel and tire to run for on-and off-road driving is an H-78-15 on at least a stock wheel. Most of these vehicles can take a 12-15 tire without clearance problems.

Medium

Toyota	Rear fenders must be cut for most tires larger than L78-15.
Bronco	Fenders must be cut for any tire wider than 8-inches.
Land Rover 88	Clearance is adequate for some 11-15 tires.
Scout II	The 10-15 tire is the limit without cutting the fender for clearance.
Commando	Cut away part of rear fender lip and body for L78-15.

Heavy

Blazer/Jimmy	Anything through 12-15 can be run some tires (like Tru-Trac) require trimming front and inside bottom of the front fender.
Trail Duster/ Ramcharger	Anything through 11-15 can be used.
Toyota Station Wagon	Anything up to 11-15 mounted on 8-inch wheels.
International Travelall	Any tire through 11-15.
Chevy Suburban	Any tire through 12-15.
Land Rover 109	Any tire through 11-15.
Wagoneer Cherokee	Bend up rear fender lip to clear L78-15 tire.

The argument is that tube-type tires are lighter than tube-less. Maybe. Dick Cepek points out that the heavy-duty, quality tube he sells weighs close to five pounds. Get the facts straight before getting into the argument.

You can buy a lot of tire these days if you go to the right dealer. Dick Cepek sells a couple of versions of the "Terra Tire" for swamp rovers.

Obsolete inner liner fits inside tubeless tire, inflates to a higher pressure than the tire itself to protect against damage from rocks and to aid in keeping extremely low-pressure tires on the rim. Liner also holds tire up when the tire is punctured. On a lightweight vehicle this is a practically fool-proof combination.

parked in the sand can be a handful for two guys too. Obviously we couldn't weigh every tire and wheel combination—but Dick Cepek did give some representative weights that might be a guide to tire weight.

The biggest tire and wheel combination in the Cepek catalog is a 14-17.5 Goodyear 8 ply which mounts on a 10.50 x 17.5 wheel. One tire and wheel assembly weighs 155 pounds.

The very popular L78-15 standard Norseman tubeless tire mounted on a 8 x 15 steel wheel weighs just under 60 pounds.

Most any 12.00-16.5 8 ply traction tread tire mounted on a 9.75 x 15 steel wheel will tip the scales at 100 pounds.

Just remember that big may be better—but big is also heavy.

INNER LINERS

Several years ago, Goodyear made a premium tubeless tire that was installed at the factory on certain luxury cars. Although the tire was tubeless it was installed with a very thick, tough odd-shaped tube called an inner liner. The liner was inflated to a higher pressure than the tire and due to the construction and shape, the inner liner tread area did not touch the inside tread area of the tire. The

theory behind this was that if the tire were punctured it would deflate quickly and the car would settle down on the inner liner which was healthy enough to carry the car many miles to the next service station. This worked slick, but due to the expense of the inner liner and the special valve and tool needed to inflate the inner liner to a different pressure than the tire, the inner liner was dropped from production. When off-road racing became popular in the late 1960's, the tire dealers having a supply of inner liners had a field day selling them off. They are a rare bird today though since they are no longer made. Installing them and inflating them is difficult for the uninitiated—another complication you don't need off-road.

GATES—NATIONAL/ARMSTRONG?

The National Sure-Trac Premium Tire we tested was manufactured by Gates. As we have pointed out, this is just another name for the Gates Commando XT—an extremely popular off-road tire. After we had completed our tests, Gates decided to get out of the tire manufacturing business and concentrate on hoses and drive belts. The Armstrong Tire and Rubber Company has now purchased the name *National*, one of the Gates tire manufacturing plants and the molds and equipment. By the time this book is in print it will be manufacturing many of the same tires formerly made by Gates. Thus if you see a tire that looks just like the National Sure-Trac—or the Gates Commando XT—but the sidewall bears the Armstrong DOT number you'll know what the story is. The tire is the same—just a change of names. It will now be called the National Commando XT.

SOMETHING TO CONSIDER

Dick and Tom Cepek are of the firm opinion the tires installed on cars and trucks as they are built are good for one thing—to allow the salesman to drive the vehicle from the showroom to the curb when the customer arrives to take delivery. The right heavy duty tire for your off-road activity is your best insurance against getting stuck, having a flat, damaging suspension or having a blowout on the way back home from an adventure. The absolute minimum tire to be on a full size vehicle going off-road should be an L78-15. This size tire is only an option on some popular off-road vehicles and light duty trucks. Get the tires first, add the rest of the gear later.

Dick and Tom tell the story of a young man who appeared with a new Blazer one day and bought a winch. The vehicle was new, the stock tires were new. The winch would be needed, he said, because he was going to Baja and might get stuck. Some months later he turned up again. He had been to Baja—and did get stuck—on the beach with nary a thing to anchor the winch to. As the waves carried sand from beneath the vehicle, the Blazer sank to the point the doors could not be opened. The vehicle was finally towed out by some Mexicans in a truck—but not before they shoved long poles under the sides of the body to help free the vehicle from the mire. The resultant damage amounted to several thousand dollars.

Camper rigs—4WD long-wheelbase pickups with a cab over camper—easily weigh 8,000 pounds. Tom Cepek's hits 9,000! This much weight is hard on any tire—and if the tire is not rated for the load, trouble is bound to happen—it's just a question of when.

Combinations of trucks, campers, trailers, 60 gallons of gas, 30 gallons of water and food and beer for four adults for a long weekend have a way of mounting up. Weigh your truck. Load up just like you would for a long weekend of fun and

drive—damn slowly!—to the nearest public scale. The Yellow Pages can help here—or try the local highway patrol office. You want three weights—each axle and the total weight. If the weight on one axle comes to 3,800 pounds, the weight carried per wheel on that axle is 1,900 pounds. You durn sure don't want any tires rated for any less than that. You take all of the weights to a tire dealer, he nods and says the weight is not excessive. He has just the tire for you. It's rated 2,230 pounds carrying capacity. That's plenty adequate right? Sure—if you keep the tire inflated to 45 psi—which is where it gets its 2,230-lb rating. If you do a little boondocking and run the pressure down to 20 psi that same tire's rating deflates to 1,390 pounds. Remember, as tire pressure goes down, so does the load capacity. Obviously in this example, you need a tire with a much greater carrying capacity or you'd better stay on the pavement and keep the pressure where it should be.

VEHICLE WEIGHT

If you are concerned with handling, tire wear and correct tire selection you should first understand vehicle weight. The one that counts is *gross load.* This is the total weight of vehicle under fully loaded conditions. For example, if you have a camper on the back of your pickup, gross load includes water in the tanks, bedding, food and all of your sporting gear. The following table is a starting point for determining gross load.

TYPICAL WEIGHTS	
ITEM	APPROX WT (LBS)
4 passengers (2 adults, 2 children)	600
Clothing for 4	100
Food	200
Sports gear	250
Spare LP gas tank, filled	50
Extra water tank (20 gal)	200
Extra fuel tank (20 gal)	160
Spare storage battery	25
Aluminum boat, 5-hp outboard	180
Golf bags, clubs, caddy carts (2)	100
Milk, gallon	12.4
24 6-8 oz bottles, box	38
12 24-32 oz bottles, box	60
Towing hitch, Class I	60
Towing hitch, Class II	105
Load-equalizing hitch platform	125
Trail bike	150-250

Tom Cepek checks over the load carried by each tire on his big rig. 4WD Ford with cabover camper runs 2500 pounds per rear wheel. Total weight of rig is 9000 lbs. Scales are not cheap—but they are accurate.

Gross loads can be measured on a commercial scale. Most large truck companies have scales and the Ma Bell's Yellow Pages list weigh stations or scales in your area. Use the table only as a starting point in determining weight and where it should be placed in a vehicle. No table of weights can be as accurate or useful as a certified scale designed specifically to weigh motor vehicles.

Commercial scales can also be used to check weight distribution. Weigh each end of the vehicle separately and you can see what percentages of the weight are on the front and rear end.

If you weigh your vehicle at a commercial scale, load it just as you normally would for a weekend trip. If you would normally run down the freeway with a 60-gallon gas tank topped off at the far rear of the vehicle and a trail bike strapped to the front bumper, I can't think of anything you would accomplish by weighing the truck without all of that in place. If the trail bike rides two feet in front of the front axle and weighs 200 pounds, rest assured its weight will completely change the handling characteristics of a vehicle. Guys concerned with building race cars lose a lot of sleep over vehicle balance and one of the things they can pass on to anyone trying to make a vehicle handle better is to get the weight *between* the axles. Think about it.

TUBE OR TUBELESS?

You can draw some arguments on this, but experience has shown that tubeless tires work as well, run cooler and are as trouble-free as tube-type tires. In fact, tubeless tires carry the advantage of being able to flex severely and hold air whereas prolonged flexing (as in very-low-pressure applications) can cause a tube to pinch and chafe and thus lose air. However, should you bend the rim, there goes the air pressure, and unless you are a metal-bending expert, you may not be able to hammer the rim contour back into the bashed rim so that the tire will again hold air. Inflating a tubeless tire off-road may also be a bear of a problem.

Here's a common case of tread separation. In most cases, the guarantee will cover this without question. Check for this sort of thing any time you rotate tires, or pull a routine maintenance check.

TIRE WARRANTIES

On January 1, 1977, the Magnuson-Moss Act of 1976 went into effect. This law says any warranty must stipulate whether it is *comprehensive* or *limited*. If a manufacturer grants the consumer a *limited* warranty, he must state how *limited* it is. That's where we are right now with tire warranties. Generally speaking, the five major tire makers will be giving improved warranties on workmanship and defective materials—and no warranty at all on road hazard and treadwear.

Obviously, there will be some exceptions as the various companies try to figure out how to attract buyers with a warranty and how not to go broke at the same time because of it. I understand Goodyear and General will replace a radial tire at no cost up to 12 months with 75% of the tread remaining, when presented with a sales document as proof of purchase.

Where does this leave the off-roader? Basically, this means an end to getting a tire replaced free (or at an adjusted cost) after you have gouged a sidewall with a rock or rim. If this means a great deal to you, and is a factor in the brand of tire you buy then we would suggest getting a full explanation of the new warranty law from the dealer you would be buying the tires from.

Within reason we consider the performance of the tire to be the most important factor for off-roading—not the price, or the warranty.

OVERSTEER/UNDERSTEER

Understeer—Describes vehicle attitude or characteristics when the rate of change in the tire slip angle is greater at the front than in the rear. In a turn of constant radius, increased speed beyond the limits of tire adhesion will cause the front of the car to move out from the path of the turn as traction is lost.

Oversteer—Describes vehicle attitude or characteristics when the rate of change in the tire slip angle is greater at the rear than in the front. In a constant-radius turn, increased speed beyond the limit of tire adhesion will cause the rear of the car to move out from the path of the turn as traction is lost.

Understeer and oversteer are two of the most misunderstood terms in use in the automotive world today. At the rate things are going though, they'll soon be replaced with EGR and PCV. Until that day arrives we would offer that understeer is present when the front wheels possess less cornering power than the rear wheels. Oversteer happens when the rear wheels possess less cornering power than the fronts. Another way of looking at this is what happens when you exceed the limit of adhesion in a corner. An understeering car fails to respond to the steering and plows off the road nose first on the outside of the corner. An oversteering car spins out when it is pushed beyond the limit of adhesion.

Any number of factors contribute to understeer/oversteer characteristics. Oversteer may be caused by: Rearward weight bias—more weight in the rear—wider front tires, under- or overinflated rear tires, or independent rear suspension causing positive camber on the rear wheels in a turn. Other more complicated factors enter the picture too such as roll center heights, roll stiffness, and roll steer geometry in the suspension. These are much too complicated to get into here. We will confine our remarks on understeer/oversteer to how it affects the off-roader and some of the basic things you can do to help certain situations.

Tires, more than any other single factor, contribute most to your vehicle's cornering power. If you have 6.70 x 15 tires on your pickup now and go directly to 11.00 x 15 and wider wheels you'll gain more cornering power than you could have by adding several thousand dollars of specialized, race car oriented work to the suspension. In fact, chances are suspension changes alone would never give the cornering power you can get by using larger tires. Just as the tires are capable of contributing greatly to the cornering power of a vehicle; the weight bias of the vehicle can have profound effect on whether the vehicle basically understeers or oversteers.

Let's say you have a Chevy pickup that's several years old and equipped with a very tired small-block V8. Instead of rebuilding the tired engine, you opt to bolt in a big-block V8. Now the vehicle handles entirely different than it did with the old engine. The rear end of the pickup always broke away in a hurry under power; now it's worse because of the added horsepower. The large-block engine added about 150 pounds almost directly over the front suspension making the truck even more of an understeering vehicle than it was with the small engine. Putting a heavier, more powerful engine in a pickup is the wrong move towards better handling. If you are carrying very heavy loads in the rear all of the time, a big block

might balance things out nicely, but when running empty the handling problems will be aggravated. Pickups usually have a pretty fair power to weight ratio, but terrible weight distribution when they are empty or close to empty. The situation gets even worse in the dirt because a little too much throttle can just about eliminate any rear-wheel traction.

When the throttle is nailed in a dirt curve the rear end comes around in a big hurry. The tires are broken loose in the rear by the throttle application, the front tires are overloaded by all that weight in the nose, and the entire truck is leaning over due to the high center of gravity. This is a bad situation that takes extreme care on the part of the driver. If too much power is applied the truck will spin out. If the brakes are applied the lightly loaded rear tires will instantly lock up, again causing a spinout. If the driver just heads into the turn without any throttle at all, chances are the truck will plow straight off into the ditch because of the nose-heavy understeering tendency. An expert driver can perhaps get the truck through a corner with just the right balance of throttle and steering control, but a novice is more likely to end up tangling with a ditch, tree, fence post, etc.

In other words, a pickup is no Grand Prix car, particularly in the dirt. Any abrupt or unconcious moves on the controls such as backing off the throttle, jerking the steering wheel, or applying the brakes in a turn are apt to get you into an uncontrolled spin. It is all due to the extreme nose-heavy weight bias combined with a high power-to-weight ratio. A pickup running empty has all the wrong characteristics for fast cornering.

If you like to rowdy about in the dirt with a pickup and have survived your share of spins, you are probably thinking that heavy-duty rear springs and shocks will help the cornering power. No way! This makes the cornering worse with an empty truck. The rear springs on a pickup are designed to work properly with some load in the truck. Empty, the rear springs are already too stiff for it. The lightly loaded rear end tends to bounce and hop off the road in a bumpy corner, even with the stock set-up. Heavy-duty rear springs will make this situation worse! The benefit of heavy springs is in allowing a heavier load to be carried. That is where they will help, period!

An anti-sway bar in the rear of the truck will not help much. It will tend to reduce the initial understeer in a turn, but it will increase the tendency to lose traction at the rear when the throttle is applied. Also the high-speed stability may suffer. Better leave these modifications to the sports cars. About the only way to really get the pickup to handle better is to lower the CG and move weight towards the rear. Both of these mods reduce the pickup's ability to go off road and to carry big loads.

A pickup being driven close to the limit of adhesion—on any surface—should be treated with utmost respect. Just keep in mind that although it may be a heavy understeering vehicle entering the curve, it can switch to violent oversteer with little warning or provocation. The driver must be very careful with the throttle and the brakes in such a situation.

Seemingly subtle changes to a pickup can have a big effect on handling. I used to drive an unloaded pickup over a certain road day after day. I thought I knew the road well and felt confident in the truck. Day after day I built up speed in a longsweeping curve until I had the speed built up right to the point of breaking the rear end away. After working up to that point I drove the truck at a constant given speed in that turn. One day I bolted a 30-pound steel pushbar to the front bumper. The very next time I entered the curve in the truck I swapped ends in the middle of the curve. That pushbar hanging off the front bumper was just enough weight far enough in front of the front wheels to make the difference between sticking and not sticking. The point here is to alter your driving habits with the load you are carrying and stay far back from driving a truck at the limit.

Wider tires and wheels, close to a 50-50 weight distribution between the axles and prudent driving are the biggest aids to improving the handling of a truck. Never lose sight of the fact a truck is not a sports car in the handling department!

And neither is a van! Vans have very similar handling characteristics to a pickup. Everything I've just said about pickup handling can also be applied to a van.

RADIAL TIRES FOR CAMPERS

Do not be tempted to install a set of radial tires on your pre-1975 camper or motor home wheels. In mid-1974 one manufacturer of motor homes sent all of its dealers a bulletin warning against using radials on the vehicles. It seems that radials are not a good match for wheels already in use with bias-ply tires. As of 1973-74, only Ford had introduced wheels suitable for use with radials. These came on their SuperCab trucks. *Camper Coachman* magazine's good article on this subject in the August 1974 issue quoted Doug MacIntre, manager of Kelsey-Hayes wheel engineering. He said, "Some of the wheels in current use are suitable—for use with radials—and others are not. Those radial tires were not available for our testing until recently and when we did get them all the manufacturers started to fail wheels. The wheels are tested under high overload conditions and radial tires are harder on wheels due to a variety of factors including higher bead loads—pressure of the bead against the rim—and additional cornering forces exerted on the disc."

"There are so many variables," said McIntre "It's impossible to go back through wheels made during the past several years and single out suitable ones from those which are not. The only safe attitude we can take is that all the wheels made by the whole industry, except those made recently, are suspect." He said testing with radial-ply tires began in earnest early in 1974. He did say the 9.75 x 16.5-inch wheels Kelsey-Hayes supplied Ford for their 12-16.5 bias-ply optional tires in 1973 passed radial-tire testing without problems.

GM and Dodge are also expected to offer radials as original-equipment options starting in 1975. You can be sure these will be OK for use with radials designed for camper use.

One last thing about radials—be sure to use them on all four wheels—not on just the front or just the back. The steering response of radials is so sharp that they should never be used on the front with conventional tires on the back.

FLATS

The first time I went to Baja, I broke the front-axle housing in a Jeep, replaced a fuel pump and broke an axle/spring U-bolt clamp. A battery went dead and by the time I got to La Paz—ever have a three-day trip turn into a nine-day trip?—an exhaust manifold was cracked, too. Naturally I didn't have a flat. Three trips and one race later

Tube repair kits are a must for the off-road tool box. For about three bucks you can have one whale of a lot of tire repair equipment.

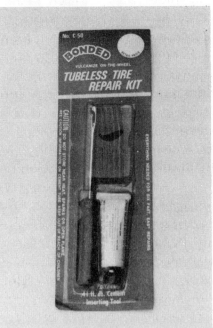

Tubeless tire repair kits are inexpensive and will normally allow a tire to be repaired without removing tire and wheel from the vehicle.

"El booto" south of the border and a mighty handy thing to have when you really cut a sidewall. If you take a boot, take a big one, they can always be trimmed down.

I still had not experienced a flat. By the time I got around to congratulating myself on superb driving skills, the beginner's luck had worn off and I refrained from saying the word "camshaft" for fear all its lobes would go flat. If you drive off-road, you will have flats. It's just a matter of time.

I advise taking everything you need to fix a flat. Secondly, I advise working like the dickens to avoid having to take the tire off the rim and fix it.

When you have a flat—remember, it's just a matter of time—don't go into a panic to jack up the vehicle, yank the tire and wheel off, lose half the lug nuts in the sand and try to break a 10.00 x 15 off the rim with a claw hammer and big screw driver. All of this takes a lot of energy—and we should conserve energy—any kind of energy. Most punctures in tubeless tires can be temporarily fixed without ever taking the tire and wheel off the vehicle—much less taking the tire off the wheel.

If you cut the sidewall, you'll need to take the tire off and insert a boot, but if you've just picked up a nail, thorn or hunk of cactus and it took the tire five or six minutes to go completely flat you can probably be on your way by squirting in some pressurized goop or by removing the of-

fending item and inserting a rubber plug with a "plug gun." This can be done regardless of where the puncture is. Like anything and everything else you take off-road, be very familiar with all of your tire fixin' hardware. A plug gun with no plugs is like a can of get-me-home tire sealant without some way to get the valve core out. If you get a slow leak and don't have a plug gun, don't get excited about finding the nail/thorn/wire/cactus and pulling it out. Leave it in place and pour in the sealant—then inflate the tire. With a spark-plug tire pump or one of the little electric compressors, I'd rather stop a couple of times a day to build the pressure back up than to break the tire off the rim and repair it.

If you are running a tube and have a flat or happen to gouge a really big hole in a tubeless tire then you will have to break the tire off the rim. In the case of the tubeless tire, you'll have to insert a boot—large rubber patch—or a tube and in the case of a tube-type tire, you'll have to locate the puncture, patch it and get the tube back in the tire and the tire back on the rim.

Fixing a leaking tube or even putting a boot in a tire—tube or tubeless—ain't no big deal; getting the tire off the rim is where the sweat starts. If for

Tire irons are indispensible when it comes to getting a tire off the rim. You should practice this once in your driveway to make a judgement of how it's done and how big a hammer you need to help the job along.

There are several types of mini-compressors on the markets. If the spark plug type pumps are difficult to use on your vehicle (vans) you should consider one of these devices which plug into a cigarette lighter.

some reason you can't make it back to civilization without breaking the tire off the rim, you may as well go to work.

Remove the valve core from the stem. This ensures you are not working against any pressure in the tire.

Break the bead seat by using a tire iron—as illustrated—or by wapping the sidewall area with a mighty big hammer. Due to their size and stiffness, off-road tires are some of the most difficult tires to dismount you are likely to encounter. You can save a lot of time in this procedure, if you'll move the tire and wheel assembly to a flat area and have a buddy drive over the sidewall of the tire with his vehicle. Another trick is to place the tire/wheel under your vehicle so you can set a jack on the sidewall, jack against the frame and thus force the bead to break away from the rim.

Once the bead of the tire is broken away from the rim, you can go to work with the tire irons and big hammer to force one of the beads over one lip of the rim. Unless you really think that working on flats is a lot of fun, you'll now take a close look at the tire or pull the tube out and figure out to patch up the damage without having to completely separate the tire from the wheel.

Dial type pressure gauges are usually more accurate than other types. A pressure gauge should be kept in the vehicle at all times—how a tire looks can be deceiving—the pressure could be off by 10 pounds or so.

Auxiliary Lights—Automotive lighting laws in the United States are incredibly old-fashioned. What you are allowed to run legally on a vehicle is just one notch above sitting on the hood holding a candle with a pie pan for a reflector.

The good stuff like quartz halogen and quartz iodine is illegal in most—if not all—states as this is being written. Guys that do off-road racing run such lights to help them make it through the night. If you drive on public roads you had best have the good lights covered or disconnected to avoid tickets.

Unless I'm racing, I ain't too keen on doing much off-road driving at night. However, on those occasions I did subject myself to the dark, I found a hand-controlled spotlight (either on the roof or windshield post) to be of most benefit. This allows you to stop, move the light around and slowly get a perspective on the situation. If you think it would be nifty keen to have some driving lights hung on your off-roader, be my guest. Consider the following:

1. Nothing works as good in fog as a fog light, preferably with directional baffles to keep the light from glaring back at you.
2. For maximum coverage, have a pencil beam *and* a wide flat beam.
3. Any light mounted above the windshield will glare on the hood to a certain extent. Install shields under the light or paint the hood flat black to reduce this annoying glare.
4. A hand-controlled spot light is your best single buy to light your nighttime off-roading.

This all-time-great off-road buff's wish book is put out by Dick Cepek. All kinds of goodies plus good tire information. Free from Cepek.

When installing a tube, inflate it ever so slightly with lung power before trying to shove it in place. This makes it go a little easier. After getting the tube in place, pull the stem through the hole in the rim and run the inflation pressure up just a touch more to help hold the tube in place while you get the tire bead back under the lip of the rim—tire irons and hammer again! When the tire and rim assembly is going back together, liquid hand cleaner, detergent or soapy water on the rim lip and bead will help the tire slide back in place. When putting the tire back on the rim where a tube is involved, keep an eye on the stem to make sure it doesn't move out of the hole. Make durn sure your tire irons are not shoved in so far and

"BAJA-PROVEN"® **TIRES & OFF-ROAD EQUIPMENT**

FOR
DUNE BUGGIES
JEEPS
MINI PICKUPS
VANS
CAMPERS
RV'S
and more

1977 FREE CATALOG

Dick CEPEK®

angled so they damage the tube.

The actual process of patching a tube or putting a plug or boot on a tire is simple and straightforward in comparison to the romance you must go through in getting tire and rim apart and then back together again.

If you have never broken a tire off a rim and plan to go off-road, I would make two suggestions. First go down to the local service station and watch a guy go through the process with all of the air-actuated equipment. Then I would suggest you go home, lay out all of your tire/tube repairing equipment and actually remove a tire from a rim. What you learn in an hour—or two—session in the driveway about the use of tire irons and hammer will show you what you are up against when your time comes. Maybe most important of all you will learn where to place your shins in relation to where you swing the hammer.

LIQUID SEALANTS

There are all sorts of liquid tire sealants on the market—and most of them claim to stop most normal punctures with little or no loss of air. The procedure for installing the sealants is to deflate the tire with the weight off the wheel—vehicle jacked up—and pour the sealant down the valve stem—valve core removed. The tire is then spun to distribute the sealant evenly about the inside of the tire—or tube. Most of the stuff is pretty good for keeping air in the tire if you shove a nail or cactus thorn through the tread. Most of the tire problems off-road though come through sidewall damage. Sealant does little if any good here because centrifugal force plasters the stuff on the inside of the tread area.

Despite manufacturers claims to the contrary there are often problems with balancing a tire loaded with sealant. Dick Cepek points out for the sealant to be effective in a large tire a quart of the sealant must be used. With that much weight added to the inside of the tire, balance simply cannot be achieved.

If a vehicle stays off the highway 95% of the time, the liquid tire sealant can be a good buy. If you run the vehicle on the highway, then take another look at whether you really need the stuff.

Don't confuse the liquid tire sealant with the pressurized cans of sealant which contain enough inert gas to inflate the tire *after* you have a flat. These are handy little cans that can get you out of a bind when the tire goes flat. You still have to fix the flat since the sealant is temporary in nature.

Large amounts of most any tire sealant will cause imbalance at freeway speeds. Sealants can be of real benefit for vehicles running in cactus or brush—but not operating on the highway.

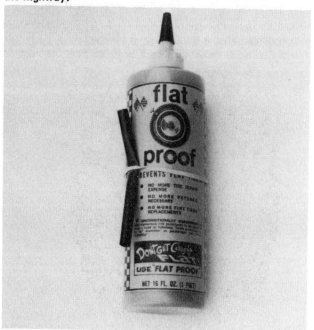

Don't confuse inflator/sealers like this with sealants designed to stay in the tire and prevent flats. This device is designed to be a temporary fix—allowing you to get back to civilization (or camp) before having to fix the tire.

WHAT'S NEW IN TIRES & WHEELS FOR 1977

EDITOR'S NOTE: I consulted Dick and Tom Cepek to gain the following information just before sending this revised edition back to the presses in mid-1977. As owners of Dick Cepek, Inc., both men are uniquely qualified to give up-to-the-minute information on tires for recreational vehicles.

PRICES & AVAILABILITY

Like everything else in today's world, prices are still rising. You can fully expect to pay 15% more for tires this year than last year. Tires are about 80% petroleum—and you know what is continuing to happen with petroleum prices. The tire-pricing picture was clouded still further by the industry-wide strike in 1976 when all tire-making facilities in the U.S. closed for 120 days. Due to the strike and 1977's worst winter in history, there is a distinct possibility some recreational-vehicle tires may be in short supply.

NEW TIRES FOR 2WD & 4WD RIGS

The big tire news for 1977 is B.F. Goodrich's all-new 12R15 LT Radial All-Terrain T/A. Aside from the fact they managed to get most of this nomenclature on the sidewall of the tire in raised white lettering, the real news here is a big—32.4-inch-diameter—true radial designed just for the off-road market. Tread pattern is aggressive and 10-inches wide. Flip back to our tire-test section and check the Sears-radial footprint, noting how it becomes quite long as the pressure goes down. The All-Terrain T/A does the same thing—but it starts with a wider tread and gets even longer because of the extremely flexible sidewall. B.F. Goodrich has taken the lead in at least one other area of recreational-vehicle tires. I believe they are the first company to publish load ratings for the tire at various inflation pressures. For instance, the maximum load for the Radial All-Terrain T/A at 35 PSI is 2,250 lbs. Goodrich lists the load capability in 5-PSI increments down to 15 PSI where maximum

Top-of-the-line tire for the 1977 RV market is this radial All-Terrain T/A from B.F. Goodrich. It can rightfully be termed a *second generation radial for off-roading*—and shows the way the industry is headed in the off-road marketplace.

New for 1977 is Dick Cepek's Big Boss Bruiser in 10-15, 11-15 and 12-15, load-range C, 6-ply rating, nylon construction. Overall diameter of the 12-15 is 32.8 inches.

Dick Cepek's grandson Ryan says, "Boy Grandpa . . . what big tires you have!" These tires are designed for superior performance in gumbo mud, deep snow, soft sand, Alaskan tundra and the rocky terrain of Baja. Gumbo Monster Mudder 14/35-16.5, at right, was made to clear front disc-brake calipers on 1976 Ford F250 4 x 4's. It is 35.5-inches tall and 14-inches wide. At left is the 12-15 Gumbo Wide Mudder, a 32-inch tall, 12.5-inch wide tire which gives you the diameter of a 12-16.5 tire without changing wheels. A 4-ply Load Range B 12-16.5 is available to fit rigs with no camper or just a shell. Super-aggressive tread on these tires is "relatively quiet," according to Cepek and he claims good wear characteristics under normal highway use.

At 12-inch width, Cepek's Off-Roader offers the widest tread available for use on 15 x 10 or 16.5 x 9.75 wheels. Tires are 14-inches wide with a 32-inch diameter. 14/32-15 is available in Load Range B or C. 14/32-16.5 is available in Load Range C.

load is 1,180 lbs. per tire. This is useful information for the off-roader. Hopefully, other manufacturers will follow suit.

The Armstrong Tru-Trac is still extremely popular and will eventually be released as a radial. **Armstrong** continues to sell the ever-popular Norseman—but only in three versions. The L78-15 is now available in a bias-ply 4-ply Nylon black-wall, a bias-ply 4-ply polyester whitewall and a bias-ply 6-ply—8-ply-rating Nylon blackwall. Gone are the puncture-sealant version—and the steel radial. Production costs are blamed for the demise of the latter two tires.

Armstrong has a complete line of eight tires called the Rhino line. Sizes available are 10-15 and 12-15 in load range B or C with a traction tread similar to the Tru-Trac. A highway tread called the SD-200 is also offered. 10-15 sizes are approximately 30 inches outside diameter with a 9.5-inch tread.

The 12-15 size is actually taller and wider than any other 12-16.5 we know of. They have the added advantage of being lighter than the 12-16.5 size.

The traction tread makes some noise but the SD-200 is extremely quiet. Our own testing confirmed the fact that tread style is not nearly as important as how much rubber you lay down in off-road performance. If you want the biggest 15-inch tire on the market—and your vehicle can accept it—the 12-15 is the answer.

Firestone offers two All-Terrain tires introduced in 1974. The polyester All-Terrain T/C town and country version has been available as an option on the Blazer since 1974. The size is 10-15 with a B load range. The dog-bone highway tread is on a tubeless carcass with raised white letters. The Nylon version is identifiable because there's no T/C after the name and it has a 9-inch-wide tread instead of the T/C's 8.5-inch tread.

Formula Tire Co. now has a load range C Desert Dog PCV tire to go with their load range B tire. It is bigger and will wear better. You'll find this bias-ply Nylon tire equipped with—believe it or not—raised white letters!

Goodyear now has the Tracker A/T in a 10-15 size in a load-range rating of B or C. Construction is polyester cord. This tire is seen everywhere because it comes as original equipment on much of the four-wheel-drive machinery built in the United States.

Jetzon is marketing a tire very similar to the Tru-Trac and made by Mansfield Rubber Co. This one is called Dune Digger in raised white letters on the sidewall. Sizes are 11-15 and 11-16 in load range C. The 11-16 fills a void in the market for all the guys running 16 x 8 inch wheels with 7.50-16 tires or 11-16 High Flotations. The 11-16 size is 32 inches outside diameter with an 8.75-inch tread width.

Lee still has a 11-15LT tire with only 28-inch outside diameter. It would appear that they took their L60-15 traction tire and remarked it 11-15 LT! More on this later.

Winston has an 11-15 Fun & Mud tire with a size and tread style almost like the 10-15 Firestone All-Terrain dog-bone highway tread. I guess this is only natural because Firestone makes the tire for Winston. It is tubeless, blackwall, load range B bias-ply.

National Sure Track Special is a Nylon 10-15 load range B or C featuring the ever-present raised white letters. It has been around for about four years now and combines many good features such

Armstrong's Rhino tires are available in two sizes as shown here: 10-15 and 12-15. The 12-15 is great for ground clearance.

Cepek's all-new Ground Hawg features a super-aggressive tread for peak performance in mud, snow and rock. Of the seven available sizes, the 12-15 at 33.2 inches is the largest currently available 12-15.

Duster Super Cargo is new in 1977. The only size available is an 11-15 in load-range B or C with or without raised white letters.

Cepek makes paddle tires for sand drags and hill climbs. 48 paddles are arranged in three different heights and thicknesses. Available in five sizes with tread width all the way to 21 inches!

as rugged—yet quiet—tread design, low cost, long-wearing tread, good traction—and it fits most vehicles.

DOES THE SIZE ON THE SIDEWALL MEAN ANYTHING?

We don't think it does and the novice tire buyer may not get what he wants if he goes by that number. Take the popular 11-15 size as an example. About 14 years ago Armstrong introduced their straight-groove Highway Flotation tire. It is slightly over 30 inches tall—outside diameter. In 1971 they introduced their 11-15 Tru-Trac—a tube-type tire almost 33 inches tall. Partly because so many tire bandits were selling the tube-type tire as tubeless, Armstrong now only offers the tire in tubeless configuration in load range B or C. The tubeless version is about 32-inches tall.

Now along comes Lee making a tire marked 11-15—but it's only 28-inches tall! 28 inches may be fine for a low-horsepower buggy or an old four-banger military Jeep, but in my opinion it is just too short for a Blazer used off-road. You need ground clearance and 28 inches just won't give it to you.

The best advice I can give you as a tire buyer is to shop carefully, ask a lot of questions, read test reports, talk to other owners—and carry a tape measure.

WHAT'S IN THE FUTURE?

Radials for sure—they are better—and that's all there is to it! But they will cost more money. A trend may be developing away from aggressive treads back to quieter conventional highway-truck treads.

Shortages—There is no let up in sight because the auto companies are selling more trucks, Jeeps, Blazers, etc. than they can produce and the tire companies just can't expand production fast enough to keep up. Wide tires take special presses which take two to three years from the time the order is placed until they are at work in the tire factory.

Big Tires—The trend is toward taller tires. When you install tires larger than 12-15's, a suspension kit to move tires away from chassis and sheet metal is *mandatory*. Dick Cepek says it is now commonplace for a set of huge tires and wheels and the necessary suspension kit to cost $1,300 to $1,600.

One of the first really tall tires to become popular after the 32-inch-tall Tru-Trac was the Gumbo Monster Mudder which gets everyone's attention with a diameter of 35.5 inches and a 14-inch-wide tread. The Mudder's popularity suggested a less-aggressive tread pattern for highway use and sure enough, Cepek is now making just that as the Quiet Giant.

It's a bird . . . it's a plane . . . it's a Dodge W-200 pickup on its way to about $2700 worth of damage. Truck was flown by Bill O'Roake, one of Cepek's salesmen, for an Armstrong Tire TV commercial. Tom Cepek says, "This was the fifth of a series of jumps, so the actual repair cost per jump works out to about $540 per."

SOURCES FOR SHOP MANUALS

If you have trouble locating a shop manual for your particular vehicle, it usually helps to go directly to the source of supply. Prices will vary anywhere from $5 to $15. In some cases you may need 2 manuals for complete coverage of your vehicle. Sometimes the manuals will not be as complete or informative as you'd like because the manufacturer is covering several vehicles in each manual. Send a stamped, self-addressed envelope to the source and you'll get a price listing or advice on where the manuals can be obtained closer to home.

CHEVY

Helm Inc.
Chevrolet Manual Distribution
P. O. Box 7706
Detroit, MI 48207

DODGE

Chrysler Motors Corp.
Dodge Division Service Department
P. O. Box 857
Detroit, MI 48231

FORD

Ford Service Publications
P. O. Box 7750
Detroit, MI 48231

JEEP

Jeep Corporation
Owner Relations
14250 Plymouth Road
Detroit, MI 48232

TOYOTA

Allied Graphics, Inc.
P. O. Box 4339
Whittier, CA 90607

INTERNATIONAL

International Harvester Co.
401 North Michigan Ave.
Chicago, IL 60611

DATSUN

Nissan Corporation
P. O. Box 191
Gardena, CA 90247

EARLY MILITARY 4WD SERVICE MANUALS

Post-Era Motor Books
Arcadia, CA 91006

Argus Publishing
131 Barrington Place
Los Angeles, CA 90049

WHEELS

On the surface, it would appear that since the wheel was invented several thousand years ago, all possible manufacturing problems would have been solved by now. They have—but the basic human frailty (greed) interferes and the unwary off-roader suffers. It's this way. A man builds a quality wheel and after figgerin' till way past midnight comes to the conclusion: The wheel should sell for $19.95 to make a decent profit. Sure as shootin' just as soon as the wheels hit the RV dealers, Jay Cheapwheel—most likely someone without any wheel building experience —sees the "immense profits to be made." The entire market can be ripped off by selling the same product for $18.50, he thinks. But of course, the wheel is not quite the same—nothing major, mind you—just *little* things. Instead of using a *new* rim and *new* center, use a new rim and *used* center. Who'll know the difference? Getting used centers can sometimes be a pain, so a lower cost new stamping must be found. This likely boils down to a center stamped from lighter-gauge material. If three minutes a wheel can be saved by not making a full weld between center and rim surely we can justify spending more money on *advertising* or giving a bigger discount to the dealer to shut

While you're looking at custom-made wheels check the welding between rim and center. Look to see if the weld is continuous or in short sections; check the penetration. Off-road pounding is hard on wheels, don't settle for less than the best.

out the quality manufacturer. And so it goes. So it is. Wheels are pieced together in the rim, partially welded to a used center on a surplus lathe manned by an alcoholic who couldn't drive a nail —much less a four-wheeler.

The point we're trying to make: There is far more to buying a wheel than meets the eye. Perhaps the safest posture to assume is that the guy making and selling the wheels was just driven out of the used car business by the Better Business Bureau. Harsh words? Yes. Necessary? We think so. Consider this: Several years ago greed began permeating wheel advertising copy in the form of "creating" wider wheels. . . all on paper. You ordered a 15 x 10 wheel; you paid for a 15 x 10 wheel, but when it was delivered it measured only 15 x 9. But 15 x 10 sounded bigger and better . . . everyone *knows* bigger is better! We will assume at least half of this advertising was honest error— a lot of wheel builders simply didn't (perhaps still don't) know the correct way to measure rim width is inside *bead-to-bead*. Customers became

Homemade wheel with ten-inch—true measurement—width was accomplished by welding two rims together. Lateral runout on this homemade job was close to 3/16-inch. Think of the wasted effort. Junk.

confused, other wheel dealers followed suit in their advertising, or simply remained confused . . . or both!

One dealer—Dick Cepek—bent over backwards to be honest, but finally had to revise his catalog to the effect that his 14 x 7 wheels were actually 6-inches inside bead-to-bead. This way he could compete with other wheeler dealers and inform the customer exactly what he was buying. This simple measuring problem will not easily be solved. In the wheel, tire and related automotive industries the correct method of expressing rim width is the inside bead-to-bead measurement. Anyone expressing rim width with the outside-to-outside measurement is in error. It's that simple.

LATERAL RUNOUT

From time to time you'll see a vehicle with a wheel wobble from side to side as it goes down the road. This is called *lateral runout* and it is caused by a bent drum, bent axle, loose or bent wheel, or a crooked wheel.

A severe side blow such as sliding into a rock or curb can bend a wheel which had, up to the point of contact, been straight. When this happens discard the wheel! Never try to correct lateral runout by straightening the wheel. New wheels to be mounted on a vehicle should be

checked for lateral runout *before mounting the tires.*

If you have access to a remote spin balancer—that's a unit which spins the wheel with tire off the car—this can be used for checking lateral runout. We'd check it for true by mounting what appears to be a straight wheel in several positions and checking the lateral runout with a dial indicator in each position. If everything seems straight, that spin balancer is a good arbor to mount wheels on for checking their lateral runout.

Or, bolt the wheel to a front drum, torque it down evenly and mount a dial indicator to something solid—like an axle housing. Always make sure the wheel is being measured on a straight drum or axle without runout. Measure how much the rim moves from side to side as it rotates. If it is off more than 0.030-inch then you have a legitimate gripe and should not be forced to pay for the wheel.

Excessive lateral runout is created by sloppy manufacturing procedures in mating the center to the rim. The more the lateral runout, the more rapid the tire wear.

OFFSET

Wheel offset is confusing to the first-time wheel buyer and as a consequence he may wind up buying from heart and not from head. Assume the stock wheels on your machine are six inches wide—remember that's inside bead-to-bead—with *zero* offset. That is, exactly one-half of the rim width—3 inches—hangs outside or away from the face of the brake drum and the other 3-inch rim-width half goes back toward the backing plate. It is important to remember that the starting point or reference is the wheel mounting surface. Stock wheels can have *any* offset, this one happens to be *zero*. Now assume you are buying a ten-inch wheel to mount on this same vehicle.

The man building the wheel can place the center in the rim and weld the two together with *zero* offset like your stock wheel—or he can place the rim farther outboard in relation to the mounting surface on the drum—thereby creating *positive* offset and a wider tread. This is the "bulldog stance" many people like to see.

Or, the wheel maker can shove the rim further inboard to make a wheel with *negative* offset.

Here's how a wheel is measured and descriptions for the measurements.

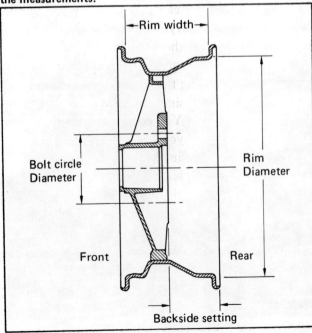

Rim width

Bolt circle Diameter

Rim Diameter

Front

Rear

Backside setting

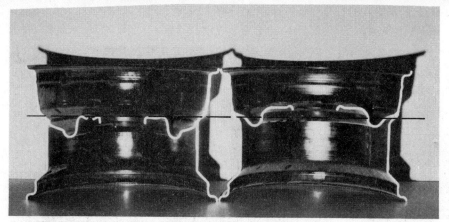

Notice dramatic difference in offset. Wheel on right will hang farther out on the spindle by more than an inch. Both wheels were built to fit the same vehicle . . . cost per item was the same.

Now you are faced with a decision concerning *offset.* Do you need positive, negative or zero? Measure the stock offset if you're looking for a clue.

Keep in mind: Positive offset adds to total tread width of the vehicle; negative offset subtracts from total tread width.

Sometimes the wheel builder or off-road supply house will help the buyer make the right choice, but often he will just sell whatever he has in stock. He has to eat, too. And he may want to buy groceries before he builds, buys or waits for the truck to come in with more wheels having just the offset you prefer—or need!

The wheel builder and tire stores solve part of their inventory problems by building and stocking more wheels with more positive offset than is really needed. A wheel with lots of positive offset easily clears disc-brake calipers, tie-rod ends and steering knuckles. Wheels and tires stick out further, giving the vehicle a wider stance and making it look *tough.* This in turn sells wheels and the dealer and manufacturer both smile all the way to the bank.

To preserve front-suspension geometry, an accessory wheel should have as close to stock offset as possible, whether *zero, positive* or *negative.* Retaining stock offset is sometimes impossible because of interference between rim and brake calipers or various steering components. Any amount of positive offset essentially turns the wheel into a lever applying load through the bearing and into the spindle. Component loading soars and life goes down the drain.

Consider a front spindle carrying a static 2,000-pound load. You drive your Blazer onto a scale and find out how much weight rests on one tire and wheel combination. Then you install wider rims and—naturally—larger tires weighing more than stock. Your new wheels have a two-

inch positive offset. The spindle still supports a 2,000-pound loading, but you moved it two inches outboard. Sort of like changing from holding a one-pound brick near your body and then doing it at arm's length.

The added strain caused by positively offset wheels causes bearings to fail quickly and feeds extreme loadings into the spindle. Keep that in mind when your heavier front wheels and tires come off the ground or go down hard in a hole.

Don't misread us. A wheel builder is not necessarily building a bad wheel if you have to trim the sheet metal on the outside portion of the fender to gain clearance. If he tells you the 10-inch wheel has two inches positive offset this is not saying it is a bad wheel. Depending on the vehicle, that much offset might be needed to clear a tie-rod end. However, you should know if the two inches of offset is really necessary before buying

Valve stems should be located so you can get to them. Check that before you buy a wheel. You don't want to crawl under the vehicle to check air pressure. Sure you can weld up one hole and drill another, but why?

Just go in and ask them for an eight-inch rim and bolt it on, right? Here are two Blazer wheels. One on right will shove the wheel and tire 1¼-inches farther out the spindle than the other. With some tires this could mean fender trimming. So all steel wheels are alike, huh?

the wheel. There should be at least ¼-inch clearance between any part of the wheel and such things as tie-rod ends, brake calipers, etc. Due to the drop in the rim section, a two-inch positive off-set may be needed to clear everything. Bolt on a rim and check it out.

WHEEL CONSTRUCTION

Factory wheels—those supplied on the vehicle

There is a complete, professional electric weld on this wheel joining center to rim. Weld is so even a casual observer might have a bit of trouble locating it in this photo—hence the arrows.

—most always have the center *riveted* to the rim. Accessory wheels usually have the center *welded* to the rim. The reason for the difference is simple economics. A small manufacturer simply cannot afford the kind of equipment it takes to rivet the center and rim together precisely. Welding is low-cost, easy and quite acceptable. Make sure the rim and center are really *welded* together all the way and not just tacked at several points. If you don't really know a good weld from a bad one, take along a buddy who does savvy welding and let him judge whether the welder achieved full penetration during the operation.

Wheels rarely fail under normal usage, but when you start pounding around off-road, the term *normal* really doesn't hold much water, does it?

Three basic methods are used in building non-stock wheels. First, new, wider-than-stock rims may be purchased and welded to new or used centers. The procedure is to clamp the center to be used on a mandrel in a large lathe, shove the rim over the center, determine the offset, align it, check the wheel for lateral runout, tack-weld it, check it again for lateral runout and possibly concentricity—whether the end product will be round—and weld the center to the rim. There are some disadvantages here. Unless the builder can buy in bulk, new rims can be expensive—so can new centers. There is a limit to the rim width. Currently the widest one-piece 15-inch rim available is 10 inches. The advantage of this type construction is that it is quite fast because there are only two pieces to deal with; safe because we are only joining two components and not really modifying either of them. The construction is relatively low cost even though new components are involved because little labor is used.

The second popular method of building a wide rim is to cut up two rims to build one, welded in the center by the method previously outlined. The problems involved here are obvious. Cuts on both rims must be straight and even. We're now faced with two welds instead of one; both lateral runout and concentricity are now even more difficult to control. Cost is up somewhat because more handling is involved, more welding, more time. The only advantage which comes to mind is that piecing two rims together allows making a wider rim than can be obtained by using one rim.

The third method of building a wide rim is actually a variation of piecing two rims together. One rim is sliced in two and a rolled band of steel is inserted between the two rim sections and welded in place. The rim is welded in two locations instead of one; then the center is welded into place. The advantage here is that the band can be three inches wide or three-feet wide! Any rim width can be constructed in this fashion. Quality of the welding, lateral runout and concentricity are up to the builder. Weight soars with this type wheel as a lot of steel is used. You may want to get a good idea of what the weight will be before you buy. When you want really wide wheels, consider the spun-aluminum type made by Cragar and Chassis Engineering.

We could call this Brand X, but actually it's just an inferior wheel. Note that the weld between rim and center is not continuous. A large amount of weld "splatter" is evident. More importantly, notice the two very short "welds" we've indicated—more like a couple of mistakes.

STEEL-SPOKE

Although relatively new on the market, these wheels are basically the same old "Hollywood" or "California" hoorah with a new look. This time the new look is white paint and flame-cut spokes. It all boils down to cosmetics. The wheels do look nice and because the centers are flame cut from 3/8 or 5/16-inch steel plate, it is easy to convince the unwary that these wheels are stronger. Than what? They are not stronger. Here's why. Stock-type centers are formed in a stamping press. Strengthening ribs and bows are formed by the die at the same time all holes are located exactly right. At the outer edge of the wheel center steel is flanged to give a wide area for attachment to the rim. Under severe pounding the rim will flex— a stock-type center is designed to absorb the load delivered by the rim—again, by flexing. Take a

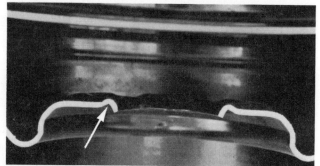

At the very center of the wheel notice how shallow this center is stamped in comparison to the one below . . . .

. . . . which has a much deeper drop in the center. The deeper turned lip is obviously a stronger design. Whether strength is needed in this area is a moot question.

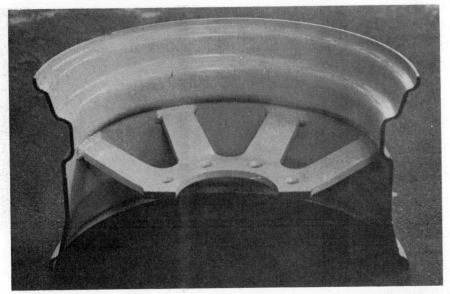

Current off-road fad is spoke wheel. Sectioned wheel reveals no magic. Selling point is strictly cosmetic. Many times weld is on one side of spoke only. Lack of lug-tensioning folds in the center section of this design makes frequent lug tightening absolutely essential.

Wheels with flat-plate centers which are not machined do not tension the lug nuts and require constant tightening. Lateral strength is also less than a stock-type center.

Dick Cepek and Appliance Plating are now marketing the Mojock spoke center wheel (bottom) with a full circumference mating to the rim. The strength advantages are obvious when compared to more usual construction of top wheel.

close look at the area immediately around the bolt holes. The area is buckled outward, called coining. That part of the wheel center deflects slightly and puts tension on the lug nut as the lug nut is torqued down. This is why a properly tightened lug nut on a stock wheel almost never loosens. Now turn your attention to the "Spoke" wheel. The center is cut from a piece of flat plate by flame cutting. On some spoke wheels the spokes are bent somewhat before being welded into place —on other designs the plate is simply left flat. This

matters little. The pilot hole and the bolt holes are drilled on a machine fixture. Bolt holes are then countersunk. On most spoke wheel centers there is nothing to keep the lug nut tight—no tension against the back side of the nut as is the case on the stock centers. Another problem arises immediately in that the holes are drilled in a piece of metal which has been flame-cut meaning there is a minimum—if any—area upon which to locate the drilling fixture accurately. Thus, it is not uncommon to have to slot a bolt hole in a spoke wheel to get the wheel on the drum. The spokes are welded to the rim. Some wheels have welding on both sides of the spoke; others on one side only. The welding of a relatively thick plate to the thinner rim metal has its own set of built-in problems called *penetration.* Any competent welder can explain this to you. Then comes the clincher. We already know that under severe loading the rim will flex and go somewhat egg-shaped; on a stock-type wheel the center will deflect in turn. On the spoke wheel the rim continues to flex—as best it can (which is not very good)—but that vertical steel plate doesn't budge. Loading is shared by the lug nuts and the spoke ends. Something has to give—and the lug nuts and rim at the area of the spoke welds get the raw end of the deal. Ditto your pocketbook.

One manufacturer of spoke wheels packs a warranty card with his wheels. In effect the card is a disclaimer—*not a warranty*—but that's beside the point. You bought the wheel, joker. Bolt it on. Installation instructions point out that the lugs must periodically be tightened and then some reasons are given. Two of the reasons are most interesting. One of them is that the wheel has no crush value—which is what we've already said. There is nothing to tension the lug nut once it's in place. The other reason is that side loads from larger tires, power steering and four-wheel drive cause excessive side load on the studs. Yup! If you are bound and determined to run spoke wheels, we'd recommend that you check the lug nuts for tightness at least twice a day when running rough stuff and a couple of times a week if your machine is a pavement runner.

Dick Cepek and Appliance Industries now market a spoke wheel with a full-circumference ring on the outer ends of the spokes. Thus the spoke ends do not contact the inside of the rim—the ring does. This gives far more strength. Looks like both Cepek and Appliance have whipped the lug-nut-loosening problem by not only stamping a bow in the center but also machining a recess on its back-side to allow the lug bolts to crush the center and thereby apply tension.

MAGS (Cast Aluminum)

Cast-aluminum wheels have been called "mags" for so long in this country—for magnesium—it is easy to forget for a moment they are still

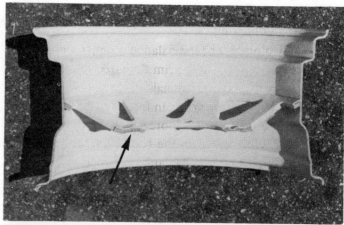

Recess machined onto backside of this Mojock spoked wheel (Appliance/Cepek) so center will tension lug nuts once they are tightened.

Mojock's full-circumference wheel center is arc-welded to the rim in short beads for minimum heat buildup and maximum strength. Area around the bolt holes has been machined to provide "coining effect" to ensure center tensions the tightened lug nuts or studs.

cast-aluminum. Their strong selling point is appearance—and we won't deny that they do look good. There are a few things you should realize before making the investment—a sizeable one for four wheels. To gain strength from the casting, mags are necessarily thicker at all points than a steel wheel. This can cause fitting problems. For instance, fitting most mags to a Blazer front end requires spacers between the hub and wheel. Or, a portion of the brake caliper must be ground off. We can't get enthusiastic about grinding on any part of the brake mechanism nor can we get excited about running spacers behind wheels because this simply adds positive offset and strains the heck out of spindles and bearings.

Only glue-on or tape balance weights will work on mags because the rim flange is far too thick to accept a conventional weight. There is a limit to how much weight can be added by this method. If a tire requires more weight than can be added with glue-ons, then the tire simply must remain out of balance. Clearance between disc brake and cast rim may not allow weights to be attached to the back of the wheel. This can mean that the wheel/tire combination cannot be dynamically balanced.

The argument will probably go on for some time as to whether mags are as strong as steel wheels. This is of relative unimportance. If you bend a steel rim in rough running it can be hammered back into a semblance of original shape. If a cast wheel is hit hard enough it will break. A steel wheel will almost never break—it will deform and then you can go to work with a large hammer or rock. Despite the very thick center section on a mag, this portion will deflect when lug nuts are being torqued down and thus some tension is provided for the nuts or bolts. But there is far less tension on the bolts than provided by a stock-type wheel—thus lug nuts must be checked frequently for tightness. If you run mags off-road and plan an extended stay in the rough you should always carry three or four extra lug nuts which fit your mags.

You should also keep in mind it can be very trying to find anyone who will mount and dismount mag type wheels when you have a flat..The reason is simple. Most bead-breaking machines are not designed to hold a mag wheel. If the wheels are clamped into a machine anyway, there is a good possibility the center will break out of the wheel. The operator knows this and avoids the problem by refusing to work on the wheel. He won't be enthusiastic about trying to remove the tire from the mag by hand either. Tire irons have a nasty way of gouging cast aluminum. Additionally, it is far more difficult to get the tire over the thicker rim flange. Tire shops and service stations that work on mag wheels charge more for their services. Can you blame them?

CHROME WHEELS

Most suppliers of stock-type steel wheels will sell the wheels painted or chromed. Except for the finish the wheel will be the same. Expect to pay $10 to $15 more for the chrome version. The reason is simple: There's a lot more labor involved. The secret to good chroming is polishing the steel before the wheel is coppered and then chrome-plated. Polishing is a super-dirty job—and time-consuming if it is done correctly. How do you know good chrome when you see it? Take one of your wife's old nylons and run it around the inside of the wheel. If it snags on something you couldn't see, you know the wheel wasn't properly polished. Any small imperfection in the surface of the metal is an instant water trap. In time it will lead to pitting, rusting, flaking and peeling. Chrome requires care. Clean them using a soft cloth and household ammonia. Wax them often with a non-abrasive carnuba wax. Do not use combination wax/polishes because these scratch the surface and could allow water to get between the layers of plating.

Chrome wheels are plated in pieces and then welded together. In effect the chrome plating is being welded to the chrome plating—which can cause a problem called hydrogen embrittlement which leads to failure of the weld. Hydrogen embrittlement can be eliminated by placing the wheel in a special oven for several hours at a given temperature—if the baking is done immediately after the welding is completed.

Like mag wheels, chrome wheels are sold because they look good—not because they are better in any way than a stock-type, painted wheel.

SUPPLIERS LIST

Advance Adapters, Inc.
13629 Talc
Santa Fe Springs, CA 90670
213/921-0702
Four-speed transmissions to transfer-case adapters. Headers & adapters for off-road vehicles.

Advanced Four-Wheel Drive
2354 E. Huntington Drive
Duarte, CA 91010
213/357-3094
Repairs, swaps and accessories.

Auto-Haus
6460 Dale Avenue
Buena Park, CA 90621
714/521-5120
Mini-truck custom accessories, lights. Catalog $2.

Big Wheels
12865 Main
Garden Grove, CA 92640
714/636-2370
Custom built wide wheels for all vehicles—some tires, free catalog 64 pages.

Dick Cepek
9201 California Ave.
South Gate, CA 90280
213/569-1675
Wheels, tires and camping gear, free catalog "Off Road Bible".

Brian Chuchua's Four-Wheel Drive Center
776 South Placentia
Placentia, CA 92670
714/528-5337
Parts and accessories for all Jeeps, some surplus items.

Custom Gas Tanks
11719 McBean Drive
El Monte, CA 91732
213/442-6258
What they don't have in stock, they will build. Free literature.

DataMotive Inc.
14041 Mt. Bismark
Reno, NV 89506
702/972-1617
Independent automotive and tire test lab for manufacturers. Write for capabilities.

Dualmatic Manufacturing Co.
PO Box 1119
Longmont, Colorado 80501
Full line of 2wd and 4wd hardware. Free catalog.

Edelbrock Equipment Co.
411 Coral Circle
El Segundo, CA 90245
213/322-7310
Intake manifolds, catalog $1.

Fairway Ford
1350 Yorba Linda
Placentia, CA 92670
213/620-9387
714/524-1200
RV accessory catalog $3.50. 4WD accessory catalog $3.50. Catalogs include $5 gift certificate.

Four Wheeler Magazine
6226 Vineland Ave.
North Hollywood, CA 91606
213/877-1195
$9 per year—monthly.

Harrah Mfg. Co.
46 W. Spring St.
Bloomfield, IN 47424
812/384-4441
"Handyman" jacks (sheepherder type), Loc-Racs and other accessories.

Hickey Enterprises Inc.
1645 Callens Road
Ventura, CA 93003
805/644-5571
Complete line of accessories and winches for Chevy/Blazer, GMC/Jimmy, Dodge/Plymouth, Ford/Bronco, Minitrucks, Catalog $1.

Hoosier Machine Products
314 S.E. 6th St.
Pentleton, OR 97801
503/276-3442
Bronco, Jeep & Scout engine & transmission hardware, free catalog.

Koenig Iron Works Inc.
Box 7726
Houston, TX 77007
713/869-6611
King winches, free literature.

Lakewood Industries
4800 Briar Road
Cleveland, OH 44135
Come-A-Longs, rollbars, metallic brake linings, catalog $1.

Man-A-Fre Co.
18736 Parthenia St.
Northridge, CA 91324
213/349-1343
Complete line of hardware for Toyota 4WD, catalog $1.

McCain Hub Winch Company
345 Mill St.
Eugene, OR 97401
No phone.
Winches, free literature.

Motorhome Life & Camper Coachman Magazine
P.O. Box 500
Calabasas, CA 91302
213/888-6000
Magazine devoted to truck camper & motor homes. $5 per year—6 issues.

Novak Enterprises
Box 1324
Whittier, CA 90609
213/921-3202
Engine-conversion hardware, free catalog. Conversion instructions.

Off-Road Vehicles Magazine
131 Barrington Place
Los Angeles, CA 90049
213/476-3004
$9 per year—12 issues

O.R.V. Magazine
7950 Deering Avenue
Canoga Park, CA 91304
Monthly magazine—four-wheel-drive oriented. $7 per year—12 issues

Perfectune
P.O. Box 26848
Tempe, AZ 85282
Quadrajet and 2G Rochester carb re-jet kits for altitude, mileage & performance. Send stamped self-addressed envelope for free details.

Pickup, Van & 4WD Magazine
1499 Monrovia Ave.
Newport Beach, CA 92663
714/646-4455
$7 per year—12 issues

Racer Brown
9270 Borden Ave.
Sun Valley, CA 91352
213/767-4062
Performance and economy camshafts, catalog $3.

Ramsey Winch Co.
P.O. Box 15829
Tulsa, OK 74115
918/835-1521
Winches, free literature.

Rancho Jeep Supply
6309 Paramount Blvd.
Long Beach, CA 90805
213/423-0477
Jeep hardware

Recreational Vehicle Accessories
2111 S. Leyden St.
Denver, CO 80222
303/756-9495
4WD accessories. Catalog $1.

Rough Country Inc.
1080 N. Marshall Ave.
El Cajon, CA 92020
Heavy-duty suspension components for most vehicles. Catalog $1.

Sand Tires Unlimited
1401 West 178th St.
Gardena, CA 90247
213/324-2996
Sand tires and dune-buggy accessories, free literature.

Smittybilt
2124 N. Lee Ave.
S. El Monte, CA 91733
213/442-1788
Off-road vehicle roll bars, tow bars, free catalog.

Trailblazer
2217 N. 36th
Boise, ID 83703
208/343-3539
Jeep, Pickup, Wagoneer, Commando, Cherokee gas tanks, skid plates, tire mounts. Free price list.

Warn Industries
19450 68th Ave. So.
Kent, WA 98031
206/854-5350
Winches, mini winches, posi-traction, locking hubs, utility hoists, free literature.

Weiand Automotive Industries
2316 San Fernando Rd.
Los Angeles, CA 90065
213/225-1346
Intake manifolds, catalog $1.

Whitco
White Automotive Corporation
Box 1209
Colorado Springs, CO 80901
303/598-3541
Soft tops for most 4WD vehicles, free literature.

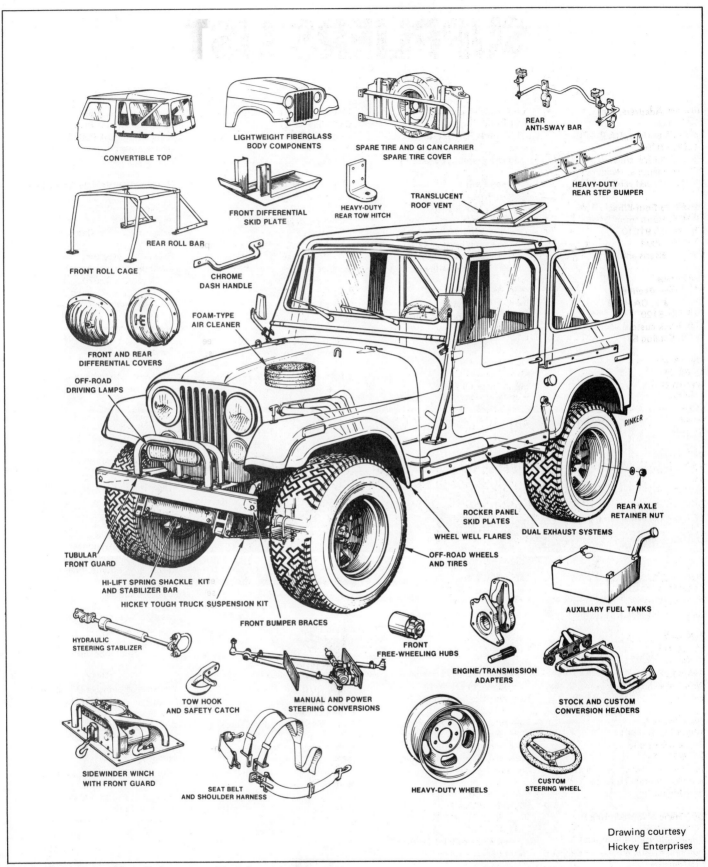

CONVERTIBLE TOP

LIGHTWEIGHT FIBERGLASS BODY COMPONENTS

SPARE TIRE AND GI CAN CARRIER SPARE TIRE COVER

REAR ANTI-SWAY BAR

HEAVY-DUTY REAR STEP BUMPER

FRONT DIFFERENTIAL SKID PLATE

HEAVY-DUTY REAR TOW HITCH

TRANSLUCENT ROOF VENT

REAR ROLL BAR

FRONT ROLL CAGE

CHROME DASH HANDLE

FOAM-TYPE AIR CLEANER

FRONT AND REAR DIFFERENTIAL COVERS

OFF-ROAD DRIVING LAMPS

RINKER

ROCKER PANEL SKID PLATES

WHEEL WELL FLARES

DUAL EXHAUST SYSTEMS

REAR AXLE RETAINER NUT

TUBULAR FRONT GUARD

OFF-ROAD WHEELS AND TIRES

HI-LIFT SPRING SHACKLE KIT AND STABILIZER BAR

HICKEY TOUGH TRUCK SUSPENSION KIT

FRONT BUMPER BRACES

AUXILIARY FUEL TANKS

HYDRAULIC STEERING STABLIZER

FRONT FREE-WHEELING HUBS

ENGINE/TRANSMISSION ADAPTERS

TOW HOOK AND SAFETY CATCH

MANUAL AND POWER STEERING CONVERSIONS

STOCK AND CUSTOM CONVERSION HEADERS

SIDEWINDER WINCH WITH FRONT GUARD

SEAT BELT AND SHOULDER HARNESS

HEAVY-DUTY WHEELS

CUSTOM STEERING WHEEL

Drawing courtesy
Hickey Enterprises

Hickey Enterprises offers all these neat things for your Jeep.

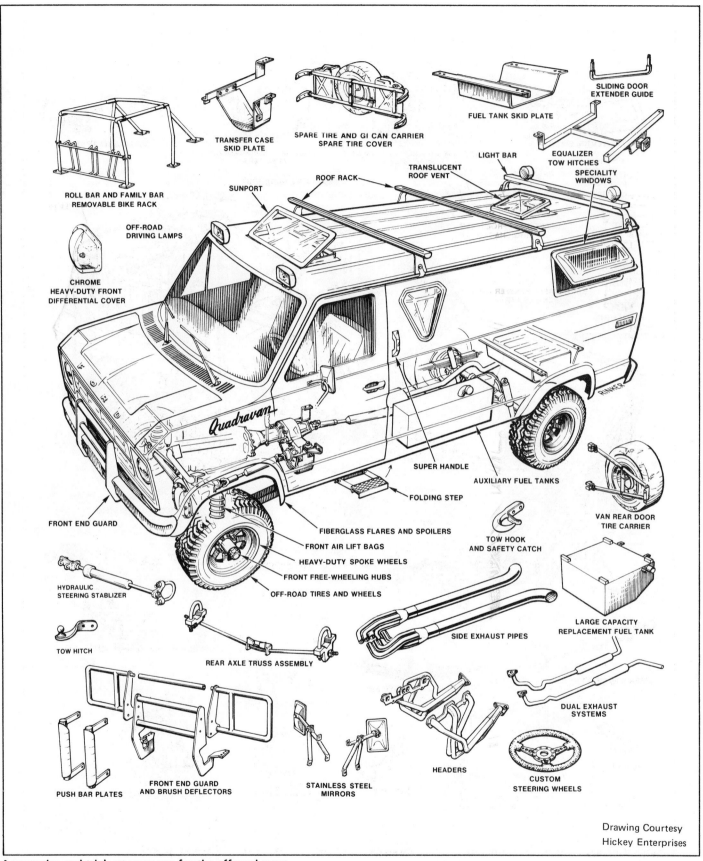

ROLL BAR AND FAMILY BAR
REMOVABLE BIKE RACK

TRANSFER CASE
SKID PLATE

SPARE TIRE AND GI CAN CARRIER
SPARE TIRE COVER

FUEL TANK SKID PLATE

SLIDING DOOR
EXTENDER GUIDE

EQUALIZER
TOW HITCHES

SPECIALITY
WINDOWS

LIGHT BAR

TRANSLUCENT
ROOF VENT

ROOF RACK

SUNPORT

OFF-ROAD
DRIVING LAMPS

CHROME
HEAVY-DUTY FRONT
DIFFERENTIAL COVER

SUPER HANDLE

AUXILIARY FUEL TANKS

VAN REAR DOOR
TIRE CARRIER

FOLDING STEP

TOW HOOK
AND SAFETY CATCH

FRONT END GUARD

FIBERGLASS FLARES AND SPOILERS

FRONT AIR LIFT BAGS

HEAVY-DUTY SPOKE WHEELS

FRONT FREE-WHEELING HUBS

OFF-ROAD TIRES AND WHEELS

LARGE CAPACITY
REPLACEMENT FUEL TANK

HYDRAULIC
STEERING STABLIZER

TOW HITCH

REAR AXLE TRUSS ASSEMBLY

SIDE EXHAUST PIPES

DUAL EXHAUST
SYSTEMS

PUSH BAR PLATES

FRONT END GUARD
AND BRUSH DEFLECTORS

STAINLESS STEEL
MIRRORS

HEADERS

CUSTOM
STEERING WHEELS

Drawing Courtesy
Hickey Enterprises

Accessorize and trick-up your van for the off-road scene.

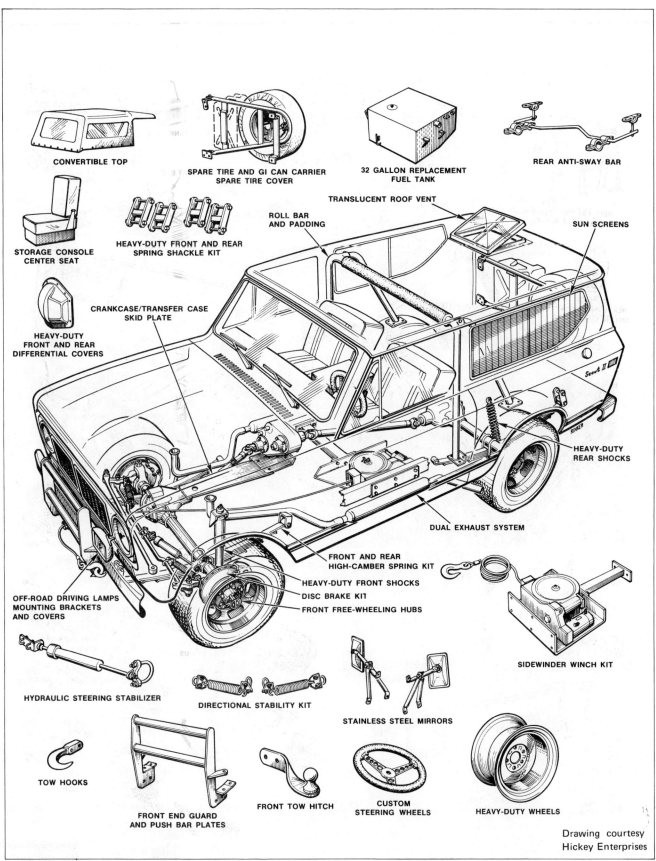

CONVERTIBLE TOP

SPARE TIRE AND GI CAN CARRIER
SPARE TIRE COVER

32 GALLON REPLACEMENT
FUEL TANK

REAR ANTI-SWAY BAR

STORAGE CONSOLE
CENTER SEAT

HEAVY-DUTY FRONT AND REAR
SPRING SHACKLE KIT

TRANSLUCENT ROOF VENT

ROLL BAR
AND PADDING

SUN SCREENS

HEAVY-DUTY
FRONT AND REAR
DIFFERENTIAL COVERS

CRANKCASE/TRANSFER CASE
SKID PLATE

HEAVY-DUTY
REAR SHOCKS

DUAL EXHAUST SYSTEM

FRONT AND REAR
HIGH-CAMBER SPRING KIT

HEAVY-DUTY FRONT SHOCKS

DISC BRAKE KIT

FRONT FREE-WHEELING HUBS

OFF-ROAD DRIVING LAMPS
MOUNTING BRACKETS
AND COVERS

SIDEWINDER WINCH KIT

HYDRAULIC STEERING STABILIZER

DIRECTIONAL STABILITY KIT

STAINLESS STEEL MIRRORS

TOW HOOKS

FRONT END GUARD
AND PUSH BAR PLATES

FRONT TOW HITCH

CUSTOM
STEERING WHEELS

HEAVY-DUTY WHEELS

Drawing courtesy
Hickey Enterprises

Looking for pieces to get real hair-on-the-chest performance for your Scout II? Start saving your pesos!

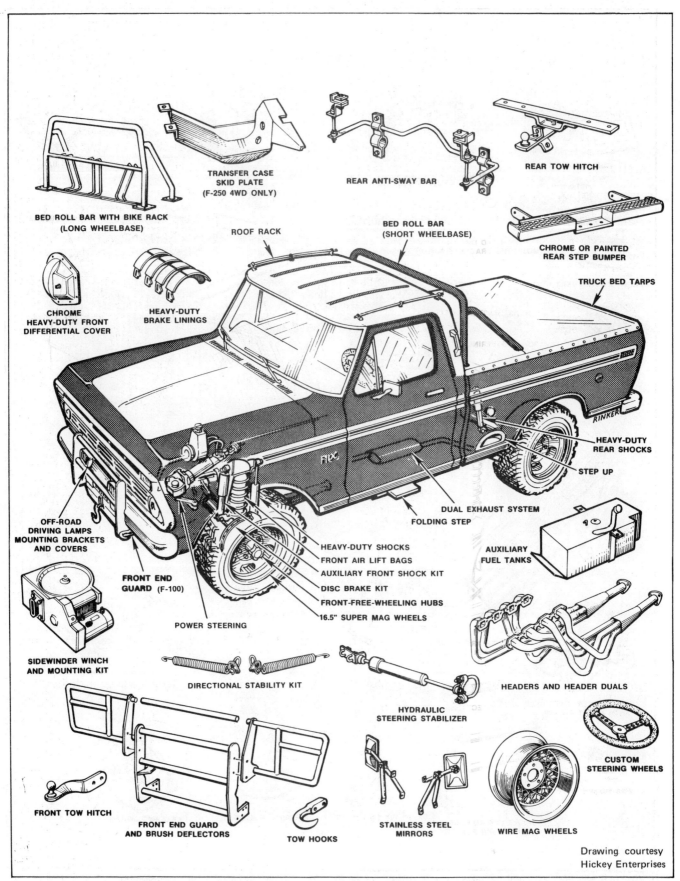

BED ROLL BAR WITH BIKE RACK
(LONG WHEELBASE)

TRANSFER CASE
SKID PLATE
(F-250 4WD ONLY)

REAR ANTI-SWAY BAR

REAR TOW HITCH

ROOF RACK

BED ROLL BAR
(SHORT WHEELBASE)

CHROME OR PAINTED
REAR STEP BUMPER

CHROME
HEAVY-DUTY FRONT
DIFFERENTIAL COVER

HEAVY-DUTY
BRAKE LININGS

TRUCK BED TARPS

HEAVY-DUTY
REAR SHOCKS

STEP UP

OFF-ROAD
DRIVING LAMPS
MOUNTING BRACKETS
AND COVERS

DUAL EXHAUST SYSTEM

FOLDING STEP

FRONT END
GUARD (F-100)

HEAVY-DUTY SHOCKS
FRONT AIR LIFT BAGS
AUXILIARY FRONT SHOCK KIT
DISC BRAKE KIT
FRONT-FREE-WHEELING HUBS
16.5" SUPER MAG WHEELS

AUXILIARY
FUEL TANKS

SIDEWINDER WINCH
AND MOUNTING KIT

POWER STEERING

DIRECTIONAL STABILITY KIT

HYDRAULIC
STEERING STABILIZER

HEADERS AND HEADER DUALS

CUSTOM
STEERING WHEELS

FRONT TOW HITCH

FRONT END GUARD
AND BRUSH DEFLECTORS

TOW HOOKS

STAINLESS STEEL
MIRRORS

WIRE MAG WHEELS

Drawing courtesy
Hickey Enterprises

To turn your Ford truck into a mean motorscooter, just start bolting on some of these fine goodies.

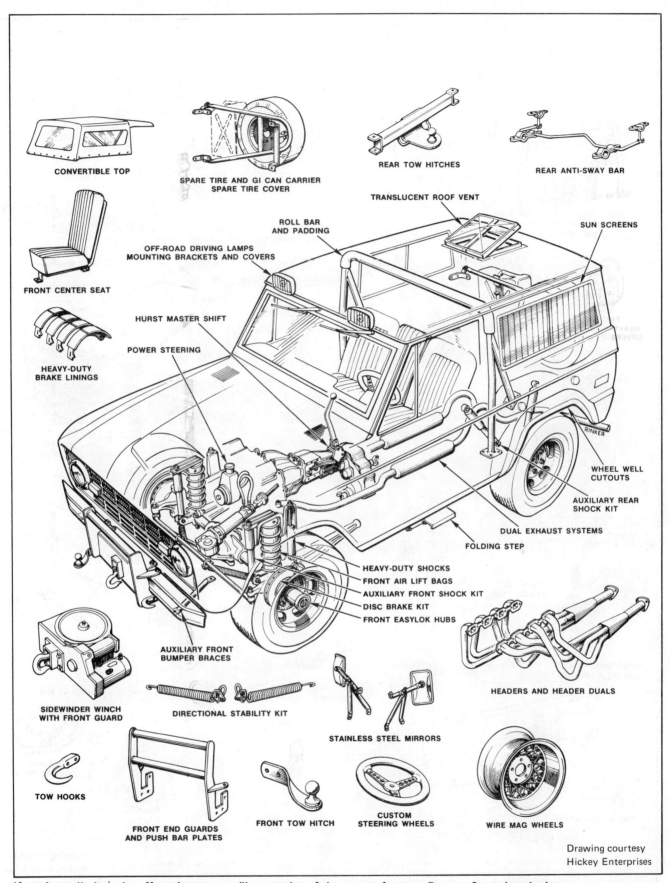

CONVERTIBLE TOP

SPARE TIRE AND GI CAN CARRIER
SPARE TIRE COVER

REAR TOW HITCHES

REAR ANTI-SWAY BAR

TRANSLUCENT ROOF VENT

ROLL BAR
AND PADDING

SUN SCREENS

FRONT CENTER SEAT

OFF-ROAD DRIVING LAMPS
MOUNTING BRACKETS AND COVERS

HURST MASTER SHIFT

POWER STEERING

HEAVY-DUTY
BRAKE LININGS

WHEEL WELL
CUTOUTS

AUXILIARY REAR
SHOCK KIT

DUAL EXHAUST SYSTEMS

FOLDING STEP

HEAVY-DUTY SHOCKS
FRONT AIR LIFT BAGS
AUXILIARY FRONT SHOCK KIT
DISC BRAKE KIT
FRONT EASYLOK HUBS

AUXILIARY FRONT
BUMPER BRACES

HEADERS AND HEADER DUALS

SIDEWINDER WINCH
WITH FRONT GUARD

DIRECTIONAL STABILITY KIT

STAINLESS STEEL MIRRORS

TOW HOOKS

FRONT END GUARDS
AND PUSH BAR PLATES

FRONT TOW HITCH

CUSTOM
STEERING WHEELS

WIRE MAG WHEELS

Drawing courtesy
Hickey Enterprises

If you're really into the off-road scene, you'll want a lot of these parts for your Bronco. Start choosing!

189

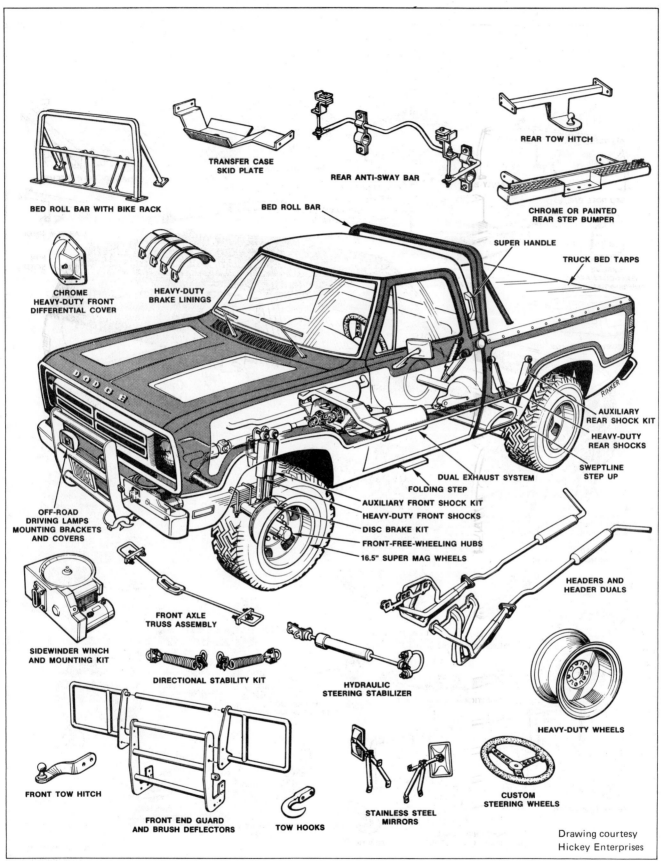

BED ROLL BAR WITH BIKE RACK

TRANSFER CASE SKID PLATE

REAR ANTI-SWAY BAR

REAR TOW HITCH

CHROME OR PAINTED REAR STEP BUMPER

BED ROLL BAR

SUPER HANDLE

TRUCK BED TARPS

CHROME HEAVY-DUTY FRONT DIFFERENTIAL COVER

HEAVY-DUTY BRAKE LININGS

AUXILIARY REAR SHOCK KIT

HEAVY-DUTY REAR SHOCKS

SWEPTLINE STEP UP

DUAL EXHAUST SYSTEM

FOLDING STEP

AUXILIARY FRONT SHOCK KIT

HEAVY-DUTY FRONT SHOCKS

DISC BRAKE KIT

FRONT-FREE-WHEELING HUBS

16.5" SUPER MAG WHEELS

OFF-ROAD DRIVING LAMPS MOUNTING BRACKETS AND COVERS

HEADERS AND HEADER DUALS

SIDEWINDER WINCH AND MOUNTING KIT

FRONT AXLE TRUSS ASSEMBLY

DIRECTIONAL STABILITY KIT

HYDRAULIC STEERING STABILIZER

HEAVY-DUTY WHEELS

FRONT TOW HITCH

FRONT END GUARD AND BRUSH DEFLECTORS

TOW HOOKS

STAINLESS STEEL MIRRORS

CUSTOM STEERING WHEELS

Drawing courtesy
Hickey Enterprises

Dodge pushers can dream of what Santa Claus can stuff into their large Christmas stockings to improve their trucks for the rough stuff.

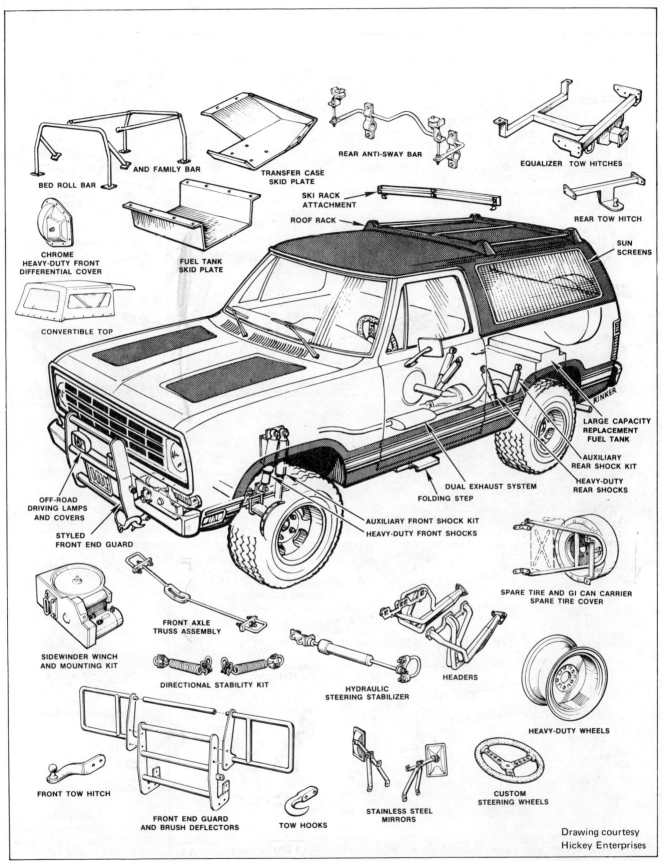

BED ROLL BAR

AND FAMILY BAR

TRANSFER CASE
SKID PLATE

REAR ANTI-SWAY BAR

EQUALIZER TOW HITCHES

CHROME
HEAVY-DUTY FRONT
DIFFERENTIAL COVER

FUEL TANK
SKID PLATE

SKI RACK
ATTACHMENT

ROOF RACK

REAR TOW HITCH

SUN
SCREENS

CONVERTIBLE TOP

LARGE CAPACITY
REPLACEMENT
FUEL TANK

AUXILIARY
REAR SHOCK KIT

HEAVY-DUTY
REAR SHOCKS

OFF-ROAD
DRIVING LAMPS
AND COVERS

STYLED
FRONT END GUARD

DUAL EXHAUST SYSTEM

FOLDING STEP

AUXILIARY FRONT SHOCK KIT
HEAVY-DUTY FRONT SHOCKS

SPARE TIRE AND GI CAN CARRIER
SPARE TIRE COVER

SIDEWINDER WINCH
AND MOUNTING KIT

FRONT AXLE
TRUSS ASSEMBLY

DIRECTIONAL STABILITY KIT

HYDRAULIC
STEERING STABILIZER

HEADERS

HEAVY-DUTY WHEELS

FRONT TOW HITCH

FRONT END GUARD
AND BRUSH DEFLECTORS

TOW HOOKS

STAINLESS STEEL
MIRRORS

CUSTOM
STEERING WHEELS

Drawing courtesy
Hickey Enterprises

Trail Duster and Ramcharger enthusiasts are offered a wealth of accessories for enhanced enjoyment of back-country travel.

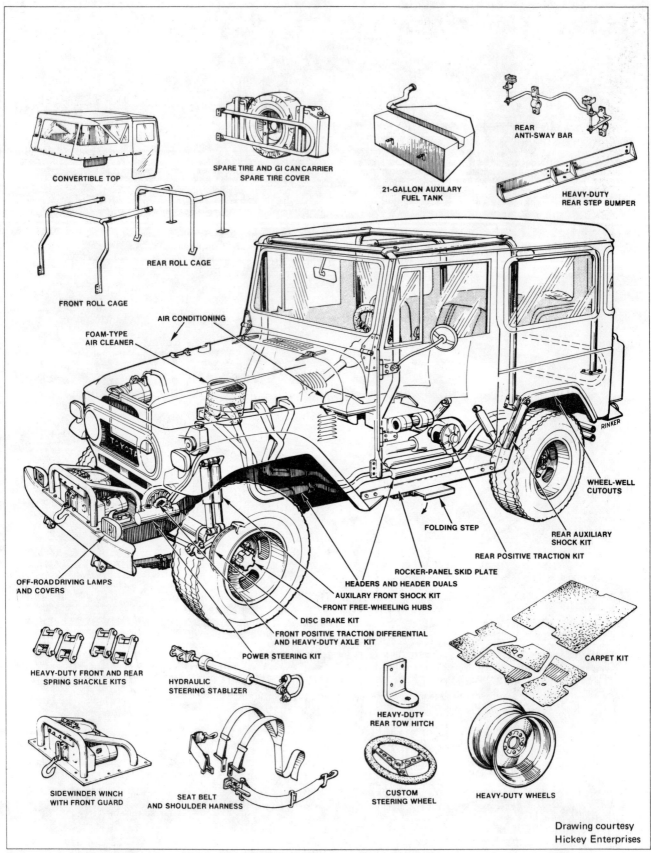

CONVERTIBLE TOP

SPARE TIRE AND GI CAN CARRIER
SPARE TIRE COVER

21-GALLON AUXILARY
FUEL TANK

REAR
ANTI-SWAY BAR

HEAVY-DUTY
REAR STEP BUMPER

REAR ROLL CAGE

FRONT ROLL CAGE

AIR CONDITIONING

FOAM-TYPE
AIR CLEANER

RINKER

WHEEL-WELL
CUTOUTS

FOLDING STEP

REAR AUXILIARY
SHOCK KIT

REAR POSITIVE TRACTION KIT

ROCKER-PANEL SKID PLATE

HEADERS AND HEADER DUALS

AUXILARY FRONT SHOCK KIT

FRONT FREE-WHEELING HUBS

DISC BRAKE KIT

FRONT POSITIVE TRACTION DIFFERENTIAL
AND HEAVY-DUTY AXLE KIT

POWER STEERING KIT

OFF-ROAD DRIVING LAMPS
AND COVERS

CARPET KIT

HEAVY-DUTY FRONT AND REAR
SPRING SHACKLE KITS

HYDRAULIC
STEERING STABLIZER

HEAVY-DUTY
REAR TOW HITCH

SIDEWINDER WINCH
WITH FRONT GUARD

SEAT BELT
AND SHOULDER HARNESS

CUSTOM
STEERING WHEEL

HEAVY-DUTY WHEELS

Drawing courtesy
Hickey Enterprises

Toyota Land Cruiser owners can utilize these accessories to improve their off-road fun.